D G R E DU I N
S T R E E T   A T L A S

Contents

Layout of Map Pages — See Opposing Page
Greater Dublin Map Pages — 2-73
City Centre Maps — Inside Back Cover + 39
Street Index — 74-104
Road Map of Ireland — Back Cover

Legend

Motorway		Parks & Playing Fields	
Main Roads/Streets	DAME STREET	Luas Line/Station	— — ○ — —
Other Roads/Streets		Railway Line/Stations	
One Way Streets	← PEARSE ST	Built-up Areas	
Pedestrianised Streets	GRAFTON STREET	Public Buildings / Church	

Scale of maps is 1:15,000 (4.2 inches to 1 mile or 6.66cm to 1 kilometre)

```
0        250m      500m      750m       1km
|----------|----------|----------|----------|
```

The maps on pages 2 to 73 are based on Ordnance Survey of Ireland by permission of the Government. © Government of Ireland Permit Number 8423

Great care has been taken throughout this publication to be accurate but the publishers cannot accept responsibility for any errors which appear, or their consequences.

Printed in Ireland by Graham & Heslip Ltd. Compiled by Paul Slevin. Comments, suggestions and inquiries should be sent to him at the address below.

Published by Causeway Press (N.I.), 17 Osborne Park, Bangor, N.Ireland BT20 3DJ. Phone UK 07768 172442. E-mail paulslevin@talk21.com

Distributed by Eason Wholesale Books Ltd (phone Dublin 844 8888) and Argosy Libraries Ltd (phone Dublin 823 9500). Quote ISBN 1 872600 34 4.

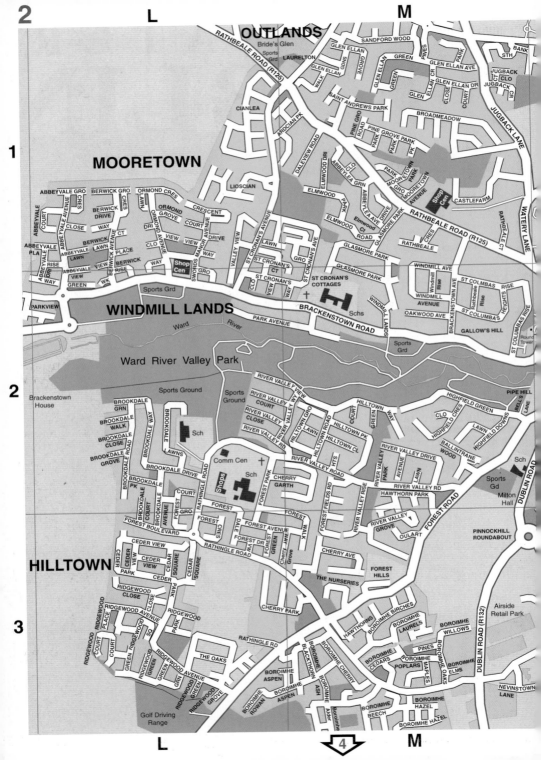

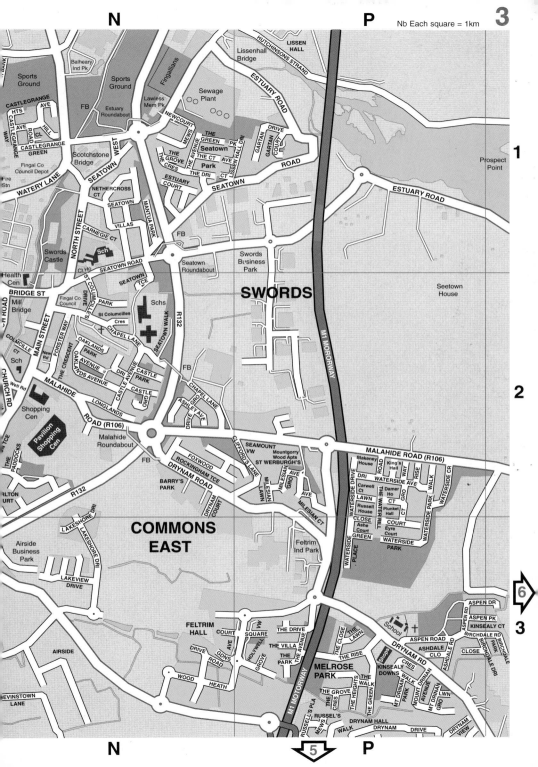

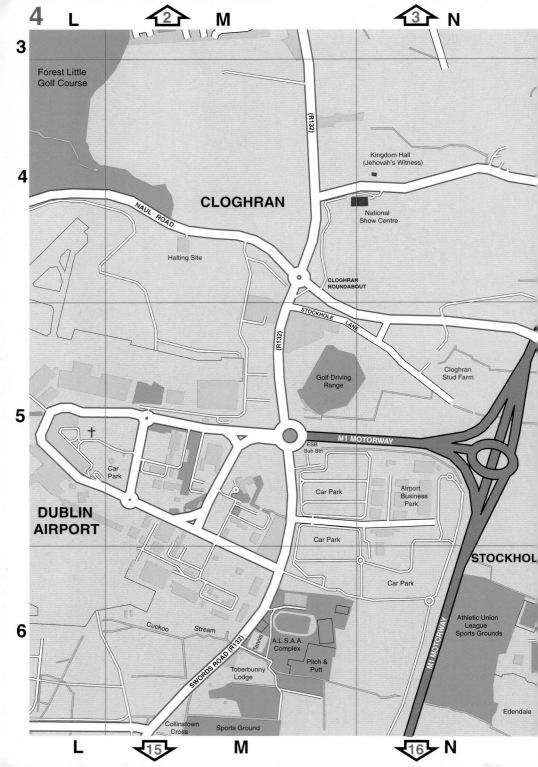

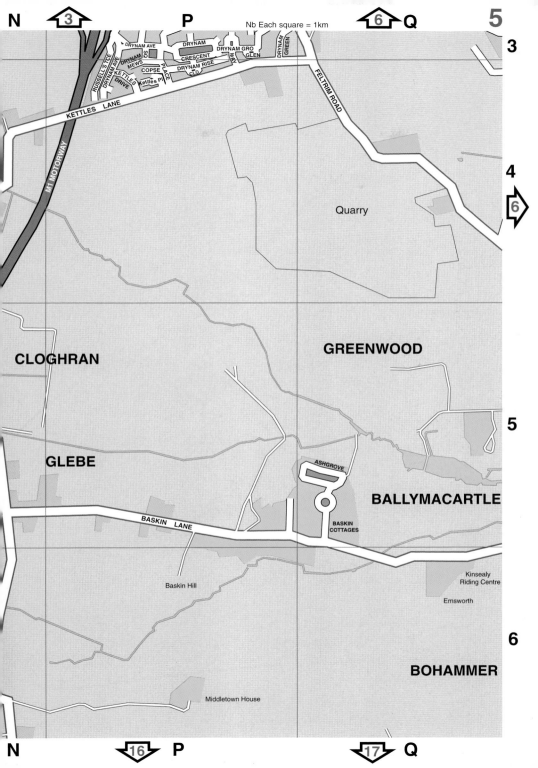

Nb Each square = 1km

DRYNAM AVE
DRYNAM
DRYNAM GRO
DRYNAM
GREEN
RUSSELL'S TCE
DRYNAM
MEWS
CRESCENT
GLEN
DRYNAM AVE
KETTLES
COPSE
DRYNAM RISE
DRIVE
PLACE
CTO
Kettles Pk

KETTLES LANE

FELTRIM ROAD

M1 MOTORWAY

Quarry

CLOGHRAN

GREENWOOD

GLEBE

ASHGROVE

BALLYMACARTLE

BASKIN LANE

BASKIN
COTTAGES

Baskin Hill

Kinsealy
Riding Centre

Emsworth

BOHAMMER

Middletown House

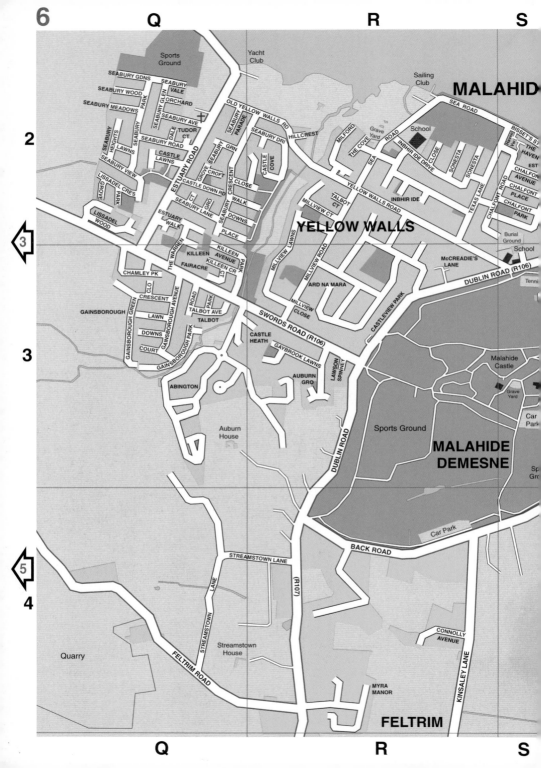

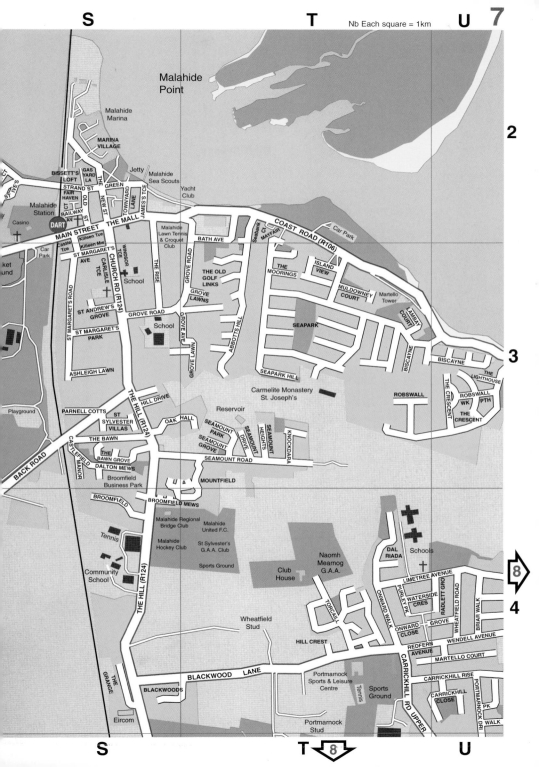

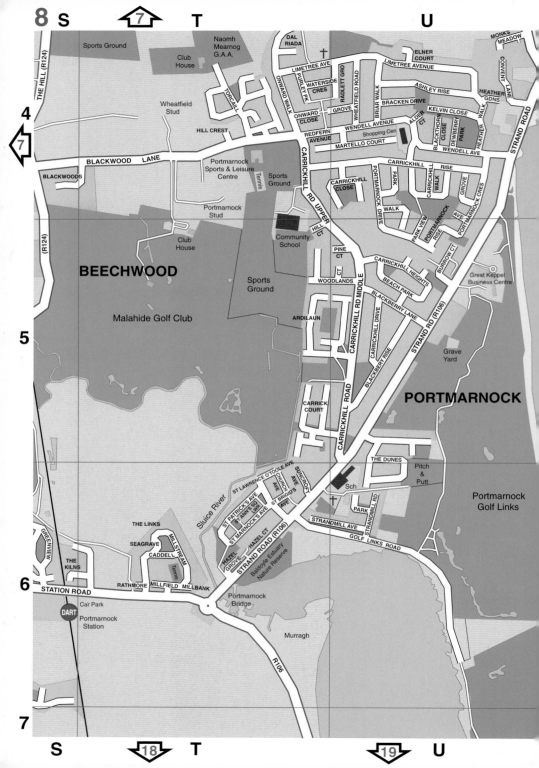

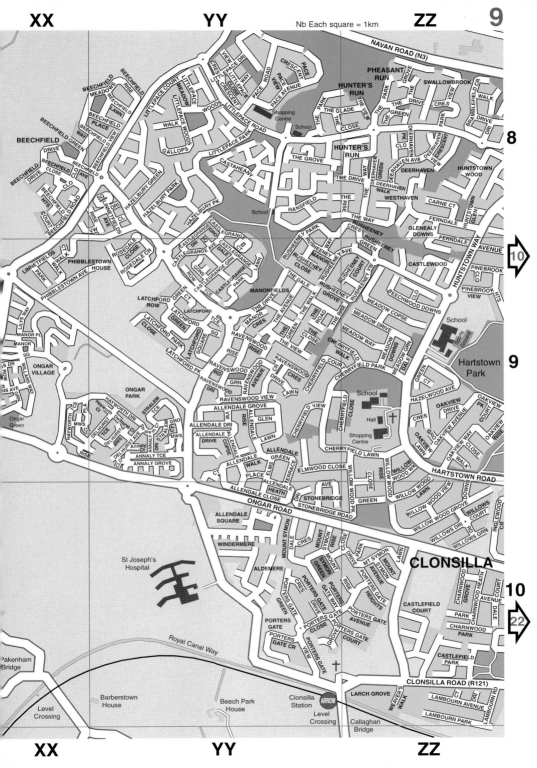

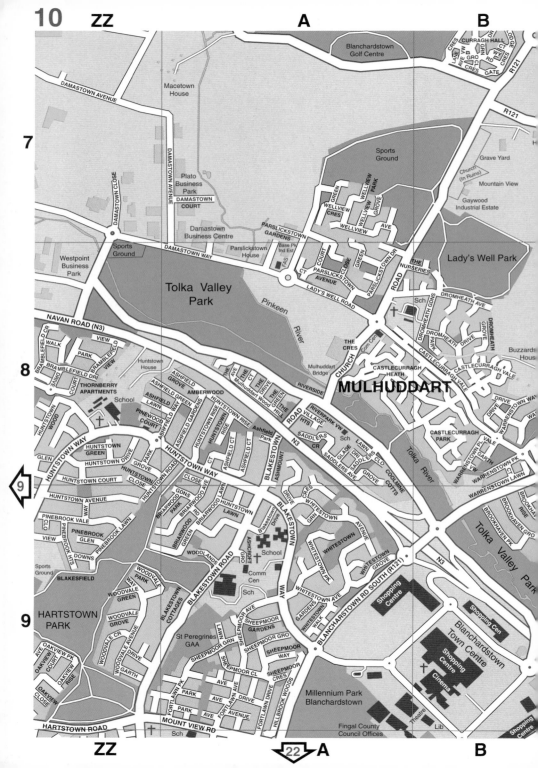

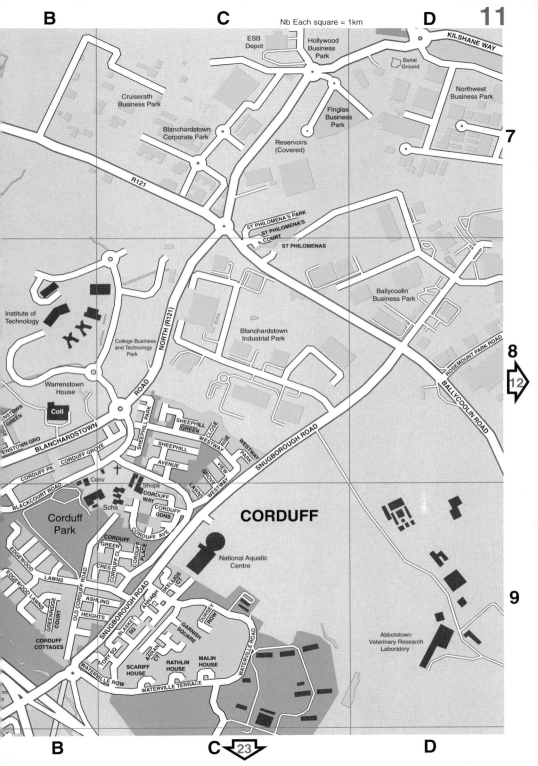

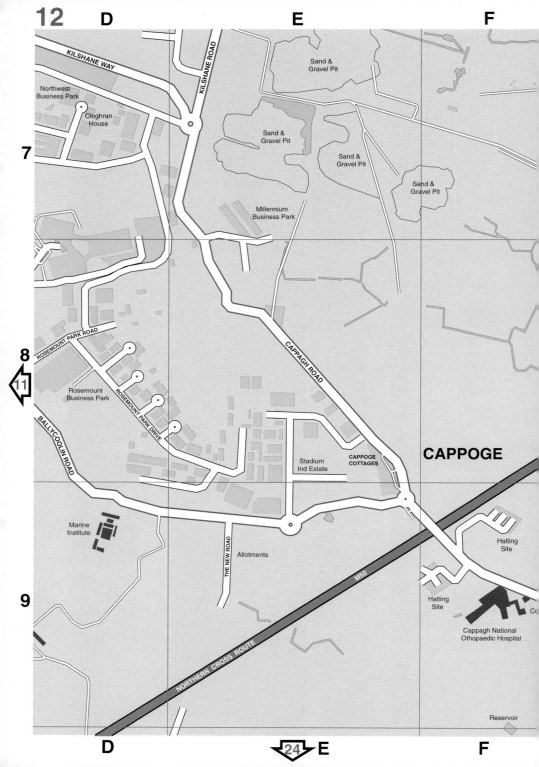

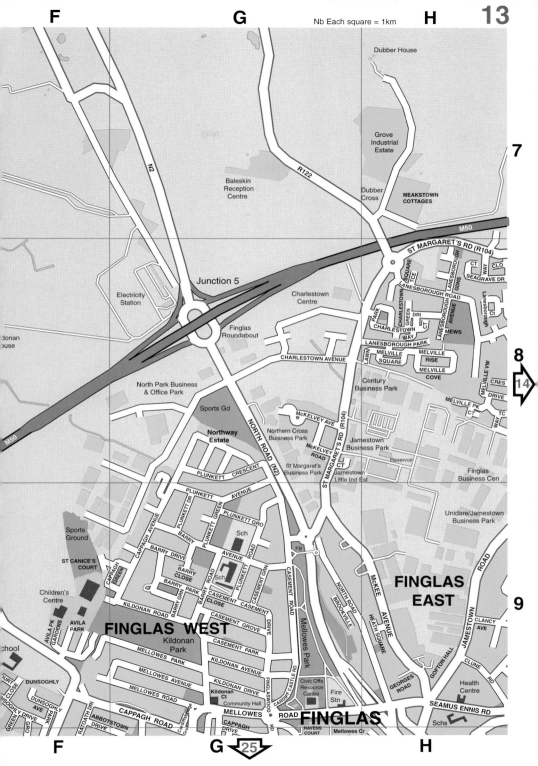

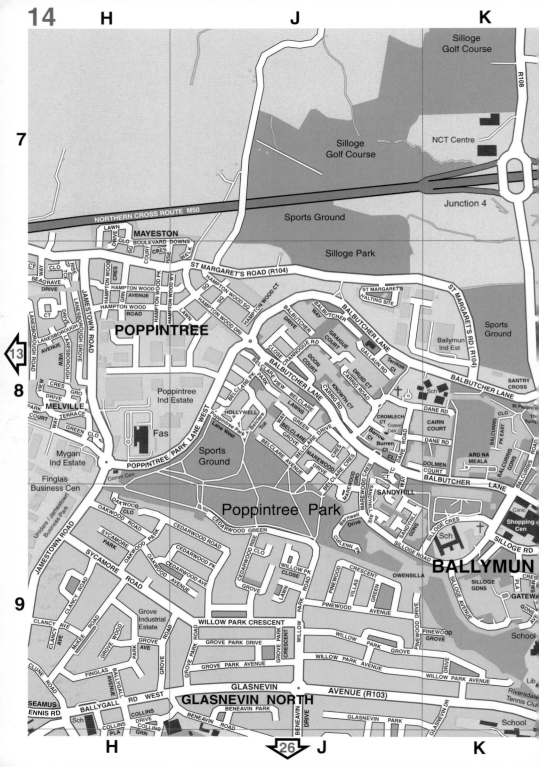

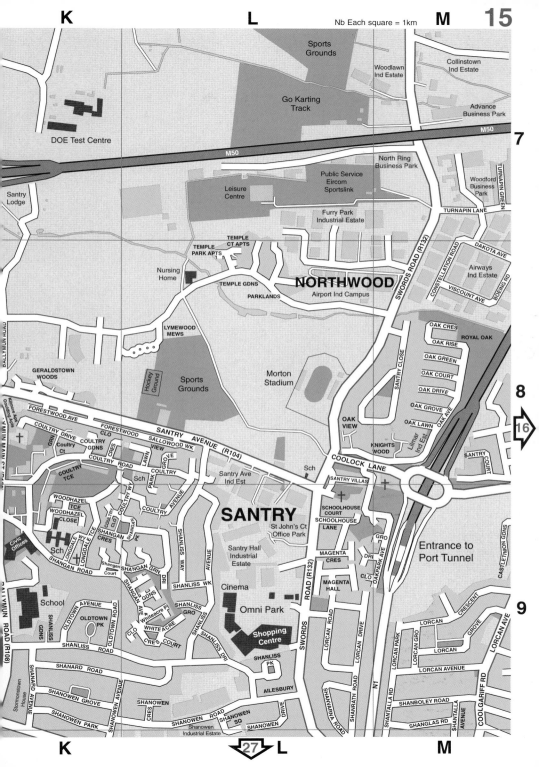

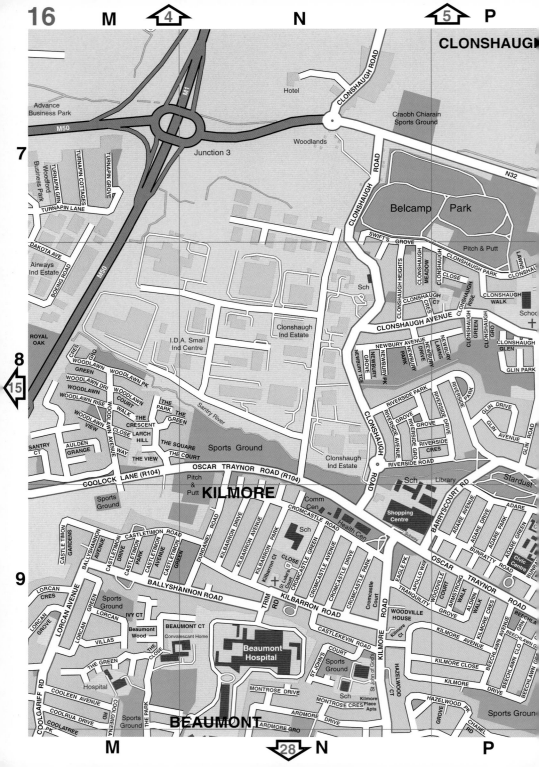

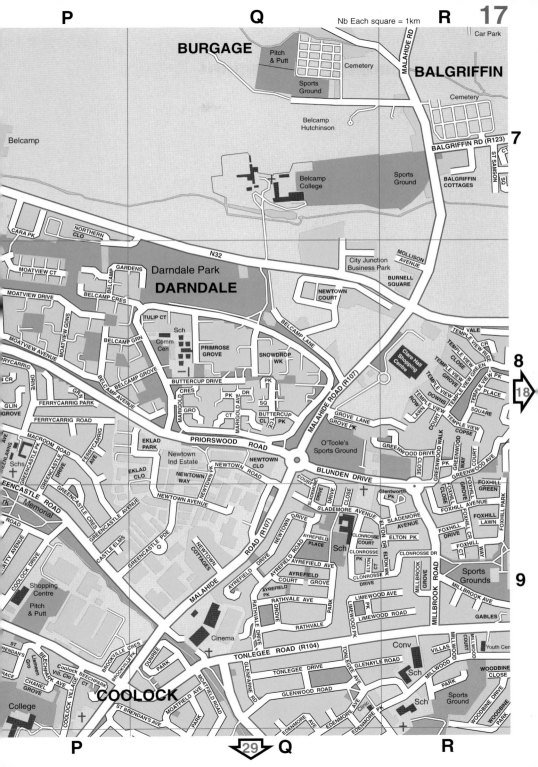

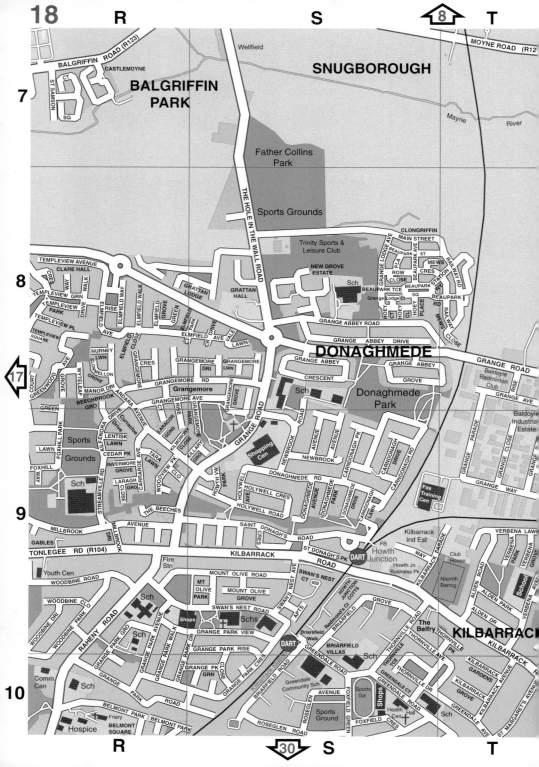

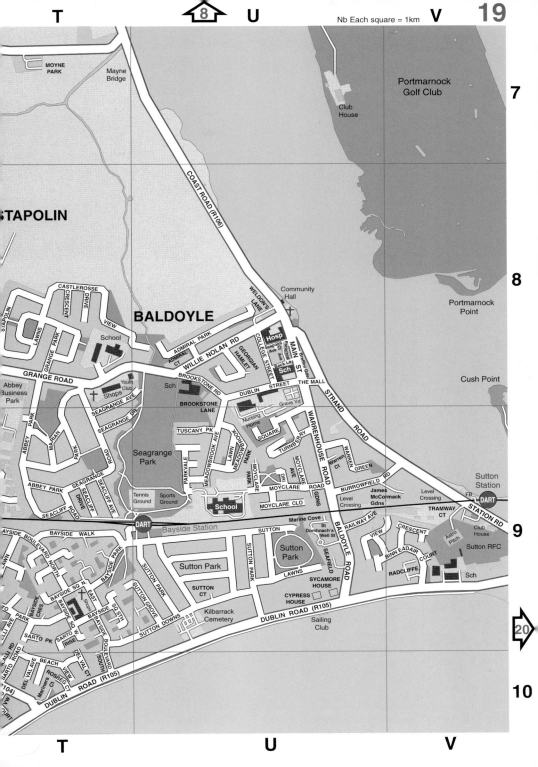

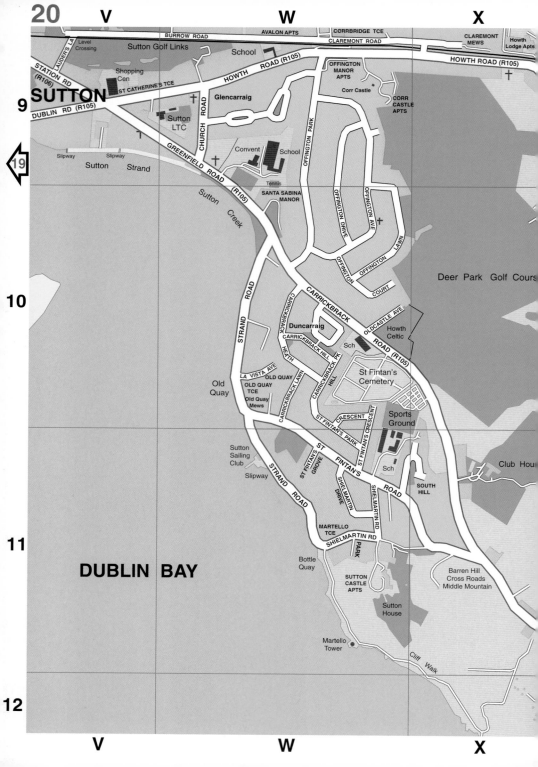

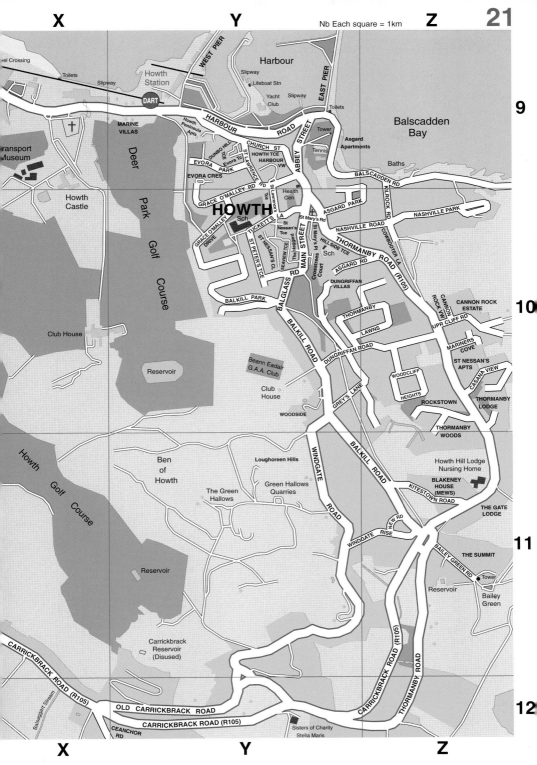

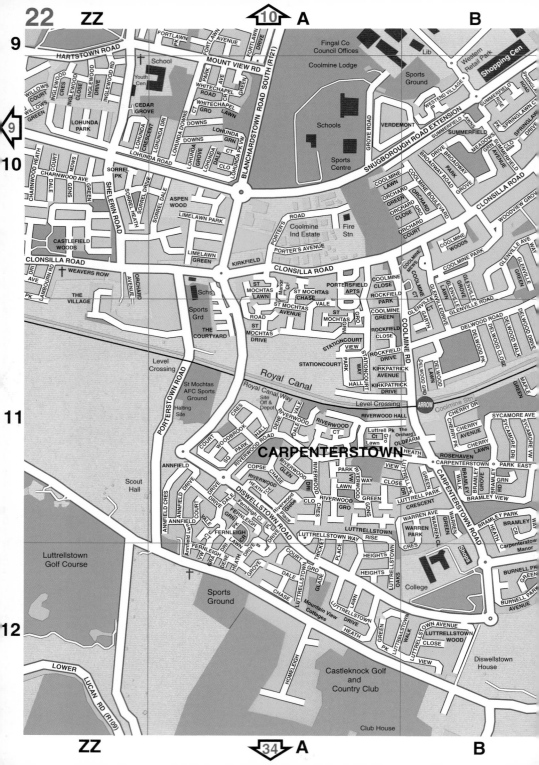

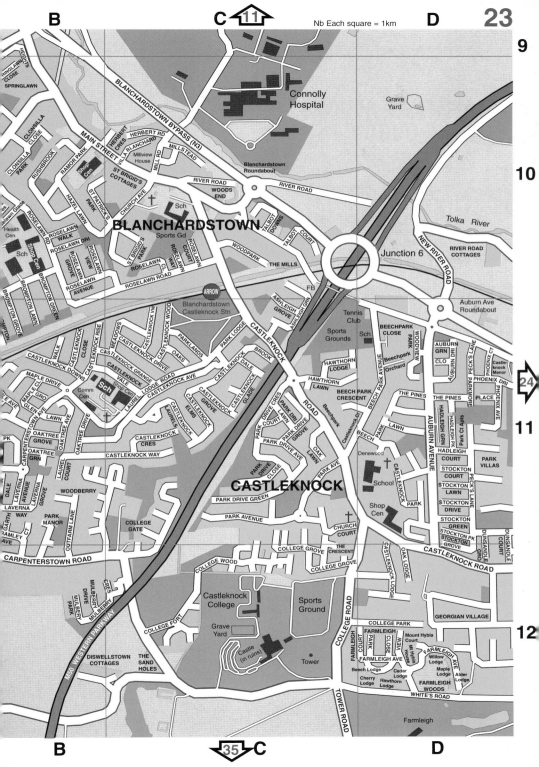

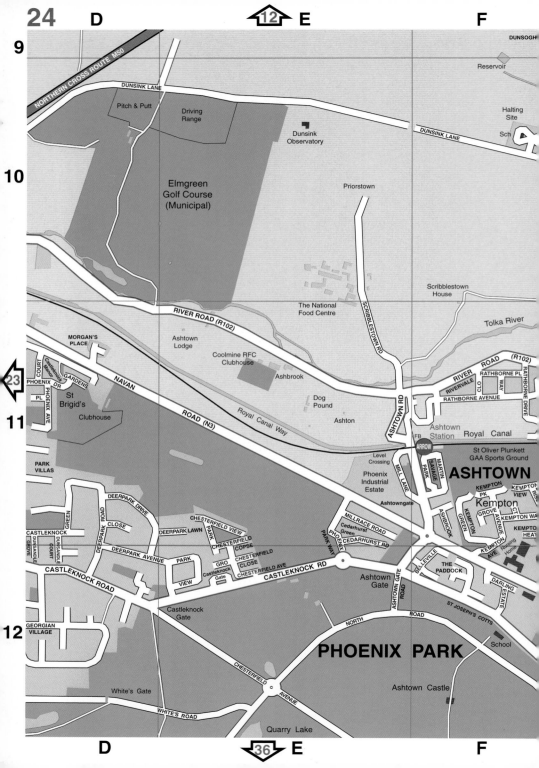

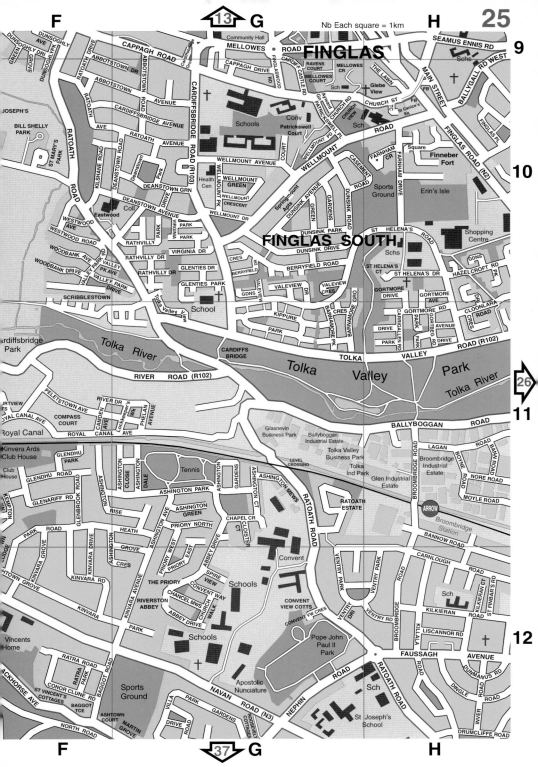

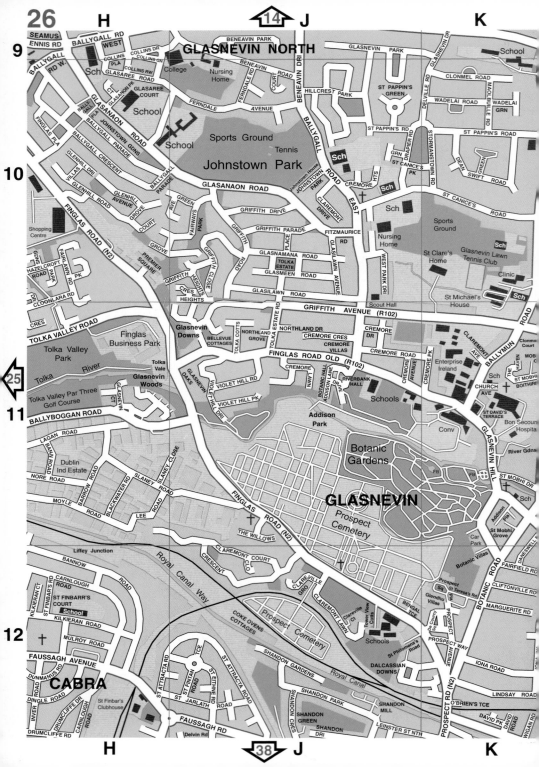

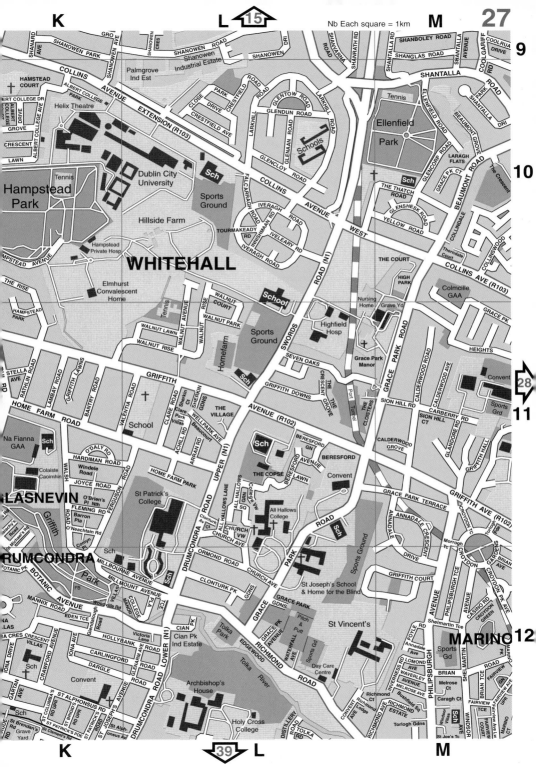

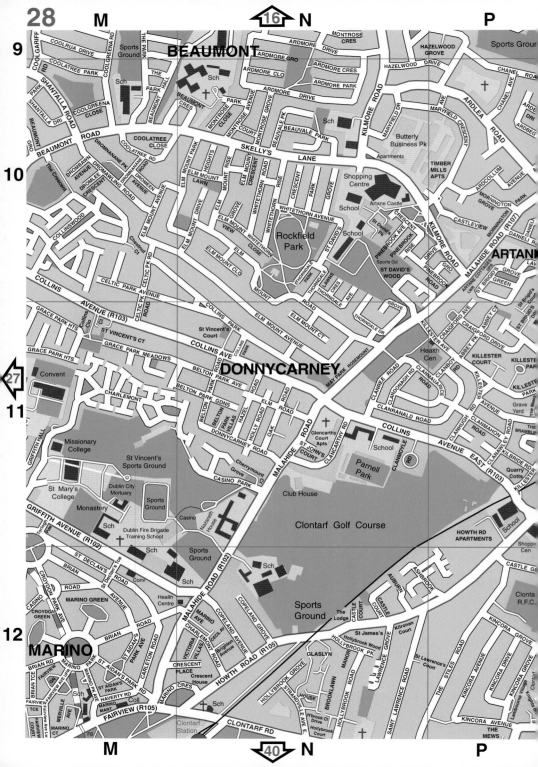

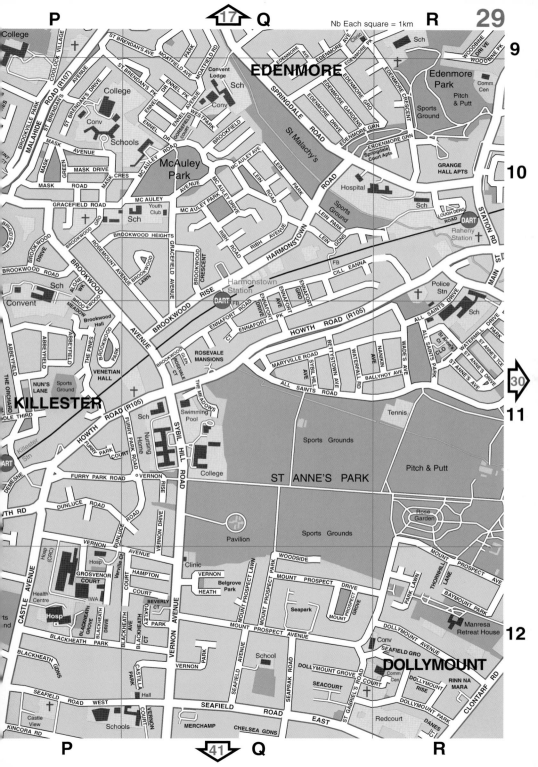

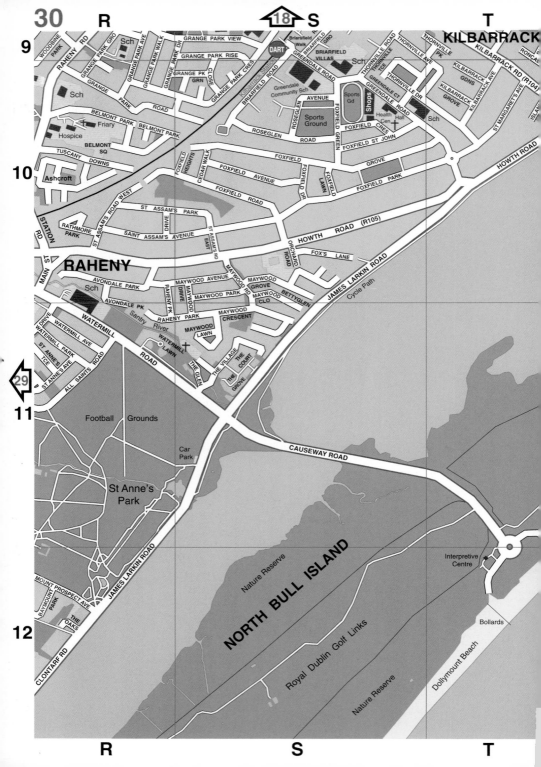

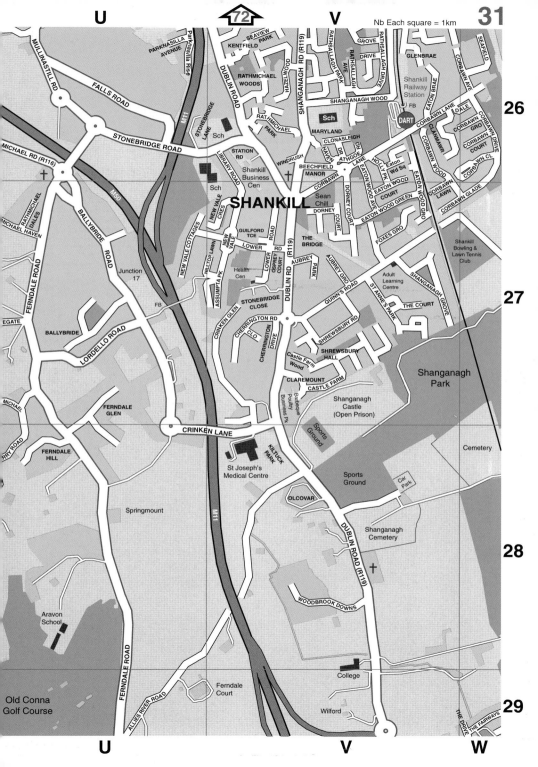

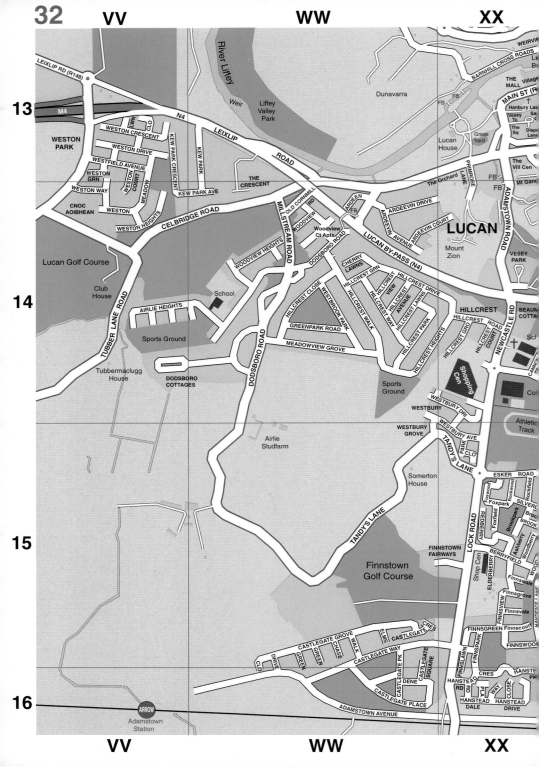

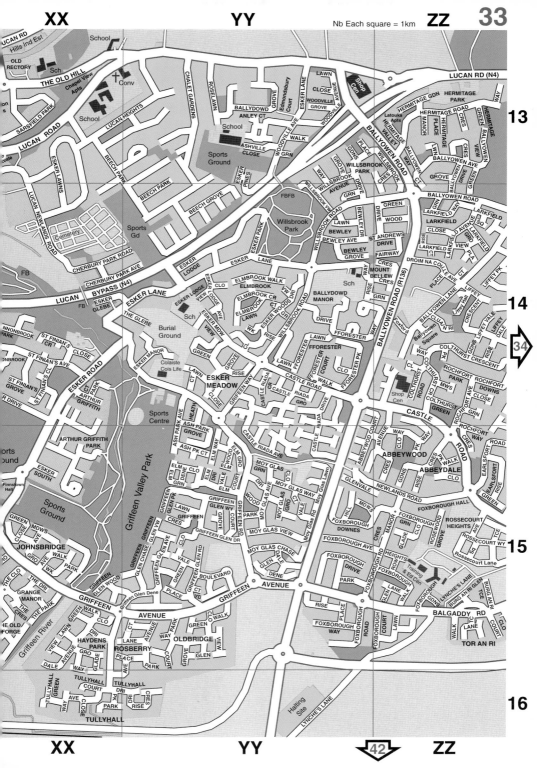

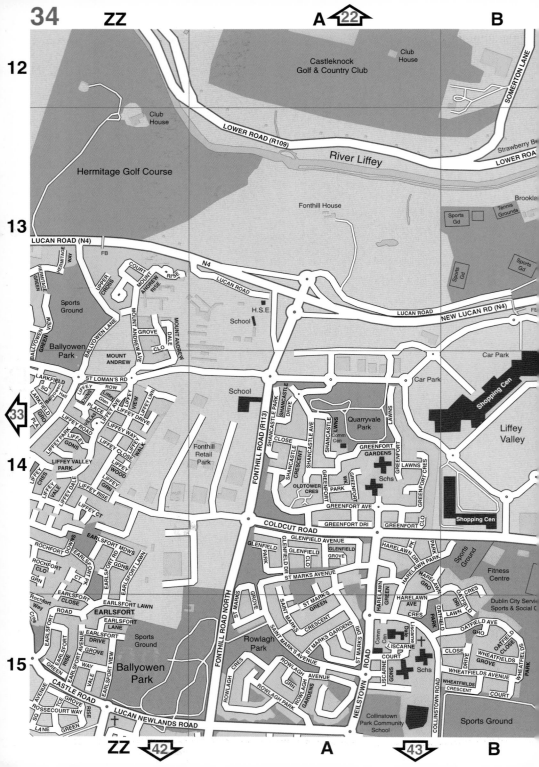

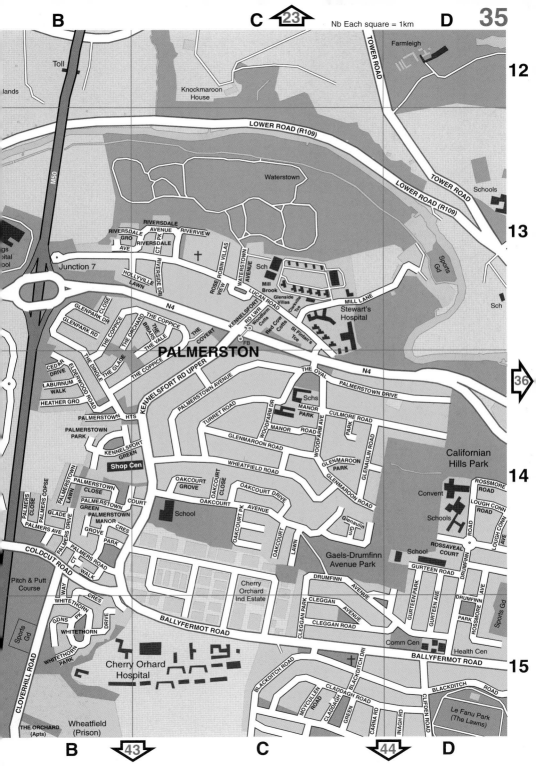

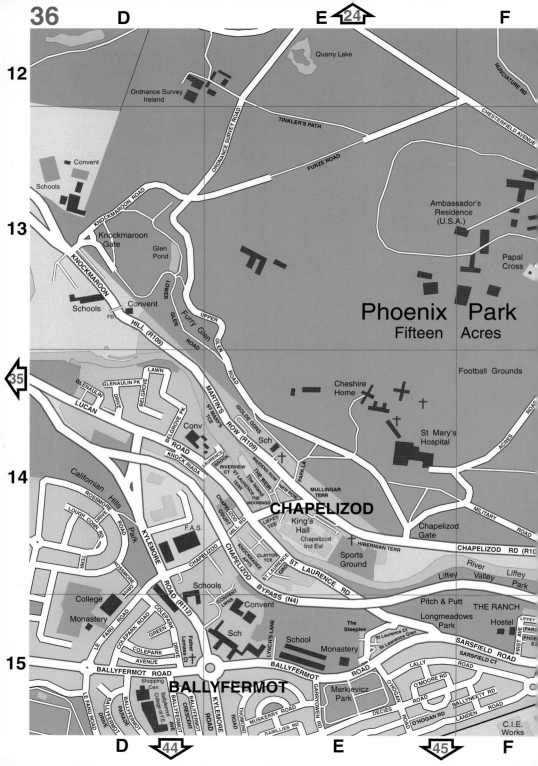

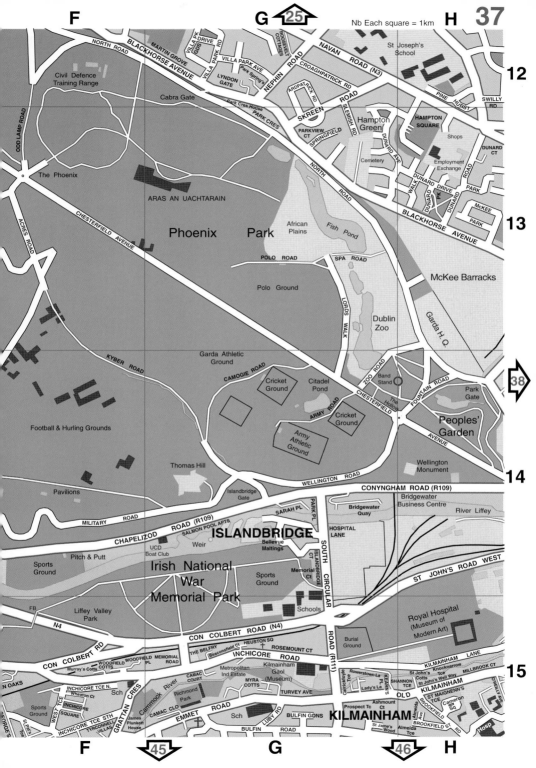

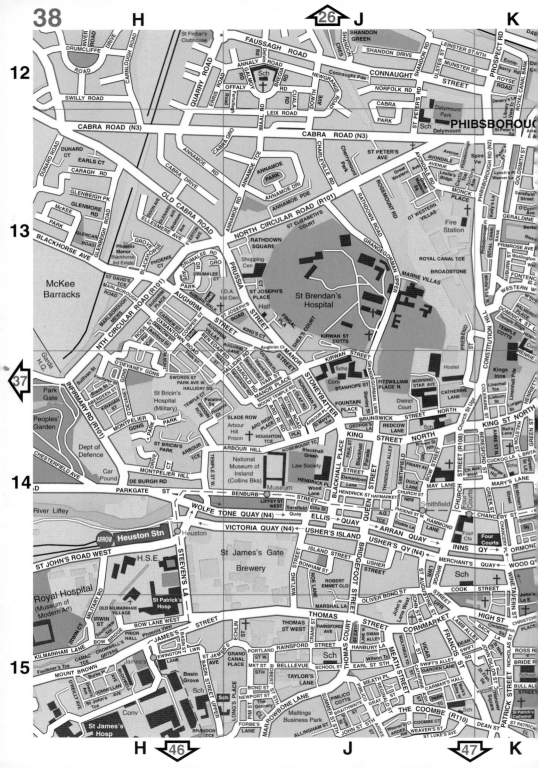

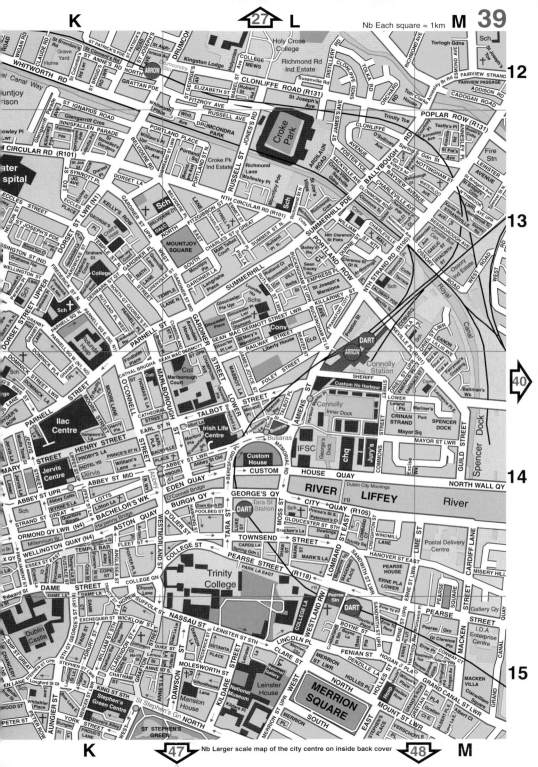

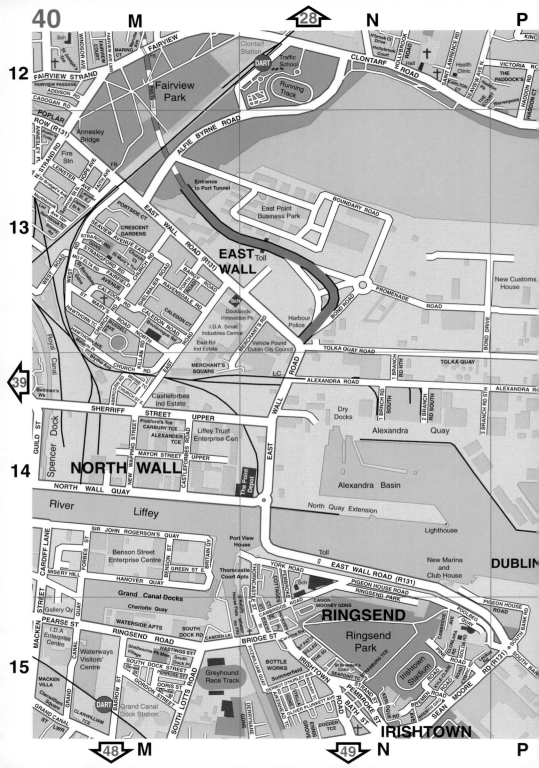

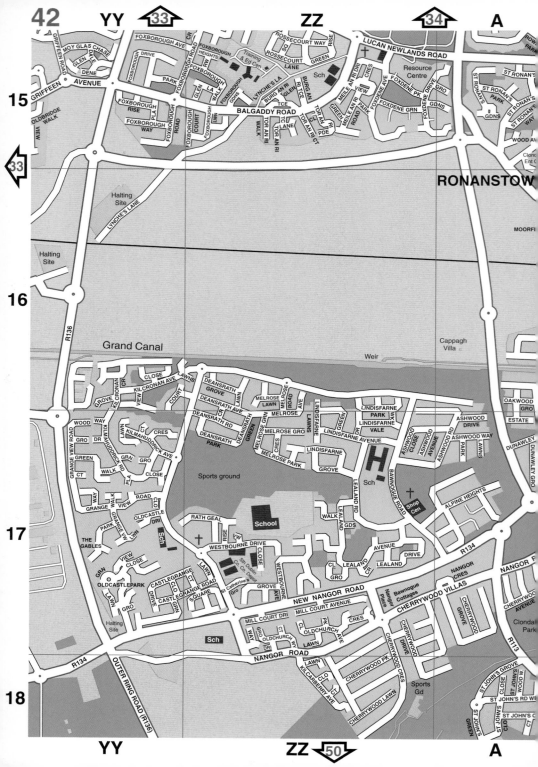

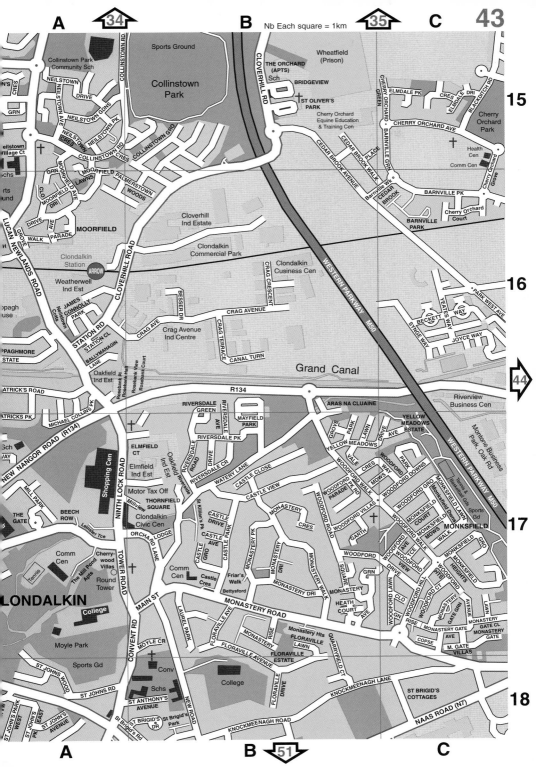

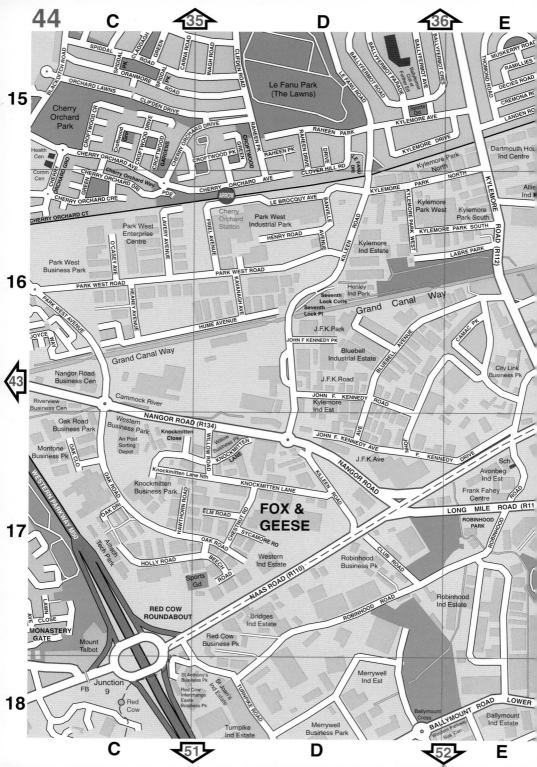

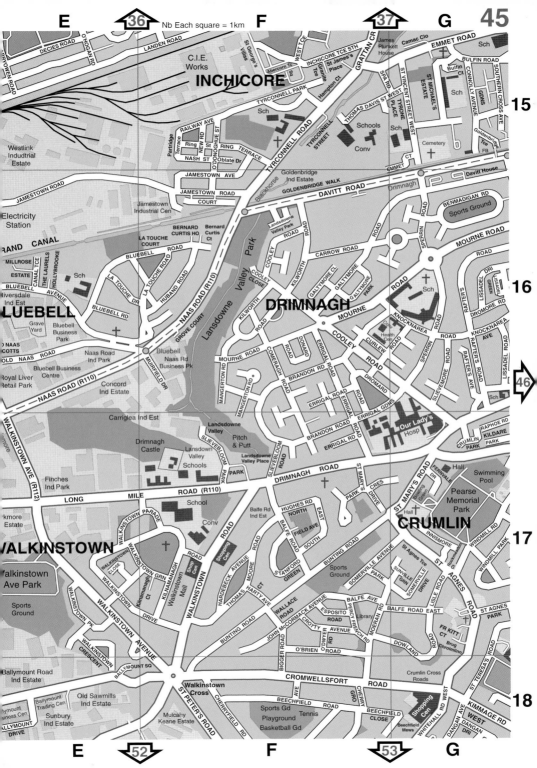

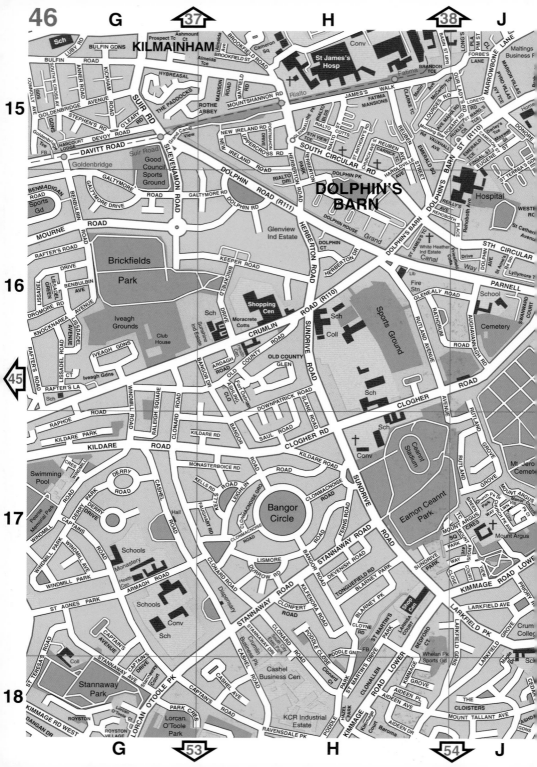

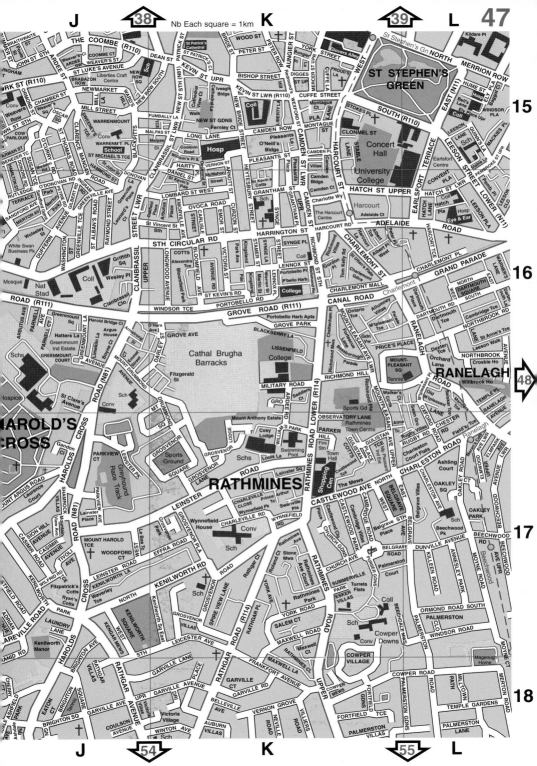

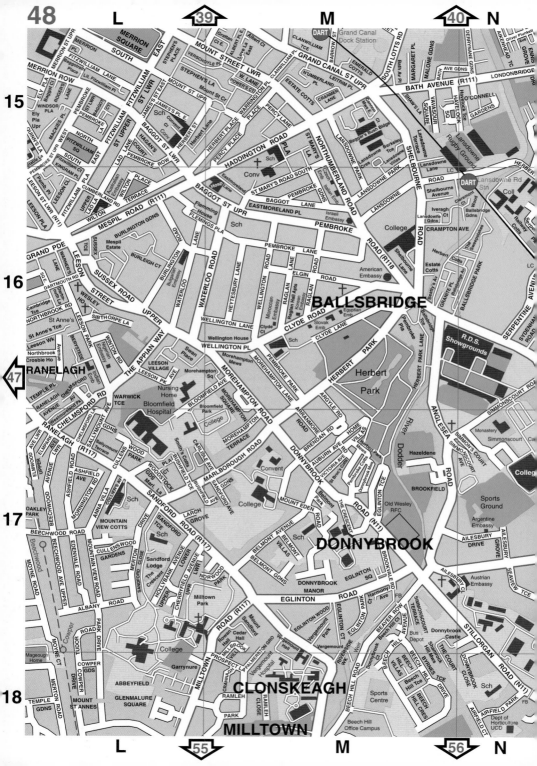

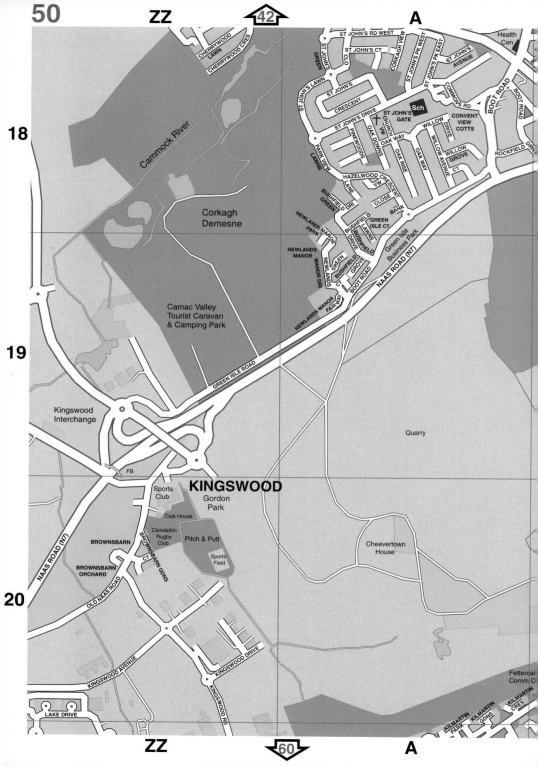

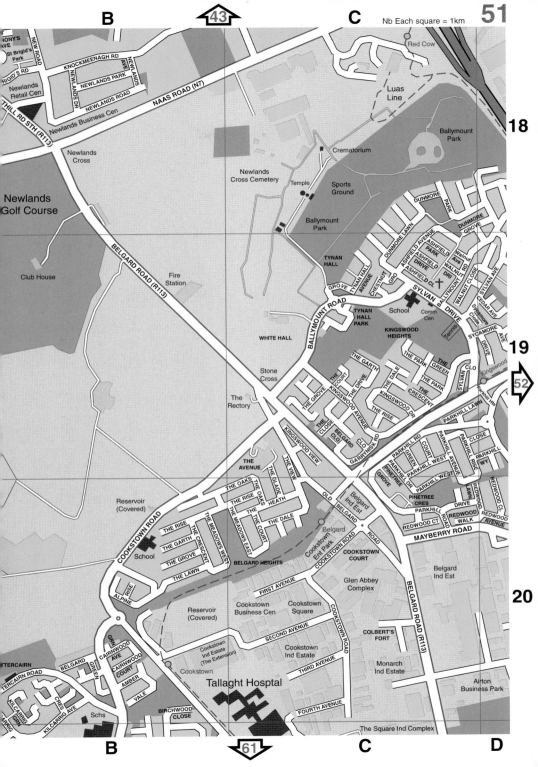

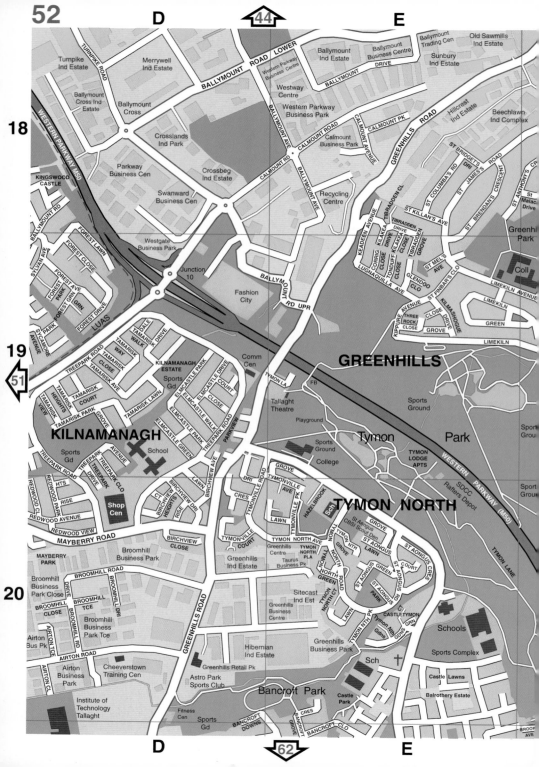

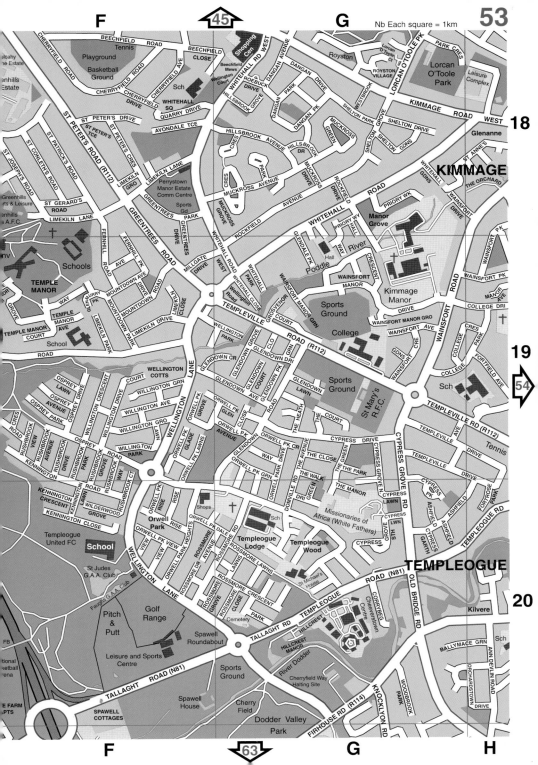

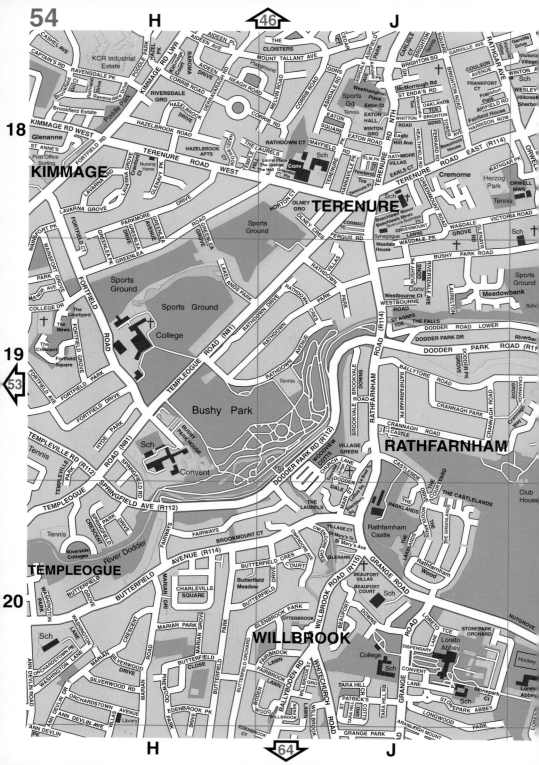

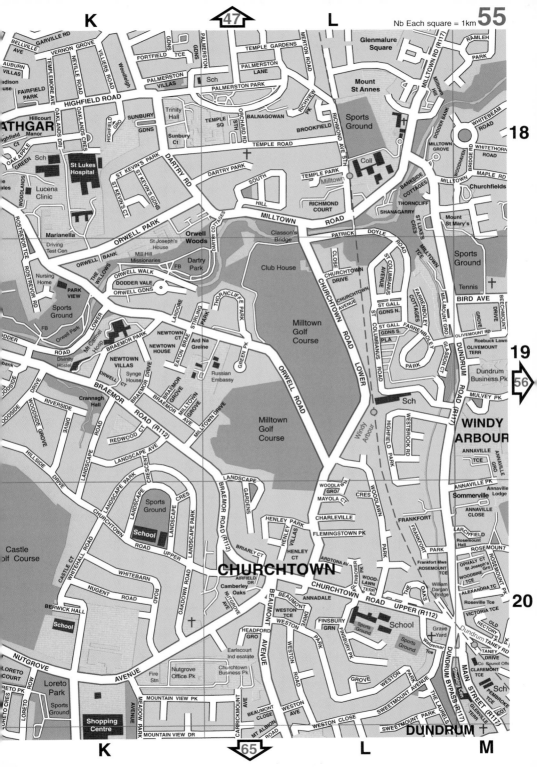

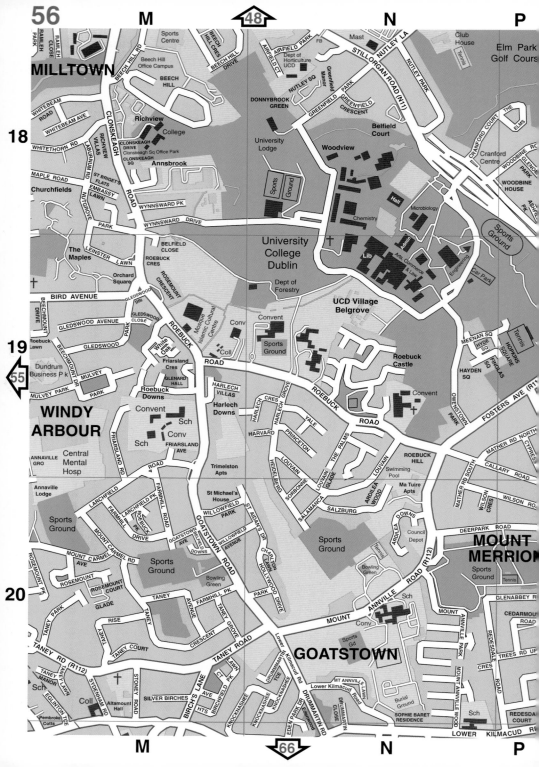

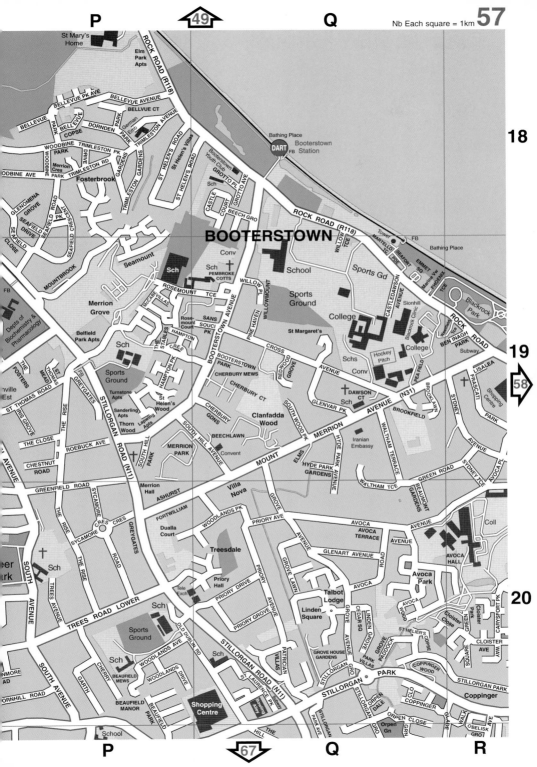

BOOTERSTOWN

18

19

58

20

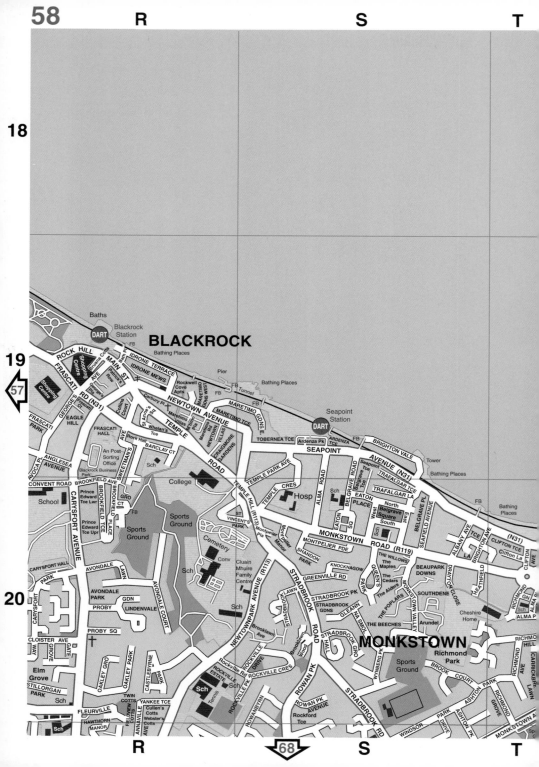

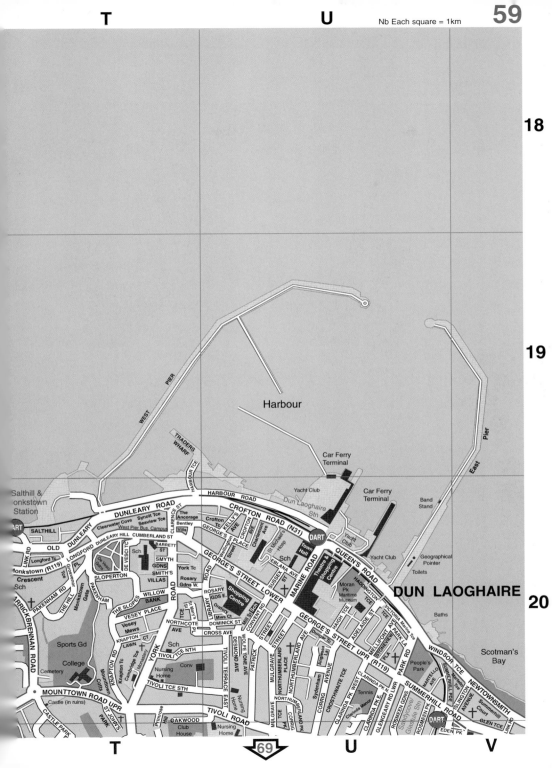

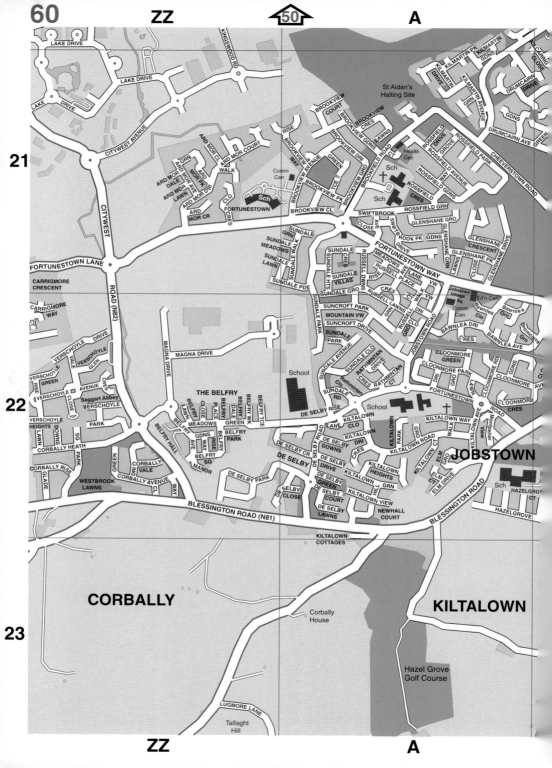

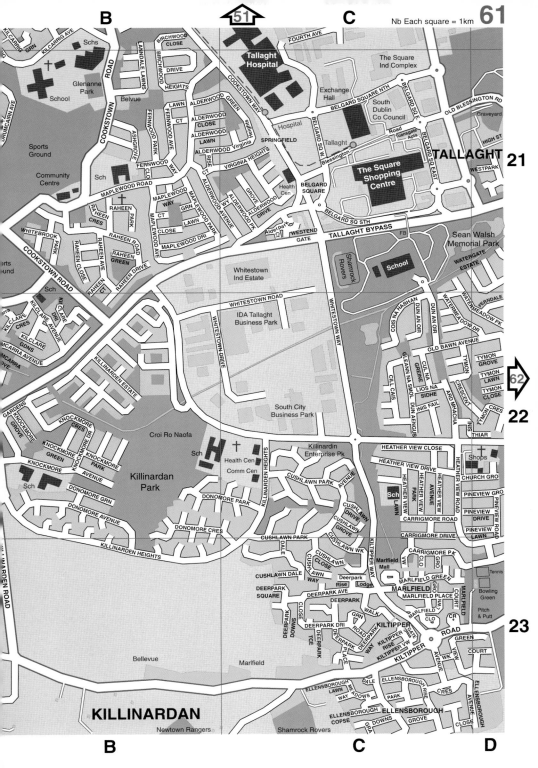

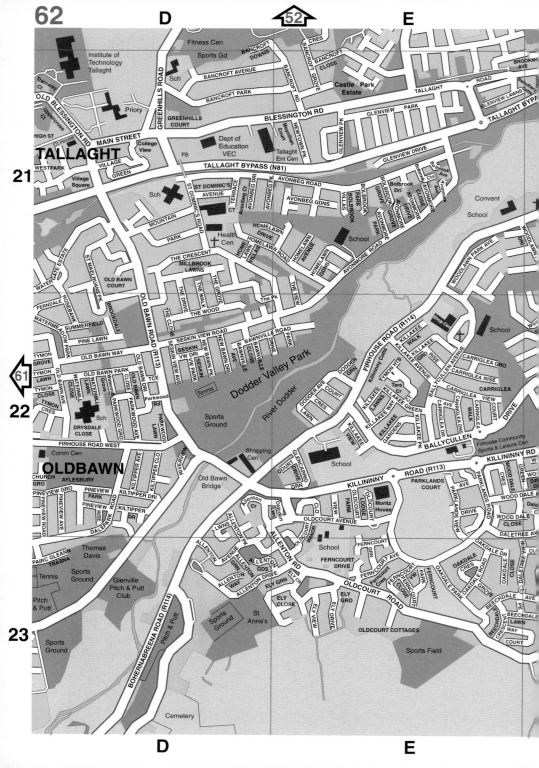

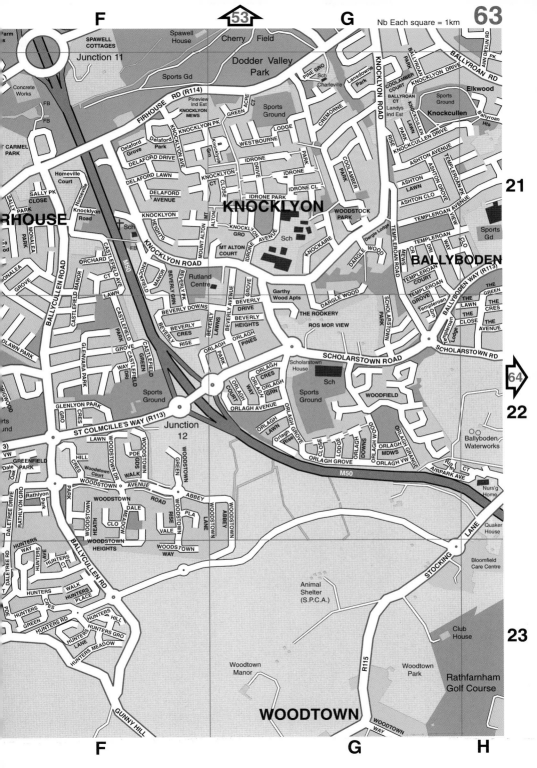

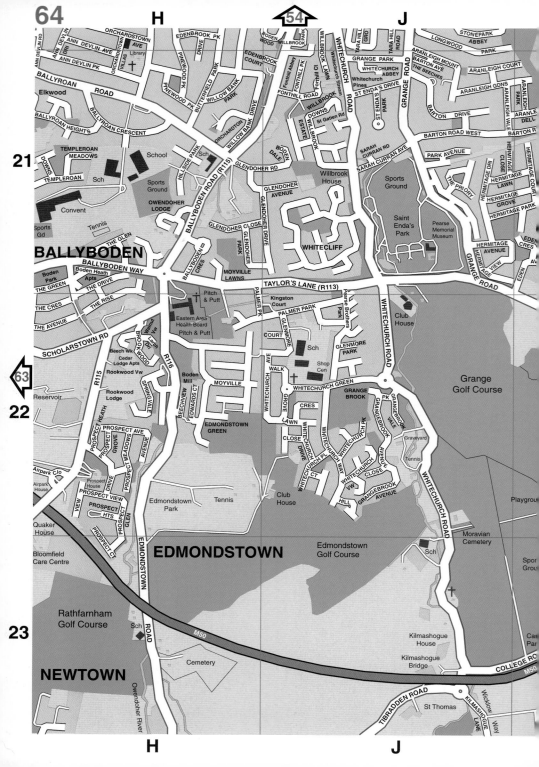

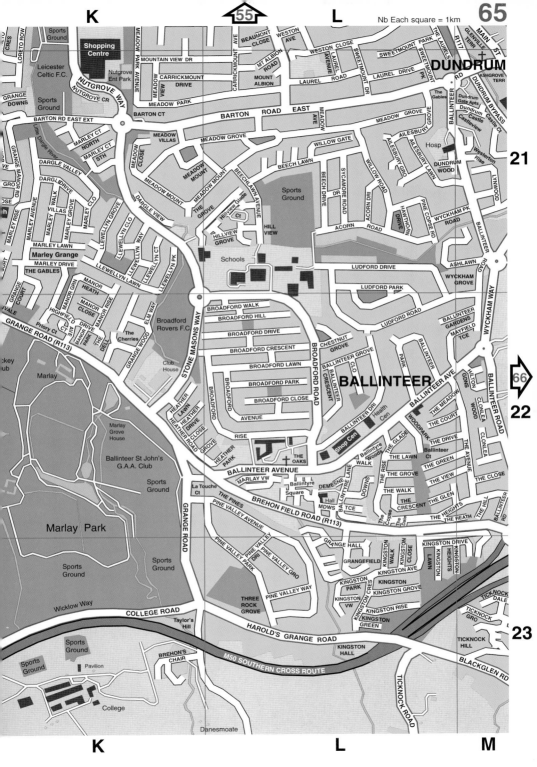

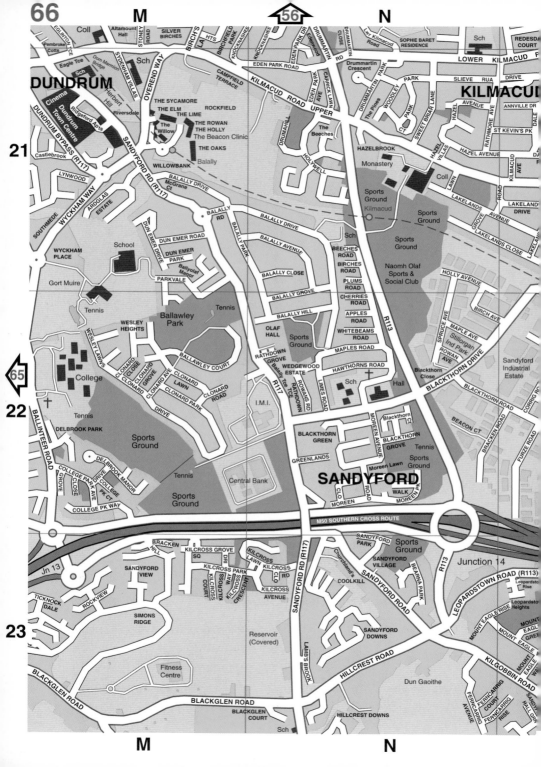

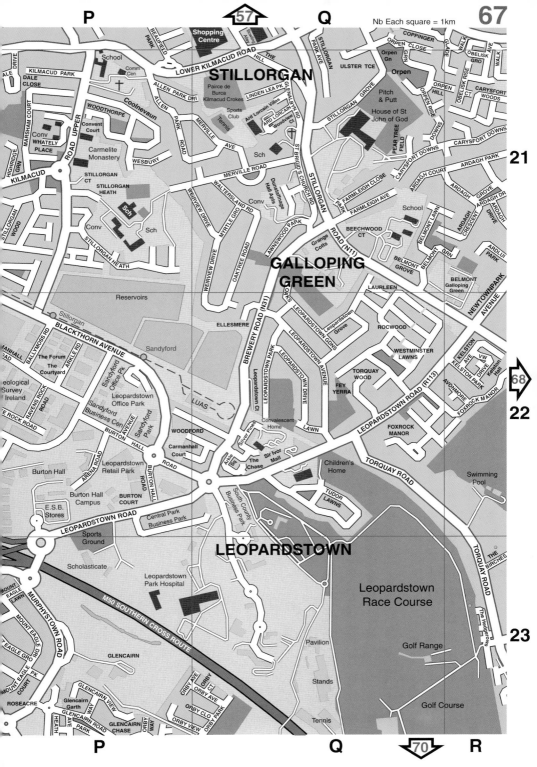

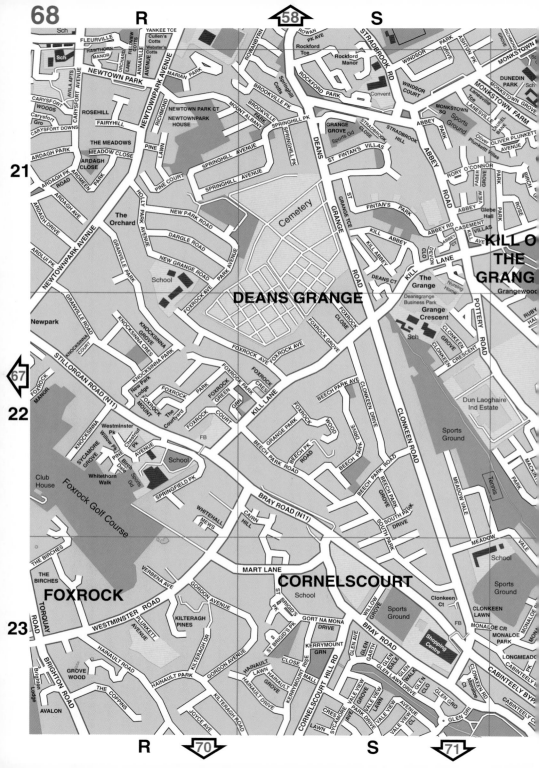

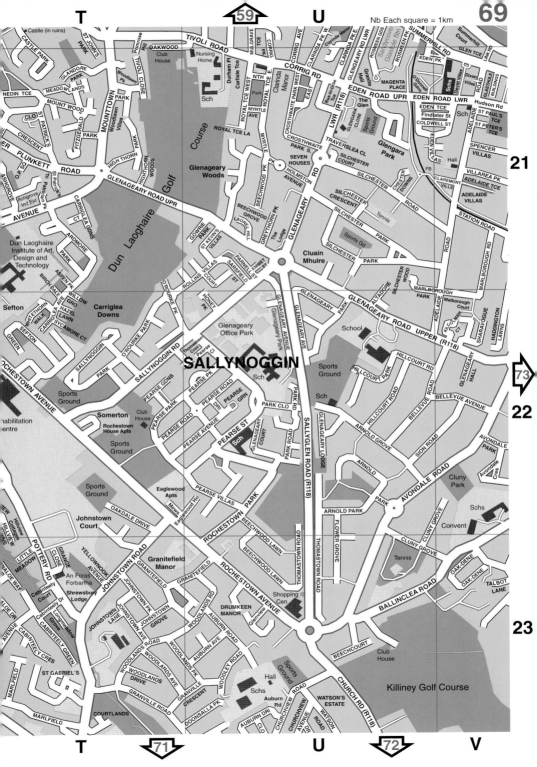

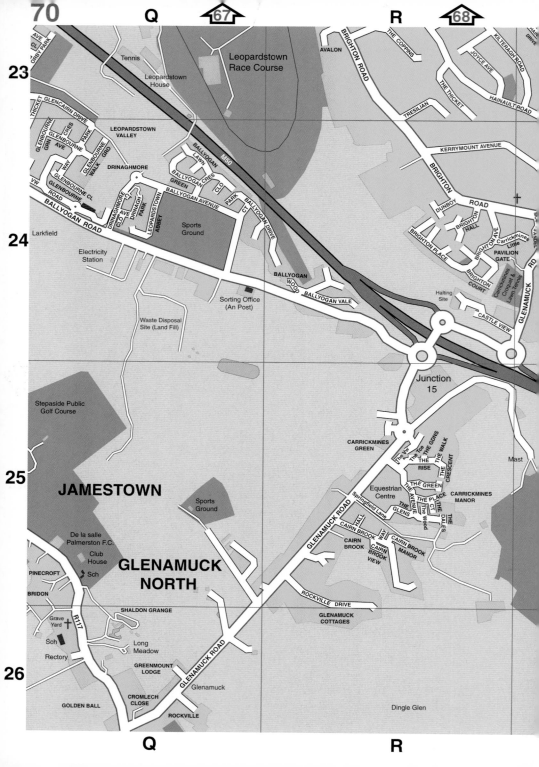

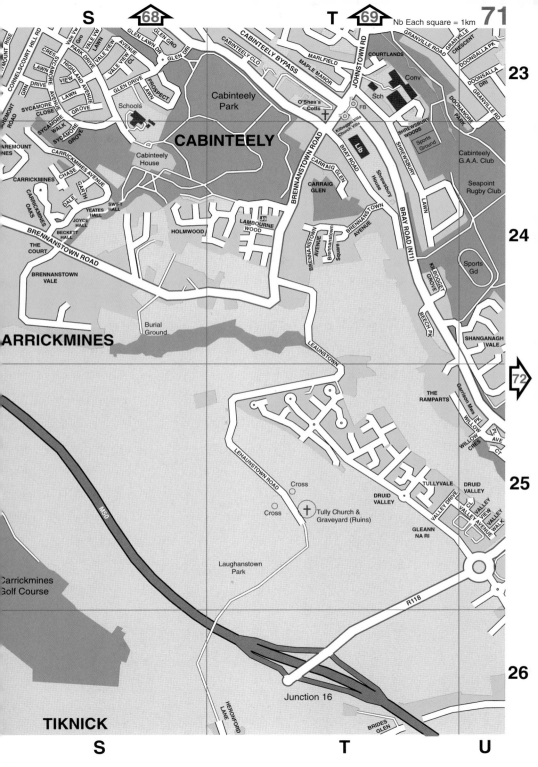

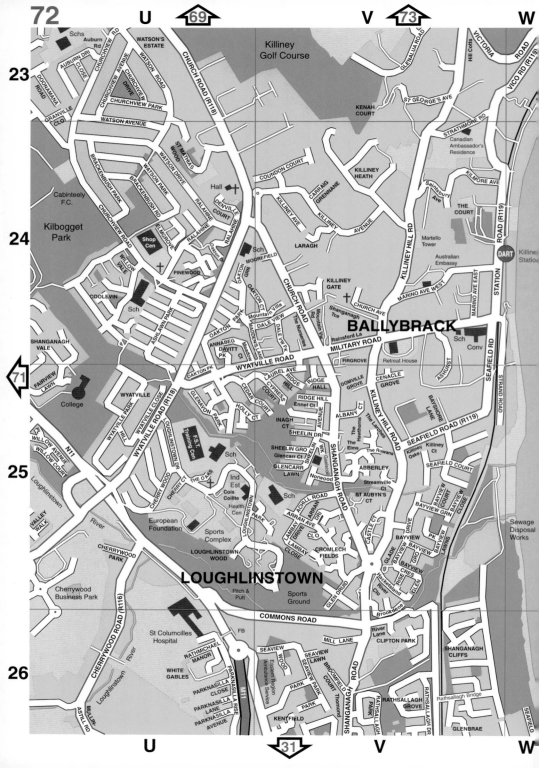

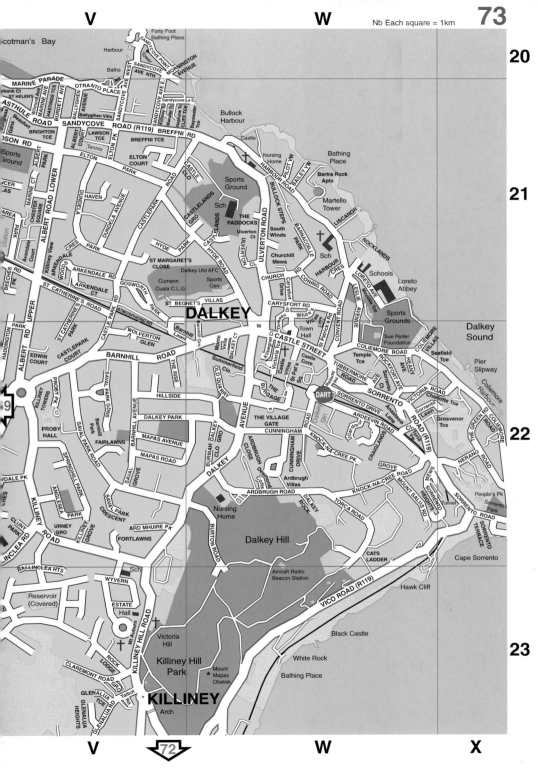

Due to insufficient space, some streets and/or their names have been omitted from the street map. Street names below which are prefixed by a * are not represented on the map, but they can be located by referring in the index to the name of the street which follows in brackets.

Page   **Grid Ref**

40 1 Branch Road Nth **N14**
40 1 Branch Road Sth **N14**
41 2 Branch Road Nth **P14**
40 2 Branch Road Sth **N14**
40 3 Branch Road Sth **N14**
41 4 Branch Road Sth **P14**
54 *A.W. Pugin House **J20**
   (Stonepark Court)
72 Abberley **V15**
39 Abbey Cottages **K14**
28 Abbey Ct (Killester) **P11**
68 Abbey Ct (Monkstown) **S21**
25 Abbey Drive **G12**
19 Abbey Pk (Baldoyle) **T9**
68 Abbey Park **S21**
   (Kill O' the Grange)
28 Abbey Pk (Killester) **P11**
68 Abbey Road **S21**
21 Abbey St (Howth) **Y9**
39 Abbey St Lower **L14**
39 Abbey St Middle **K14**
39 Abbey St Old **L14**
39 Abbey St Upper **K14**
21 *Abbey Tce **Y9**
   (Harbour Road)
68 Abbey View **S21**
33 Abbeydale **ZZ15**
33 Abbeydale Close **ZZ15**
33 Abbeydale Crescent **ZZ15**
33 Abbeydale Gardens **ZZ15**
33 Abbeydale Park **ZZ15**
33 Abbeydale Rise **ZZ15**
33 Abbeydale Walk **ZZ15**
48 Abbeyfield (Clonskeagh) **L18**
29 Abbeyfield (Killester) **P11**
2 Abbeylea Ave **M1**
2 Abbeylea Close **M1**
2 Abbeylea Drive **M1**
2 Abbeylea Green **M1**
2 Abbeyvale Ave **L1**
2 Abbeyvale Close **L1**
2 Abbeyvale Court **L1**
2 Abbeyvale Cres **L1**
2 Abbeyvale Drive **L1**
2 Abbeyvale Green **L1**
2 Abbeyvale Grove **L1**
2 Abbeyvale Lawn **L1**
2 Abbeyvale Place **L1**
2 Abbeyvale Rise **L1**
2 Abbeyvale View **L1**
2 Abbeyvale Way **L1**
33 Abbeywood **ZZ15**
33 Abbeywood Ave **ZZ15**
33 Abbeywood Close **ZZ15**
33 Abbeywood Court **YY15**
33 Abbeywood Cres **ZZ15**
33 Abbeywood Pk **ZZ15**
33 Abbeywood Way **ZZ15**
7 Abbots Hill **T3**
25 Abbotstown Ave **F10**
13 Abbotstown Drive **F9**
25 Abbotstown Rd **G10**
40 Abercorn Road **M14**
45 Abercorn Square **F15**
45 Abercorn Terrace **F15**
38 Aberdeen Street **H14**
6 Abington **Q3**
27 Achill Rd (Drumcondra) **L11**
72 Achill Road **V25**
   (Loughlinstown)
65 Acorn Drive **L21**
65 Acorn Road **L21**
36 Acres Road **F14**
49 Adair **N16**
39 *Adair Lane **K13**
   (off Dorset Street)
39 *Adair Terrace **K13**
   (on St Joseph's Parade)
39 *Adam Court **K13**
   (off Grafton Street)
32 Adamstown Ave **WW16**
32 Adamstown Rd **XX14**
16 Adare Avenue **P9**
16 Adare Drive **P9**
16 Adare Green **P9**
16 Adare Park **P9**
16 Adare Road **P9**
26 Addison Drive **J11**
26 Addison Lane **J11**
26 Addison Park **J11**
26 Addison Place **K11**

40 Addison Road **M12**
47 Adelaide Ct **K16**
48 Adelaide Mews **P17**
69 Adelaide Road **V22**
   (Dun Laoghaire)
47 Adelaide Road **K16**
   (Leeson Street)
59 Adelaide Street **U20**
69 Adelaide Terrace **V21**
   (Dun Laoghaire)
37 *Adelaide Terrace **H15**
   (off Brookfield Road)
69 Adelaide Villas **V21**
   (Dun Laoghaire)
19 Admiral Court **U8**
19 Admiral Park **U8**
47 Adrian Avenue **J17**
61 *Aengus Hall **C21**
   (Belgard Square)
46 Aideen Avenue **H18**
46 Aideen Drive **H18**
46 Aideen Place **H18**
40 Aikenhead Tce **N15**
15 Ailesbury **L9**
48 Ailesbury Close **M17**
48 Ailesbury Drive **N17**
49 Ailesbury Gardens **P17**
48 Ailesbury Grove **N17**
   (Donnybrook)
65 Ailesbury Grove **L21**
   (Dundrum)
49 *Ailesbury Lane **N17**
   (off Ailesbury Road)
65 Ailesbury Lawn **L21**
48 Ailesbury Mews **P17**
49 Ailesbury Park **P17**
49 Ailesbury Road **N17**
49 Ailesbury Wood **N17**
48 Airfield Court **N18**
55 Airfield Drive **L20**
48 Airfield Park **N18**
54 Airfield Road **J18**
32 Airlie Heights **VV14**
63 Airpark Avenue **G22**
64 Airpark Close **H22**
63 Airpark Court **G22**
64 *Airpark House **H22**
   (Airpark Close)
63 Airpark Rise **G22**
3 Airside **N3**
52 Airton Close **D20**
52 Airton Road **D20**
52 Airton Terrace **D20**
58 Albany Avenue **S20**
72 Albany Court **V25**
48 Albany Road **L17**
27 Albert College Ave **K10**
27 Albert College Court **K10**
27 Albert College Cres **K10**
27 Albert College Drive **K10**
27 Albert College Grove **K10**
27 Albert College Lawn **K10**
27 Albert College Park **K10**
39 Albert Court **M15**
   (Grand Canal St Lower)
73 Albert Court **V21**
   (Sandycove Road)
73 Albert Park **V21**
39 Albert Place East **M15**
47 Albert Place West **K16**
73 Albert Road Lower **V21**
73 Albert Road Upper **V22**
47 Albert Terrace **K16**
   (Charlemont Street)
59 *Albert Terrace **U20**
   (Kelly's Avenue)
39 *Aldborough House **L13**
   (St Joseph's Mansions)
39 Aldborough Parade **L13**
39 Aldborough Place **L13**
39 *Aldborough Square **L13**
   (off Aldborough Road)
39 Aldemere **YY10**
18 Alden Drive **T9**
18 Alden Park **T9**
18 Alden Road **T9**
8 Alder Court **U4**
23 Alder Lodge **D12**
61 Alderpark Court **C21**
61 Alderwood Ave **B21**
61 Alderwood Close **B21**

61 Alderwood Court **B21**
61 Alderwood Drive **C21**
61 Alderwood Green **B21**
61 Alderwood Grove **C21**
61 Alderwood Lawn **B21**
61 Alderwood Park **C21**
61 Alderwood Rise **B21**
61 Alderwood Way **C21**
16 Aldrin Walk **P9**
61 *Alen Hall **C21**
   (Belgard Square)
40 Alexander Terrace **M14**
   (North Wall)
55 *Alexandra Court **M20**
   (Alexandra Terrace)
40 *Alexandra Quay **N14**
   (York Road)
40 Alexandra Road **N14**
41 Alexandra Road Ext **Q14**
55 Alexandra Terrace **M20**
   (Dundrum)
47 Alexandra Tce **K16**
   (Portobello)
54 Alexandra Terrace **J18**
   (Terenure)
55 *Alexandra Villas **M20**
   (Alexandra Terrace)
40 Alfie Byrne Rd **M13**
27 All Hallows Green **L11**
27 All Hallows Lane **L11**
29 All Saint's Close **R11**
29 All Saints Drive **R11**
29 All Saints Park **R11**
29 All Saints Road **Q11**
67 Allen Park Drive **P21**
67 Allen Park Road **P21**
38 *Allen Terrace **J13**
   (off Avondale Ave)
9 Allendale Close **YY10**
9 Allendale Copse **YY9**
9 Allendale Court **YY9**
9 Allendale Drive **YY9**
9 Allendale Elms **YY9**
9 Allendale Glen **YY9**
9 Allendale Green **YY9**
9 Allendale Grove **YY9**
9 Allendale Heath **YY10**
9 Allendale Lawn **YY9**
9 Allendale Place **YY9**
9 Allendale Rise **YY9**
9 Allendale Square **YY10**
9 Allendale Terrace **YY9**
9 Allendale View **YY9**
9 Allendale Walk **YY9**
62 Allenton Avenue **D23**
62 Allenton Crescent **D22**
62 Allenton Drive **D23**
62 Allenton Gardens **D23**
62 Allenton Green **D23**
62 Allenton Lawns **D22**
62 Allenton Park **D22**
62 Allenton Road **E23**
62 Allenton Way **D23**
31 Allies River Rd **U29**
38 Allingham Street **J15**
58 Alma Park **T20**
58 Alma Place **T20**
58 Alma Road **S20**
47 Alma Terrace **K17**
58 Almeida Avenue **H15**
37 Almeida Terrace **H15**
29 Alone Walk **P10**
42 Alpine Heights **A17**
51 Alpine Rise **B20**
69 Altadore **U22**
56 Altamont Hall **M20**
40 Alverno **P12**
51 Amber Vale **B20**
10 Amberwood **A8**
39 Amiens Street **L14**
73 Anastasia Lane **W22**
48 *Anglers Rest **M17**
   (Simmonscourt Terrace)
58 Anglesea Avenue **R19**
59 Anglesea Lane **U20**
73 Anglesea Rd **V22**
58 Anglesea Road **N17**
58 Anglesea Row **K14**
39 Anglesea Street **K14**
57 Anley Court **YY13**
54 Ann Devlin Ave **H20**

54 Ann Devlin Drive **H22**
64 Ann Devlin Park **H21**
54 Ann Devlin Rd **H20**
48 Anna Villa **L17**
72 Annabeg **U24**
55 Annadale **L20**
27 Annadale Ave **M12**
27 Annadale Cres **M11**
27 Annadale Drive **M11**
11 Annagh Court **C9**
9 Annaly Close **YY9**
9 Annaly Court **YY9**
9 Annaly Drive **YY9**
9 Annaly Grove **YY9**
38 Annaly Road **J12**
38 Annaly Terrace **YY9**
38 Annamoe Drive **H13**
38 Annamoe Parade **J13**
38 Annamoe Park **J13**
38 Annamoe Road **J13**
38 Annamoe Terrace **J13**
58 Annaville Avenue **R21**
55 Annaville Close **M19**
55 Annaville Grove **M19**
55 Annaville Lodge **M20**
55 Annaville Park **M20**
55 Annaville Terrace **M19**
14 Anne Street North **K14**
39 Anne Street South **K15**
46 Anner Road **G15**
39 Anne's Lane **K15**
39 Annesley Avenue **M13**
39 Annesley Bridge Rd **M12**
47 Annesley Park **L17**
40 Annesley Place **M13**
22 Annfield **A10**
22 Annfield Court **A10**
22 Annfield Cres **A10**
22 Annfield Drive **A10**
22 Annfield Lawn **A11**
56 Annsbrook **M18**
66 Annville Drive **P21**
16 Apollo Way **N9**
48 *Appian Close **L16**
   (on Leeson Park)
66 Apples Road **N22**
64 Aranleigh Court **J21**
64 Aranleigh Dell **K21**
64 Aranleigh Gardens **J21**
54 Aranleigh Mount **J20**
64 Aranleigh Park **K21**
64 Aranleigh Vale **J21**
43 Aras na Cluaine **B16**
38 Arbour Hill **J14**
38 Arbour Place **J14**
38 Arbour Terrace **H14**
47 Arbutus Avenue **J16**
47 Arbutus Place **K16**
67 Ard Lorcain **Q21**
67 Ard Lorcain Villas **Q21**
61 Ard Mhacha **C22**
73 Ard Mhuire Park **V22**
60 Ard Mor Avenue **ZZ21**
60 Ard Mor Close **ZZ21**
60 Ard Mor Court **ZZ21**
60 Ard Mor Crescent **ZZ21**
60 Ard Mor Dale **ZZ21**
60 Ard Mor Drive **ZZ21**
60 Ard Mor Green **ZZ21**
60 Ard Mor Lawn **ZZ21**
60 Ard Mor Park **ZZ21**
60 Ard Mor Walk **ZZ21**
55 Ard Na Greine **K19**
6 Ard na Mara **R3**
14 Ard na Meala **K8**
38 Ard Ri Road **J14**
38 Ard Righ Place **J14**
68 Ardagh Avenue **R21**
68 Ardagh Close **R21**
67 Ardagh Court **Q21**
67 Ardagh Crescent **R21**
68 Ardagh Drive **R21**
67 Ardagh Grove **R21**
68 Ardagh Park **R21**
68 Ardagh Park Road **R21**
46 Ardagh Road **H16**
18 Ardara Avenue **R8**
29 Ardbeg Crescent **P10**
28 Ardbeg Drive **P10**
28 Ardbeg Park **P10**
28 Ardbeg Road **P10**

Page		Grid Ref
73	Ardbrugh Close	W22
73	Ardbrugh Road	W22
73	Ardbrugh Villas	W22
2	Ardcian Park	M1
28	Ardcollum Avenue	P10
47	Ardee Grove	K16
47	Ardee Road	K16
38	Ardee Row	J15
38	Ardee St	J15
32	Ardeen	WW14
32	Ardeevin Avenue	WW14
32	Ardeevin Court	WW14
32	Ardeevin Drive	WW14
73	Ardeevin Road	W22
73	*Ardeevin Terrace	W22
	(off Ardeevin Road)	
58	Ardenza Park	S19
58	Ardenza Terrace	S19
66	Ardglas Estate	M21
8	Ardilaun	T5
39	Ardilaun Road	L13
39	*Ardilaun Square	L13
	(off Sackville Avenue)	
56	Ardilea Downs	N20
56	Ardilea Wood	N20
28	Ardlea Road	P10
67	Ardlui Park	R21
68	Ardmeen Park	R21
47	Ardmore Avenue	H13
28	Ardmore Close	N10
28	Ardmore Cres	N10
28	Ardmore Drive	N9
28	Ardmore Grove	N9
28	Ardmore Pk (Artane)	N10
69	Ardmore Park	T21
	(Kill O' the Grange)	
37	Ardpatrick Road	G12
55	Ardtona Avenue	L20
67	Arena Road	P22
47	Argus House	J16
48	Argyle Road	M16
73	Arkendale Court	V21
73	Arkendale Road	V21
73	Arkendale Woods	V21
67	Arkle Road	P22
67	Arkle Square	Q22
38	Arklow Street	H13
46	Armagh Road	G17
47	Armstrong Street	J16
16	Armstrong Walk	P9
37	Army Road	G14
69	Arnold Grove	U22
69	Arnold Park	U22
47	Arnott Street	K16
72	Arran Avenue	V25
72	Arran Close	V25
11	Arran Court	C9
72	Arran Drive	V25
38	Arran Quay	J14
38	Arran Quay Tce	J14
27	Arran Road	L11
38	Arran Street East	K14
38	*Arran Street West	J14
	(Arran Quay)	
38	Arranmore Avenue	K12
48	Arranmore Road	M17
28	Artane	P10
28	Artane Cottages Lwr	P10
28	Artane Cottages Upr	P10
33	Arthur Griffith Ct	XX14
33	Arthur Griffith Pk	XX14
58	Arundel	S20
39	*Asdill's Row	K14
	(off Temple Bar)	
21	Asgard Apts	Y9
21	Asgard Park	Y10
21	Asgard Road	Y10
38	*Ash Grove (Meath St)	J15
33	Ash Park Avenue	YY15
33	Ash Park Court	YY15
33	Ash Park Grove	YY15
33	Ash Park Heath	YY14
38	Ash Street	J15
32	Ashberry	XX15
24	Ashbrook (Ashtown)	F11
28	Ashbrook (Clontarf)	N12
47	*Ashbrook Tce	L17
	(Ranelagh)	
47	*Ashbrook Villas	L17
	(Ranelagh)	
30	Ashcroft	R10
47	Ashcroft Grove	A9
47	Ashdale Avenue	J18
3	Ashdale Close	P3
46	Ashdale Gardens	J18
47	Ashdale Park	J18
3	Ashdale Rd (Swords)	P3
46	Ashdale Rd (Terenure)	J18
3	Ashe Court	P3
53	Ashfield	G20
51	Ashfield Ave	C19

Page		Grid Ref
	(Clondalkin)	
48	Ashfield Ave (Ranelagh)	L17
51	Ashfield Cl (Clondalkin)	C19
10	Ashfield Ct (Mulhuddart)	A8
51	Ashfield Drive	C19
10	Ashfield Gardens	A8
10	Ashfield Green	A8
10	Ashfield Grove	A8
10	Ashfield Lawn	ZZ8
56	Ashfield Pk	P18
	(Booterstown)	
51	Ashfield Pk (Clondalkin)	C19
10	Ashfield Park	A8
	(Huntstown Way)	
47	Ashfield Pk (Terenure)	J18
48	Ashfield Rd (Ranelagh)	L17
10	Ashfield Way	A8
38	Ashford Cottages	H13
38	Ashford Place	H13
38	Ashford Street	H13
5	Ashgrove (Baskin Lane)	Q5
69	Ashgrove	T21
	(Kill O' the Grange)	
61	Ashgrove (Tallaght)	B21
26	*Ashgrove Court	M21
	(Eagle Terrace)	
65	Ashgrove Terrace	M21
25	Ashington Avenue	G11
25	Ashington Close	G11
25	Ashington Court	G11
25	Ashington Crescent	F12
25	Ashington Dale	G11
25	Ashington Gardens	G11
25	Ashington Green	G11
25	Ashington Grove	G11
25	Ashington Heath	G11
25	Ashington Mews	G11
25	Ashington Park	G11
25	Ashington Rise	F11
65	Ashlawn	M21
72	Ashlawn Park	U24
23	Ashleigh Green	C11
23	Ashleigh Grove	C11
	(Blanchardstown)	
7	Ashleigh Lawn	S3
3	Ashley Avenue	N2
3	Ashley Drive	N2
3	Ashley Grove	N2
8	Ashley Rise	U4
46	Ashling Close	H16
47	Ashling Court	L17
11	Ashling Heights	B9
10	Ashmount	A8
37	Ashmount Court	G15
63	Ashton Avenue	G21
63	Ashton Close	G21
63	Ashton Green	G21
63	Ashton Lawn	G21
58	Ashton Park	S20
25	Ashtown	F11
25	Ashtown Court	F12
25	Ashtown Gate Road	E12
25	Ashtown Grove	F12
25	Ashtown Lodge	F12
24	Ashtown Road	E11
24	Ashtowngate	E11
57	Ashurst	P20
72	Ashurst (Ballybrack)	V25
33	Ashville Close	YY13
42	Ashwood Avenue	ZZ17
41	Ashwood Close	ZZ17
42	Ashwood Drive	A17
42	Ashwood Lawns	A17
42	Ashwood Park	A17
42	Ashwood Road	A17
42	Ashwood Way	A17
47	*Ashworth Place	J16
	(off Mount Drumond Ave)	
3	Aspen Drive	P3
69	Aspen Park	T21
	(Kill O'the Grange)	
3	Aspen Park (Kinsealy Ct)	P3
3	Aspen Road	P3
22	Aspen Wood	A10
31	Assumpta Park	V27
39	Aston Place	K14
31	Aston Quay	K14
31	Athgoe Drive	V26
31	Athgoe Road (Shankill)	V26
47	Atlumney Villas	K16
73	Atmospheric Road	V21
31	Aubrey Grove	V27
31	Aubrey Park	V27
28	Auburn	N12
69	Auburn Ave (Cabinteely)	U23
23	Auburn Ave	D11
	(Castleknock)	
48	Auburn Ave	M17
	(Donnybrook)	
69	Auburn Clo (Cabinteely)	U23
23	Auburn Close	D11

Page		Grid Ref
	(Castleknock)	
69	Auburn Dr (Cabinteely)	U23
23	Auburn Dr (Castleknock)	D11
23	Auburn Green	D11
6	Auburn Grove	R3
69	Auburn Rd (Cabinteely)	U23
69	Auburn Rd (Cabinteely)	U23
48	Auburn Road	M17
	(Donnybrook)	
38	Auburn Street	K13
37	*Auburn Terrace	H15
	(Old Kilmainham)	
47	Auburn Villas (Rathgar)	K18
38	Auburn Walk	H13
46	Aughavannagh Road	J16
38	Aughrim Court	J13
38	Aughrim Lane	J13
38	Aughrim Place	H13
38	Aughrim Street	H13
38	Aughrim Villas	H13
5	Aulden Grange	M8
39	Aungier Lane	K15
39	Aungier Place	K15
39	Aungier Street	K15
40	Austin's Cottages	M13
68	Avalon	R23
20	Avalon Apts	W9
49	Ave Maria Road	H15
47	Avenue Road	K16
68	Avila Apts	R21
13	Avila Park	F9
13	Avila Park Gdns	F9
57	Avoca Ave (Stillorgan)	Q20
57	Avoca Hall	R20
57	Avoca Park	Q20
57	Avoca Place	R19
57	Avoca Road	Q20
57	Avoca Terrace	Q20
57	Avoca Wood	Q20
62	Avonbeg Court	D21
62	Avonbeg Drive	D21
62	Avonbeg Gardens	E21
62	Avonbeg Park	D21
62	Avonbeg Road	D21
38	Avondale Avenue	J13
58	Avondale Ct (Blackrock)	R20
72	Avondale Ct (Dalkey)	V21
69	Avondale Crescent	V22
58	Avondale House	L13
58	Avondale Lawn	R20
69	Avondale Pk (Blackrock)	R10
30	Avondale Pk (Raheny)	R10
69	Avondale Rd (Dalkey)	U22
38	Avondale Road	J15
	(Phibsborough)	
53	Avondale Terrace	F18
67	Avonmore	Q22
62	Avonmore Avenue	E21
62	Avonmore Close	E21
62	Avonmore Drive	E21
62	Avonmore Grove	E21
62	Avonmore Park	E21
62	Avonmore Road	E21
62	Aylesbury	D22
17	Ayrefield Avenue	Q9
17	Ayrefield Court	Q9
17	Ayrefield Drive	Q9
17	Ayrefield Grove	Q9
17	Ayrefield Park	Q9
17	Ayrefield Place	Q9
17	Ayrefield Road	Q9
25	Ayward Green	G10
39	**BACHELOR'S WALK**	K14
39	Bachelors Way	K14
19	Back Lane (Baldoyle)	U8
38	Back Lane (High Street)	K15
39	*Back Lane	L15
	(off Sandwith St Upr)	
6	Back Road	R4
47	Baggot Court	L15
48	Baggot Court	L15
48	Baggot Lane	M16
25	Baggot Road	F12
48	Baggot Street Lwr	L15
48	Baggot Street Upr	M16
25	Baggot Terrace	F12
48	Baggotrath Place	L15
21	Bailey Green Road	Z11
73	Bailey View	W21
39	Bailey's Row	L13
66	Balally Avenue	N21
66	Balally Close	N21
66	Balally Drive	N22
66	Balally Grove	N22
66	Balally Hill	N22
66	Balally Park	M21
66	Balally Road	M21
66	Balally Terrace	N22
14	Balbutcher Drive	J8

Page		Grid Ref
14	Balbutcher Lane	J8
14	*Balbutcher Lane Lwr	J8
	(Balbutcher Lane)	
14	Balbutcher Way	J8
14	Balcurris Close	K8
14	Balcurris Gardens	K8
14	Balcurris Park East	K8
14	Balcurris Road	K8
19	Baldoyle	U8
19	Baldoyle Road	U9
45	Balfe Avenue	F17
45	Balfe Road	F17
45	Balfe Road East	G17
39	Balfe Street	K15
53	Balgaddy Road	Z15
21	Balglass Road	Y10
17	Balgriffin	R7
17	Balgriffin Cottages	R7
18	Balgriffin Road	R7
21	Balkill Park	Y10
21	Balkill Road	Y10
66	Ballawley Court	M22
73	Ballinclea Heights	V22
69	Ballinclea Road	U23
18	Ballinteer	L22
65	Ballinteer Avenue	L22
65	Ballinteer Close	L22
65	Ballinteer Court	L22
65	Ballinteer Crescent	L22
65	Ballinteer Drive	L22
65	Ballinteer Gardens	L22
65	Ballinteer Grove	L22
65	Ballinteer Park	L22
65	Ballinteer Road	L22
2	Ballintrane Wood	M2
65	Ballintyre Demesne	L22
65	Ballintyre Downs	L22
65	Battintyre Lane	L22
65	Ballintyre Meadows	L22
65	Ballintyre Square	L22
65	Ballintyre Terrace	L22
65	Ballintyre Walk	L22
65	Ballintyre Woods	L22
38	Ball's Lane	K14
48	Ballsbridge	M16
46	Ballsbridge Avenue	M16
46	Ballsbridge Gardens	N16
48	Ballsbridge Park	N16
48	Ballsbridge Terrace	M16
48	Ballsbridge Wood	N16
63	Ballyboden	G21
64	Ballyboden Crescent	H21
54	Ballyboden Road	J20
63	Ballyboden Way	G22
25	Ballyboggan Road	H11
39	Ballybough Avenue	L13
39	Ballybough Court	L13
39	Ballybough Lane	L13
39	Ballybough Road	L13
72	Ballybrack	V24
31	Ballybride	U27
31	Ballybride Road	U27
11	Ballycoolin Road	D8
62	Ballycullen Avenue	E22
62	Ballycullen Drive	E22
63	Ballycullen Road	F22
33	Ballydowd Grove	YY13
33	Ballydowd Manor	YY14
36	Ballyfermot	D15
36	Ballyfermot Avenue	D15
36	Ballyfermot Crescent	D15
36	Ballyfermot Drive	D15
36	Ballyfermot Parade	D15
36	Ballyfermot Road	C15
36	Ballyfermot Road	E15
14	Ballygall Avenue	H9
26	Ballygall Crescent	H10
26	Ballygall Parade	H10
26	Ballygall Place	H10
26	Ballygall Road East	J10
14	Ballygall Road West	H9
73	Ballygihen Avenue	V21
73	Ballygihen Villas	V21
29	Ballyhoy Avenue	Q11
5	Ballymacartle	Q5
53	Ballymace Green	G20
43	Ballymanagin Lane	A16
67	*Ballymoss Parade	Q22
	(Arkle Square)	
67	Ballymoss Road	P22
52	Ballymount Avenue	E18
45	Ballymount Drive	E18
51	Ballymount Road	D18
52	Ballymount Road Lwr	D18
52	Ballymount Road Upper	E19
45	Ballymount Square	E18
14	Ballymun	K9
15	Ballymun Main Street	K8
15	Ballymun Road	K8
15	Ballymun Road	K9
36	Ballyneety Road	F15

Page		Grid Ref
70	Ballyogan Avenue	Q24
70	Ballyogan Close	Q24
70	Ballyogan Court	Q24
70	Ballyogan Crescent	Q24
70	Ballyogan Drive	Q24
70	Ballyogan Estate	Q24
70	Ballyogan Green	Q24
70	Ballyogan Lawn	Q24
70	Ballyogan Park	Q24
70	Ballyogan Vale	R24
70	Ballyogan Wood	Q24
66	Ballyolaf Manor	M21
33	Ballyowen Avenue	ZZ13
33	Ballyowen Court	ZZ13
33	Ballyowen Crescent	ZZ13
33	Ballyowen Drive	ZZ13
34	Ballyowen Green	ZZ13
33	Ballyowen Grove	ZZ13
34	Ballyowen Hall	ZZ14
34	Ballyowen Lane	ZZ13
33	Ballyowen Lawn	ZZ13
33	Ballyowen Road	ZZ14
33	Ballyowen Square	ZZ14
34	Ballyowen View	ZZ13
33	Ballyowen Way	ZZ13
63	Ballyroan Court	G21
63	Ballyroan Crescent	H21
63	Ballyroan Heights	H21
63	Ballyroan Park	G21
63	Ballyroan Road	H21
16	Ballyshannon Avenue	M9
16	Ballyshannon Road	M9
54	Ballytore Road	J19
55	Balnagowan	L18
62	Balrothery Cottages	F21
52	Balrothery Estate	E20
21	Balscadden Road	Z9
62	Bancroft Avenue	D21
62	Bancroft Close	E21
52	Bancroft Crescent	E20
62	Bancroft Downs	D20
52	Bancroft Grove	E20
62	Bancroft Park	D21
62	Bancroft Road	E21
46	Bangor Circle	H17
46	Bangor Drive	H16
46	Bangor Road	H17
55	Bankside Cottages	L18
25	Bann Road	H11
47	*Bannaville	K16
	(Mountpleasant Ave Lower))	
25	Bannow Road	H11
27	Bantry Park	K11
44	Banville Avenue	D16
58	Barclay Court	R19
40	Bargy Road	M13
73	Barnacoille Park	W21
25	Barnamore Crescent	G11
25	Barnamore Grove	G11
25	Barnamore Park	G11
73	Barnhill Avenue	V22
32	Barnhill Cross Roads	XX13
73	Barnhill Grove	W22
73	Barnhill Lawn	V22
73	Barnhill Park	V22
73	Barnhill Road	V22
73	*Barnhill Villas	V22
	(on Barnhill Road)	
43	Barnville Green	C15
43	Barnville Park	C16
43	Barnville Walk	B16
14	Barnwell Drive	J9
46	Baroma	H18
49	*Barrack Lane	N15
	(off Irishtown Road)	
59	Barrett Street	T20
27	Barron Place	K11
14	Barrow Court	J8
26	Barrow Road	H11
40	Barrow Street	M15
13	Barry Avenue	G9
13	Barry Close	G9
13	Barry Drive	G9
13	Barry Green	G9
13	Barry Park	G9
13	Barry Road	G9
3	Barry's Park	N2
16	Barryscourt Rd	P9
64	Barton Avenue	J21
65	Barton Court	K21
64	Barton Drive	J21
65	Barton Road East	L21
65	Barton Road East Ext	K21
64	Barton Road Ext	K21
64	Barton Road West	J21
73	Bartra Rock Apts	W21
38	Basin Grove	H15
38	Basin Street Lower	H15
38	Basin Street Upper	H15
38	*Basin View	H15

Page		Grid Ref
	(off Basin Street Upper)	
5	Baskin Cottages	Q5
5	Baskin Lane	P5
39	Bass Place	L15
7	Bath Ave (Malahide)	T2
48	Bath Ave (Sandymount)	M15
48	Bath Avenue Gdns	M15
48	Bath Avenue Place	M15
39	Bath Lane	K13
58	Bath Place	R19
40	Bath Street	N15
60	Bawnlea Avenue	A22
60	Bawnlea Close	A22
60	Bawnlea Crescent	A22
60	Bawnlea Drive	A22
60	Bawnlea Green	A22
42	Bawnogue Cottages	ZZ17
42	Bawnogue Road	ZZ17
62	Bawnville Avenue	D22
62	Bawnville Close	D22
62	Bawnville Drive	D22
62	Bawnville Park	D22
62	Bawnville Road	D22
29	Baymount Park	R12
72	Bayshore Lane	V25
19	Bayside Boulevard Nth	T9
19	Bayside Boulevard Sth	T9
19	Bayside Crescent	T9
19	Bayside Park	T9
19	Bayside Square East	T9
19	Bayside Square North	T9
19	Bayside Square South	T9
19	Bayside Square West	T9
19	Bayside Walk	T9
73	Bayswater Terrace	W21
72	Bayview	V25
	(Loughlinstown)	
39	Bayview Avenue	L13
72	Bayview Close	V25
72	Bayview Court	V25
72	Bayview Crescent	V25
72	Bayview Drive	V25
72	Bayview Glade	V25
72	Bayview Glen	V25
72	Bayview Green	V25
72	Bayview Grove	V25
72	Bayview Lawn	V25
72	Bayview Park	V25
72	Bayview Rise	V25
49	Beach Avenue	N15
49	Beach Drive	N15
8	Beach Park	U5
49	Beach Road	N15
19	Beach View	T10
66	Beacon Court	N22
73	*Beacon Hill	X22
	(off Nerano Road)	
37	Beaconsfield Court	G15
66	Bearna Park	N23
48	Beatty's Avenue	M16
27	Beaucourt	L11
57	Beaufield Manor	P20
57	Beaufield Mews	P20
57	Beaufield Park	P20
73	Beaufort	V21
54	Beaufort Court	J20
54	Beaufort Downs	J20
54	Beaufort Villas	J20
16	Beaumont	N9
55	Beaumont Avenue	L20
55	Beaumont Close	L20
32	Beaumont Cottages	XX14
16	Beaumont Court	M9
55	Beaumont Drive	L20
57	Beaumont Gardens	Q20
28	Beaumont Grove	M10
28	Beaumont Hall	M10
54	Beaumont House	J18
28	Beaumont Road	M10
16	Beaumont Wood	M9
18	Beaupark Avenue	S8
18	Beaupark Close	S8
18	Beaupark Crescent	S8
58	Beaupark Downs	S20
18	Beaupark Mews	S8
18	Beaupark Place	S8
18	Beaupark Road	S8
18	Beaupark Row	S8
18	Beaupark Square	S8
18	Beaupark Street	S8
18	Beaupark Terrace	S8
28	Beauvale Park	N10
39	Beaver Close	L13
48	Beaver Row	M17
39	Beaver Street	L13
71	Beckett Hall	S24
43	Beckett Way	C16
46	Bedford Court	H17
39	*Bedford Lane	K14
	(off Aston Quay)	

Page		Grid Ref
39	*Bedford Row	K14
	(off Aston Quay)	
65	Beech Drive	L21
57	Beech Gro (Blackrock)	Q18
33	Beech Grove (Lucan)	YY14
56	Beech Hill	M18
48	Beech Hill Avenue	M18
48	Beech Hill Court	M17
48	Beech Hill Crescent	M18
48	Beech Hill Drive	M18
48	Beech Hill Road	M18
48	Beech Hill Terrace	M18
48	Beech Hill Villas	M18
65	Beech Lawn	L21
23	Beech Lodge	D12
71	Beech Pk (Cabinteely)	T24
23	Beech Pk (Castleknock)	C11
33	Beech Park (Lucan)	YY14
23	Beech Park Avenue	D11
	(Castleknock)	
68	Beech Park Avenue	S22
	(Deans Grange)	
23	Beech Park Crescent	C11
68	Beech Park Drive	S22
68	Beech Park Grove	S22
23	Beech Park Lawn	D11
68	Beech Park Road	S22
44	Beech Rd (Fox & Geese)	D17
43	Beech Row (Nangor Rd)	A17
43	Beech Row	A16
	(Newlands Road)	
64	Beech Walk	H22
18	Beechbrook Grove	R8
69	Beechcourt	U23
62	Beechdale Avenue	E23
62	Beechdale Close	E23
62	Beechdale Court	E23
62	Beechdale Crescent	E23
62	Beechdale Lawn	E23
47	Beechdale Mews	K17
62	Beechdale Park	E23
63	Beechdale Place	F23
62	Beechdale Road	F23
62	Beechdale Way	E23
73	Beeches Park	V21
66	Beeches Road	N21
9	Beechfield	XX8
9	Beechfield Ave (Clonee)	XX8
45	Beechfield Ave	F18
	(Walkinstown)	
9	Beechfield Cl (Clonee)	XX8
45	Beechfield Close	F18
	(Walkinstown)	
9	Beechfield Court	XX8
9	Beechfield Drive	XX8
9	Beechfield Green	XX8
31	Beechfield Haven	V26
9	Beechfield Heights	XX8
9	Beechfield Lawn	YY8
31	Beechfield Manor	V26
45	Beechfield Mews	G18
9	Beechfield Place	YY8
9	Beechfield Rise	YY8
9	Beechfield Rd (Clonee)	XX8
45	Beechfield Road	F18
	(Walkinstown)	
9	Beechfield View	YY8
9	Beechfield Way	XX8
57	Beechlawn	Q19
65	Beechlawn Ave	L21
	(Ballinteer)	
16	Beechlawn Ave (Coolock)	P9
16	Beechlawn Close	P9
16	Beechlawn Green	P9
16	Beechlawn Grove	P9
54	Beechlawn Manor	J18
54	Beechlawn Mews	J18
55	Beechmount Drive	M18
	(Bird Avenue)	
56	Beechmount Drive	M19
	(Windy Arbour)	
17	Beechpark Avenue	P9
23	Beechpark Close	D11
17	Beechpark Court	P9
23	Beechpark Orchard	D11
64	Beechview	H22
48	Beechwood Ave Lwr	L17
48	Beechwood Ave Upper	L17
9	Beechwood Close	ZZ9
	(Hartstown)	
67	Beechwood Court	Q21
9	Beechwood Downs	ZZ9
69	Beechwood Grove	U21
31	*Beechwood House	V26
	(Corbawn Lane)	
69	Beechwood Lawn	U22
69	Beechwood Park	U21
	(Dun Laoghaire)	
47	Beechwood Park	L17
	(Rathmines)	

Page		Grid Ref
48	Beechwood Road	L17
48	Beggar's Bush Buildings	M15
48	Beggars Bush Court	M15
17	Belcamp Avenue	P8
17	Belcamp Crescent	P8
17	Belcamp Gardens	P8
17	Belcamp Green	P8
17	Belcamp Grove	P8
17	Belcamp Lane	Q8
14	Belclare Avenue	J8
14	Belclare Crescent	J8
14	Belclare Drive	J8
14	Belclare Green	J8
14	Belclare Grove	J8
14	Belclare Lawns	J8
14	Belclare Park	J8
14	Belclare Terrace	J8
14	Belclare View	J8
14	Belclare Way	J8
56	Belfield Close	M19
48	Belfield Court	N18
56	Belfield Downs	M20
57	Belfield Park Apts	P19
60	Belfry Avenue	ZZ22
60	Belfry Close	ZZ22
60	Belfry Dale	ZZ22
60	Belfry Gardens	ZZ22
60	Belfry Green	ZZ22
60	Belfry Hall	ZZ22
60	Belfry Manor	ZZ22
60	Belfry Meadows	ZZ22
60	Belfry Park	ZZ22
60	Belfry Place	ZZ22
60	Belfry Rise	ZZ22
60	Belfry Square	ZZ22
60	Belfry Terrace	ZZ22
60	Belfry Walk	ZZ22
60	Belfry Way	ZZ22
51	Belgard Close	C19
51	Belgard Green	B20
51	Belgard Heights	C20
51	Belgard Road	B19
51	Belgard Square	C21
61	Belgard Square East	C21
61	Belgard Square Nth	C21
61	Belgard Square Sth	C21
61	Belgard Square West	C21
47	Belgrave Avenue	L17
58	Belgrave Pl (Monkstown)	S20
47	Belgrave Pl (Rathmines)	K17
58	Belgrave Road	S20
	(Monkstown)	
47	Belgrave Rd (Rathmines)	K17
58	Belgrave Square	S20
	(Monkstown)	
47	Belgrave Sq (Rathmines)	K17
58	Belgrave Square East	S20
	(Monkstown)	
47	Belgrave Square East	K17
	(Rathmines)	
58	Belgrave Square North	S20
	(Monkstown)	
47	Belgrave Square North	K17
	(Rathmines)	
58	Belgrave Square South	S20
	(Monkstown)	
47	Belgrave Square South	K17
	(Rathmines)	
58	Belgrave Square West	S20
	(Monkstown)	
47	Belgrave Square West	K17
	(Rathmines)	
58	Belgrave Terrace	S20
	(Monkstown)	
47	Belgrave Villas	L17
	(Rathmines)	
36	Belgrove Lawn	D14
36	Belgrove Pk	D14
	(Chapelizod)	
29	Belgrove Park	Q12
	(Vernon Avenue)	
29	Belgrove Road	Q12
39	*Bella Ave (off Bella St)	L13
39	*Bella Pl (off Bella St)	L13
39	Bella Street	L13
37	Belleview Maltings	G14
24	Belleville	F11
47	Belleville Avenue	K18
38	Bellevue	H15
57	Bellevue Ave (Merrion)	P18
69	Bellevue Ave (Dalkey)	V22
57	Bellevue Copse	P18
26	Bellevue Cottages	J11
57	Bellevue Court	P18
57	Bellevue Park	P18
57	Bellevue Park Avenue	P18
69	Bellevue Road	U22
39	Bellman's Walk	M14
2	Bell's Lane	M2
47	Bell's Lane	L15

Page **Grid Ref**

67 Belmont (Stillorgan) **R21**
48 Belmont Avenue **M17**
48 *Belmont Court **M17**
　(off Belmont Ave)
48 Belmont Gardens **M17**
67 Belmont Green **Q21**
67 Belmont Grove **Q21**
67 Belmont Lawn **Q21**
48 Belmont Park **M17**
　(Donnybrook)
18 Belmont Pk (Raheny) **R10**
30 Belmont Park **R12**
30 Belmont Park **R10**
39 *Belmont Place **L13**
　(off Gardiner St Middle)
18 Belmont Square **R10**
67 *Belmont Terrace **Q21**
　(off Stillorgan Road)
48 Belmont Villas **M17**
27 *Belmont Court **M12**
　(Philipsburgh Avenue)
28 Belton Park Avenue **N11**
28 Belton Park Gardens **N11**
28 Belton Park Road **N11**
28 Belton Park Villas **N11**
39 Belvidere Avenue **L13**
39 Belvidere Court **K13**
39 Belvidere Place **L13**
39 Belvidere Road **K13**
38 Ben Edar Road **H13**
57 Ben Inagh Park **R19**
46 Benbulbin Avenue **G16**
46 Benbulbin Road **G16**
38 Benburb Street **J14**
26 Beneavin Court **J10**
26 Beneavin Drive **J10**
14 Beneavin Park **J9**
14 Beneavin Road **J9**
26 Bengal Terrace **J12**
45 Benmadigan Road **G16**
40 Benson Street **N14**
59 Bentley Villas **T20**
27 Beresford **L11**
27 Beresford Avenue **L11**
27 Beresford Green **L11**
39 Beresford Lane **L13**
27 Beresford Lawn **L11**
39 Beresford Place **L14**
38 Beresford Street **K14**
39 Berkeley Avenue **K13**
39 Berkeley Place **K13**
38 Berkeley Road **K12**
38 Berkeley Street **K12**
48 Berkeley Terrace **M15**
45 Bernard Curtis Court **F16**
45 Bernard Curtis House **F16**
32 Berryfield **XX15**
25 Berryfield Crescent **G10**
25 Berryfield Drive **G10**
25 Berryfield Road **G10**
2 Berwick Avenue **L1**
2 Berwick Court **L1**
2 Berwick Crescent **L1**
2 Berwick Drive **L1**
2 Berwick Grove **L1**
55 Berwick Hall **K20**
2 Berwick Lawn **L1**
2 Berwick Place **L1**
2 Berwick Rise **L1**
2 Berwick View **L1**
2 Berwick Walk **L1**
2 Berwick Way **L1**
48 Berystede **L16**
38 Bessborough Ave **M13**
47 Bessborough Pde **K16**
38 Besser Drive **B16**
43 Bethany House **P16**
39 Bethesda Place **K13**
33 Bettyglen **S10**
43 Bettysford **B17**
48 Bettystown Avenue **Q11**
63 Beverly Avenue **G22**
63 Beverly Court **Q12**
63 Beverly Crescent **F22**
63 Beverly Downs **F22**
63 Beverly Drive **G22**
63 Beverly Green **F21**
63 Beverly Grove **G22**
63 Beverly Heights **G22**
63 Beverly Lawns **G22**
63 Beverly Park **F21**
63 Beverly Rise **F22**
33 Bewley **YY14**
33 Bewley Avenue **YY14**
33 Bewley Drive **YY14**
33 Bewley Grove **YY14**
33 Bewley Lawn **YY14**
58 Bigger Road **F18**
18 Bill Shelly Park **F10**
19 Binn Eadair Court **V9**
19 Binn Eadair Crescent **V9**

19 Binn Eadair View **V9**
66 Birch Avenue **N22**
68 Birch Dale (Foxrock) **R22**
69 Birch Dale **T21**
　(Kill O'the Grange)
68 Birch Grove **T21**
3 Birchdale Close **P3**
3 Birchdale Drive **P3**
3 Birchdale Park **Q3**
3 Birchdale Road **P3**
66 Birches Road **N21**
56 Birchfield Avenue **M20**
56 Birchfield Court **M20**
56 Birchfield Heights **M20**
56 Birchfield Lawn **M20**
56 Birchfield Park **M20**
56 Birch's Lane **M20**
52 Birchview Avenue **D20**
52 Birchview Close **D20**
52 Birchview Court **D20**
52 Birchview Drive **D20**
52 Birchview Heights **D20**
52 Birchview Lawn **D20**
52 Birchview Rise **D20**
51 Birchwood Close **B20**
61 Birchwood Drive **B21**
61 Birchwood Heights **B21**
55 Bird Avenue **M19**
7 Biscayne **T3**
47 Bishop Street **K15**
6 Bisset's Strand **S2**
2 Bisset's Loft Apts **S2**
38 Black Street **H14**
8 Blackberry Lane **U5**
　(Portmarnock)
47 Blackberry Lane **K16**
　(Rathmines)
8 Blackberry Rise **U5**
54 Blackburn Square **J20**
11 Blackcourt Road **B9**
35 Blackditch Drive **C15**
35 Blackditch Road **C15**
66 Blackglen Court **M23**
65 Blackglen Road **M23**
38 Blackhall Green **J14**
38 Blackhall Parade **J14**
38 Blackhall Place **J14**
38 Blackhall Street **J14**
29 Blackheath Avenue **Q12**
29 Blackheath Court **Q12**
29 Blackheath Drive **P12**
29 Blackheath Gardens **P12**
29 Blackheath Grove **P12**
29 Blackheath Park **P12**
37 Blackhorse Avenue **G12**
25 Blackhorse Avenue **F12**
38 Blackhorse Grove **H13**
47 Blackpitts **J15**
58 Blackrock **R19**
67 Blackthorn Avenue **P22**
8 Blackthorn Lane **U4**
　(Portmarnock)
66 Blackthorn Close **N22**
　(Sandyford)
66 Blackthorn Court **N22**
66 Blackthorn Drive **N22**
66 Blackthorn Green **N22**
66 Blackthorn Grove **N22**
66 Blackthorn Road **N22**
26 Blackwater Road **H11**
9 Blackwood Crescent **XX9**
9 Blackwood Drive **XX9**
7 Blackwood Lane **T4**
7 Blackwoods **S4**
3 Blakeney House **P2**
21 Blakeney House (Mews) **Z11**
38 *Blakes Villas **J14**
　(on Grangegorman Lower)
10 Blakesfield **ZZ9**
10 Blakestown Cottages **A9**
10 Blakestown Drive **A9**
10 Blakestown Road **A9**
10 Blakestown Way **A9**
23 Blanchardstown **C10**
10 Blanchardstown Bypass **C10**
11 Blanchardstown Rd Nth **B8**
10 Blanchardstown Rd Sth **A9**
23 Blanchardstown **C10**
　Roundabout
46 Blarney Park **H17**
11 Blasket Square **C9**
39 Blessington Court **K13**
38 Blessington Lane **K13**
39 *Blessington Place **K13**
　(off St Joseph's Road)
60 Blessington Road **ZZ22**
62 Blessington Road **E21**
38 Blessington Street **K13**
48 Bloomfield Avenue **L16**
　(Donnybrook)
47 Bloomfield Avenue **K16**

　(Portobello)
47 Bloomfield Cottages **K16**
48 Bloomfield Park **M16**
　(Ballsbridge)
47 Bloomfield Park **K16**
　(Rathmines)
45 Bluebell **E16**
44 Bluebell Avenue **D16**
45 Bluebell Road **E16**
17 Blunden Drive **Q8**
40 Blythe Avenue **M14**
47 *Boardman's Lane **J15**
　(off Cork Street)
64 Boden Dale **J21**
64 Boden Heath **H21**
64 Boden Heath Apts **H21**
64 Boden Mill **H22**
64 Boden Park **H21**
54 Boden Wood **J20**
15 Boeing Road **M8**
2 Bohammer **Q6**
62 Bohernabreena Road **D23**
62 Bolbrook Avenue **E21**
62 Bolbrook Close **E21**
62 Bolbrook Drive **E21**
62 Bolbrook Grove **E21**
62 Bolbrook Park **E21**
62 Bolbrook Villas **E21**
38 Bolton Street **K14**
40 Bond Drive **N13**
40 Bond Road **N13**
38 Bond Street **J15**
38 Bonham Street **J14**
40 Boolavogue Road **M13**
50 Boot Road **A18**
57 Booterstown **Q18**
57 Booterstown Avenue **Q19**
57 *Booterstown Grove **Q19**
　(off Booterstown Avenue)
57 Booterstown Park **Q19**
2 Boroimhe Alder **M3**
2 Boroimhe Ash **M3**
2 Boroimhe Aspen **L3**
2 Boroimhe Beech **M3**
2 Boroimhe Birches **M3**
2 Boroimhe Blackthorn **M3**
2 Boroimhe Cedars **M3**
2 Boroimhe Cherry **M3**
2 Boroimhe Elms **M3**
2 Boroimhe Hawthorns **M3**
2 Boroimhe Hazel **M3**
2 Boroimhe Laurels **M3**
2 Boroimhe Maples **M3**
2 Boroimhe Oaks **M3**
2 Boroimhe Pines **M3**
2 Boroimhe Poplars **M3**
2 Boroimhe Rowan **L3**
2 Boroimhe Willows **M3**
27 Botanic Avenue **K12**
26 Botanic Hall **J11**
27 Botanic Park **K12**
26 Botanic Road **K12**
26 Botanic Villas **K12**
40 Bottle Works **N15**
40 Boundary Road **N13**
38 *Bow Bridge Place **H15**
39 Bow Lane East **K15**
38 Bow Lane West **H15**
38 Bow Street **J14**
47 Boyne Court **J16**
39 Boyne Lane **L15**
25 Boyne Road **H11**
39 Boyne Street **L15**
xxx Brabazon Cottages
46 Brabazon House **J15**
47 *Brabazon Place **J15**
　(Brabazon Row)
47 Brabazon Row **J15**
38 *Brabazon Square **J15**
　(Gray Street)
38 *Brabazon Street **J15**
　(Weaver's Street)
8 Bracken Drive **U4**
66 Bracken Hill **M23**
66 Bracken Road **N22**
72 Brackenbush Park **U24**
72 Brackenbush Road **U24**
39 Bracken's Lane **L14**
2 Brackenstown Avenue **M2**
2 Brackenstown Road **M2**
55 Braemor Avenue **K19**
55 Braemor Drive **K19**
55 Braemor Grove **K19**
55 Braemor Park **K19**
55 Braemor Road **K19**
38 Braithwaite Street **J15**
10 Bramblefield Court **ZZ8**
9 Bramblefield Crescent **ZZ8**
9 Bramblefield Drive **ZZ8**
10 Bramblefield Park **ZZ8**

10 Bramblefield View **ZZ8**
9 Bramblefield Walk **ZZ8**
23 Bramley Avenue **B11**
23 Bramley Court **B11**
22 Bramley Crescent **B11**
23 Bramley Garth **B11**
22 Bramley Green **B11**
22 Bramley Grove **B11**
22 Bramley Heath **B11**
22 Bramley Park **B11**
22 Bramley Road **B11**
22 Bramley View **B11**
22 Bramley Walk **B11**
22 Bramley Way **B11**
45 Brandon Road **F16**
45 Brandon Road **F17**
38 Brandon Terrace **H15**
68 Bray Road **S22**
71 Bray Road **T24**
41 Breakwater Rd North **P14**
41 Breakwater Rd South **P14**
19 Breffni Gardens **U8**
19 Breffni Road **V21**
65 Brehon Field Road **L22**
65 Brehon's Chair **K23**
40 Bremen Avenue **N15**
40 Bremen Grove **N15**
40 Bremen Road **N15**
39 *Brendan Behan Court **L13**
　(Russell Street)
48 Brendan Road **M17**
71 Brennanstown Avenue **T24**
71 Brennanstown Road **S24**
71 Brennanstown Square **T24**
71 Brennanstown Vale **S24**
28 Brian Avenue **M12**
41 Brian Boru Avenue **Q13**
41 Brian Boru Street **Q13**
28 Brian Road **M12**
28 Brian Terrace **M12**
47 *Briansboro Terrace **J16**
　(Washington Street)
7 Briar Walk **U4**
18 Briarfield Grove **S9**
18 Briarfield Road **S10**
18 Briarfield Villas **S9**
55 Briarly Court **L20**
18 Briarsfield Walk **S9**
10 Briarwood Avenue **A9**
10 Briarwood Close **A9**
10 Briarwood Gardens **A9**
10 Briarwood Green **A9**
10 Briarwood Lawn **A9**
10 Briarwood Park **A9**
10 Briarwood Road **A9**
46 Brickfield Drive **H16**
47 Brickfield Lane **J15**
39 Bride Close **K15**
38 Bride Road **K15**
47 Bride Street **K15**
47 Bride Street New **K15**
71 Brides Glen **T26**
40 Bridge St (Ringsend) **N15**
3 Bridge St (Swords) **N2**
38 Bridge St Lower **J14**
38 Bridge St Upper **J14**
38 Bridgefoot Street **J14**
43 Bridgeview **B15**
37 Bridgewater Quay **G14**
70 Bridon **Q25**
70 Brighton Avenue **R24**
　(Carrickmines)
28 Brighton Ave (Clontarf) **N12**
58 Brighton Ave **S20**
　(Monkstown)
47 Brighton Ave (Rathgar) **J18**
68 *Brighton Cottages **R23**
　(Brighton Road)
70 Brighton Court **R24**
54 Brighton Gardens **J18**
47 Brighton Green **J18**
70 Brighton Hall **R24**
58 Brighton Lane **S20**
68 Brighton Lodge **R23**
70 Brighton Place **R24**
68 Brighton Rd (Foxrock) **R23**
54 Brighton Rd (Terenure) **J18**
47 Brighton Square **J18**
73 Brighton Terrace **V21**
　(Dun Laoghaire)
58 Brighton Tce **S20**
　(Monkstown)
58 Brighton Vale **S19**
39 Britain Place **K13**
40 Britain Quay **M14**
65 Broadford Avenue **L22**
65 Broadford Close **L22**
65 Broadford Crescent **L22**

Page		Grid Ref
65	Broadford Drive	L22
65	Broadford Hill	L22
65	Broadford Lawn	L22
65	Broadford Park	L22
65	Broadford Rise	L22
65	Broadford Road	L22
65	Broadford Walk	L22
2	Broadmeadow	M1
38	*Broadstone Avenue	K13
	(off Royal Canal Bank)	
38	*Broadstone Place	K13
	(off Royal Canal Bank)	
22	Broadway Drive	B10
22	Broadway Grove	B10
22	Broadway Park	B10
22	Broadway Road	B10
38	Brodin Row	H14
23	Brompton Court	B11
23	Brompton Green	B10
23	Brompton Grove	B11
23	Brompton Lawn	B10
58	Brook Court	S20
62	Brookdale	D22
2	Brookdale Avenue	L2
2	Brookdale Close	L2
2	Brookdale Court	L2
2	Brookdale Drive	L2
2	Brookdale Green	L2
2	Brookdale Grove	L2
2	Brookdale Lawns	L2
2	Brookdale Park	L2
2	Brookdale Road	L2
2	Brookdale Walk	L2
2	Brookdale Way	L2
72	Brookdene	V26
57	Brookfield (Blackrock)	Q19
29	Brookfield (Coolock)	Q10
48	Brookfield (Donnybrook)	M17
32	Brookfield (Lucan)	XX15
55	Brookfield (Milltown)	L18
58	Brookfield Avenue	R20
	(Blackrock)	
58	Brookfield Court	R20
	(Blackrock)	
54	Brookfield Court	H18
	(Kimmage)	
60	Brookfield Ct (Tallaght)	A21
54	Brookfield Estate	H18
54	Brookfield Green	H18
58	Brookfield Grove	R20
58	Brookfield Place	R20
37	Brookfield Road	H15
	(Kilmainham)	
60	Brookfield Rd (Tallaght)	A21
37	Brookfield Street	H15
58	Brookfield Terrace	R19
10	Brookhaven Drive	B9
10	Brookhaven Grove	B9
11	Brookhaven Lawn	B9
10	Brookhaven Park	B9
10	Brookhaven Rise	B9
49	Brooklands	N17
57	Brooklawn (Blackrock)	Q19
28	Brooklawn (Clontarf)	N21
32	Brooklawn (Lucan)	XX15
58	Brooklawn Avenue	S20
58	Brooklawn Wood	S20
62	Brookmount Avenue	F21
54	Brookmount Court	H20
62	Brookmount Lawns	F21
32	Brookpark	XX15
19	Brookstone Lane	U8
19	Brookstone Road	U8
33	Brookvale	XX13
54	Brookvale Downs	J19
48	Brookvale Road	M17
	(Donnybrook)	
54	Brookvale Road	J19
	(Rathfarnham)	
60	Brookview Avenue	A21
60	Brookview Close	A21
60	Brookview Court	A21
60	Brookview Crescent	A21
60	Brookview Drive	A21
60	Brookview Gardens	A21
60	Brookview Green	A21
60	Brookview Grove	A21
60	Brookview Lawns	A21
60	Brookview Park	A21
60	Brookview Rise	A21
60	Brookview Terrace	A21
60	Brookview Way	A21
13	Brookville	G9
17	Brookville Crescent	P9
29	Brookville Pk (Artane)	P10
17	Brookville Pk (Coolock)	P9
68	Brookville Park	S21
	(Dean's Grange)	
64	Brookwood	H22
29	Brookwood Avenue	P10
29	Brookwood Cres	Q10

Page		Grid Ref
29	Brookwood Drive	P10
28	Brookwood Glen	Q11
29	Brookwood Grove	P10
29	Brookwood Hall	P11
29	Brookwood Heights	Q10
29	Brookwood Lawn	Q10
29	Brookwood Meadow	P11
29	Brookwood Park	P11
29	Brookwood Rise	Q11
29	Brookwood Road	P10
25	Broombridge Road	H11
7	Broomfield (Malahide)	S4
72	Broomfield Court	V26
7	Broomfield Mews	S4
52	Broomhill Close	D20
52	Broomhill Drive	D20
52	Broomhill Road	D20
52	Broomhill Terrace	D20
38	Brown Street North	JI4
47	Brown Street South	JI5
50	Brownsbarn	ZZ20
50	Brownsbarn Court	ZZ20
50	Brownsbarn Garden	ZZ20
50	Brownsbarn Orchard	ZZ20
45	Brug Chroimlinn	G17
39	Brunswick Place	M15
38	Brunswick St Nth	JI4
39	*Brunswick Villas	L14
	(Pearse Street)	
58	Brusna Cottages	R19
39	Buckingham St Lwr	L13
39	Buckingham St Upr	L13
39	Buckingham Village	L13
45	Bulfin Court	G15
37	Bulfin Gardens	G15
45	Bulfin Road	G15
38	Bull Alley Street	K15
73	Bullock Steps	W21
17	Bunratty Avenue	P9
16	Bunratty Drive	P9
16	Bunratty Road	P9
45	Bunting Road	F17
73	Burdett Avenue	V21
33	Burg an Ri Glen	ZZ15
33	Burg an Ri Terrace	ZZ15
38	*Burgess Lane	
	(Haymarket)	
39	Burgh Quay	L14
38	Burke Place	H15
48	Burleigh Court	L16
48	Burlington Gardens	L16
48	Burlington Road	L16
73	Burmah Close	W22
22	Burnell Park Avenue	B12
22	Burnell Park Green	B12
17	Burnell Square	R8
14	Burren Court	J8
38	*Burris Court	K15
	(off High St)	
8	Burrow Ct (Portmarnock)	U5
20	Burrow Road (Sutton)	W9
19	Burrowfield Road	U9
67	Burton Court	P22
67	Burton Hall Avenue	P22
67	Burton Hall Road	P22
73	Burton Road	W22
48	Bushfield Avenue	L17
50	Bushfield Drive	A18
50	Bushfield Green	A18
50	Bushfield Grove	A19
50	Bushfield Lawns	A18
48	Bushfield Place	L17
27	Bushfield Square	M12
48	Bushfield Terrace	L17
54	Bushy Park Gardens	J19
54	Bushy Park House	H19
54	Bushy Park Road	J19
17	Buttercup Close	Q8
17	Buttercup Drive	Q8
17	Buttercup Park	Q8
17	Buttercup Square	Q8
17	Buttercup Terrace	Q8
54	Butterfield Avenue	H20
54	Butterfield Close	H20
54	Butterfield Court	H20
54	Butterfield Crescent	H20
54	Butterfield Drive	H20
54	Butterfield Grove	H20
54	Butterfield Meadow	H20
54	Butterfield Orchard	H20
54	Butterfield Park	H20
38	*Byrne's Cottages	JI5
	(Francis Street)	
39	Byrne's Lane (Jervis St)	K14
39	*Byrne's Lane	M15
	(Pearse Sq West)	
71	**CABINTEELY**	S24
69	Cabinteely Avenue	T23
68	Cabinteely Bypass	T23
68	Cabinteely Close	T23

Page		Grid Ref
69	Cabinteely Court	T23
69	Cabinteely Crescent	T23
69	Cabinteely Drive	T23
69	Cabinteely Green	T23
68	Cabinteely Park	T23
68	Cabinteely Way	T23
26	Cabra	H12
38	Cabra Drive	H13
38	Cabra Grove	H13
38	Cabra Park	JI2
38	Cabra Road	H13
8	Caddell	T6
40	Cadogan Road	M12
70	Cairn Brook	R25
70	Cairn Brook Hall	R25
70	Cairn Brook Manor	R25
70	Cairn Brook View	R25
70	Cairn Brook Way	R25
14	Cairn Court	K8
68	Cairn Hill	S22
51	Cairnwood Avenue	B20
51	Cairnwood Court	B20
51	Cairnwood Green	B20
27	Calderwood Avenue	M11
27	Calderwood Grove	M11
27	Calderwood Road	M11
40	Caledon Court	M13
40	Caledon Road	M13
56	Callary Road	N19
52	Calmount Avenue	E18
52	Calmount Park	E18
52	Calmount Road	E18
37	Camac Close	G15
37	Camac Court	G15
44	Camac Park	E16
55	Camberley Oaks	L20
40	Cambridge Avenue	N15
40	Cambridge Court	N15
40	Cambridge Park	N15
47	Cambridge Road	K17
	(Rathmines)	
40	Cambridge Rd	N15
	(Ringsend)	
40	*Cambridge Square	N14
	(off Thorncastle St)	
40	Cambridge Street	N15
59	Cambridge Terrace	T20
	(Dun Laoghaire)	
48	Cambridge Terrace	L16
	(Ranelagh)	
47	Cambridge Villas	K17
25	Camden Avenue	F11
47	Camden Buildings	K15
47	Camden Court	K16
40	Camden Lock	N15
47	*Camden Market	K15
	(Camden Street Lower)	
47	Camden Place	K15
47	Camden Row	K15
47	Camden Street Lower	K15
47	Camden Street Upper	K16
47	Camden Villas	K15
37	Cameron Square	H15
46	Cameron Street	JI5
37	Camogie Road	G14
21	*Campbell Court	Y10
	(Main Street)	
38	Campbell's Court	K14
39	*Campbell's Lane	L13
	(off Belvidere Ave)	
39	*Campbell's Row	L13
	(off Portland Street North)	
66	Campfield Terrace	M21
47	Canal Road	K16
45	Canal Terrace	E16
43	Canal Turn	B16
48	Cannon Mews East	M15
21	Cannon Rock Estate	Z10
21	Cannon Rock View	Z10
33	Cannonbrook	XX14
32	Cannonbrook Avenue	XX14
32	Cannonbrook Court	XX14
33	Cannonbrook Lawn	XX14
39	Canon Lillis Avenue	M13
40	Canon Mooney Gdns	N15
39	Capel Street	K14
13	Cappagh Avenue	G9
13	Cappagh Drive	G9
13	Cappagh Green	G9
13	Cappagh Road	G8
43	Cappaghmore Estate	A16
12	Cappoge	F8
12	Cappoge Cottages	E8
46	Captain's Avenue	G17
46	Captain's Drive	G18
46	Captain's Road	G17
17	Cara Park	P7
22	Caragh Court	H12
38	Caragh Road	H13
27	Carberry Road	M11

Page		Grid Ref
58	Carbury Place	R19
40	Carbury Terrace	M14
25	Cardiff Castle Road	G10
39	Cardiff Lane	M14
25	Cardiffs Bridge	G11
13	Cardiffsbridge Avenue	G10
25	Cardiffsbridge Grove	G9
25	Cardiffsbridge Road	G10
2	Cardiffsbridge Rd	M1
39	Card's Lane (Pearse St)	L14
13	Cardiff Castle Rd	G9
28	Carleton Road	K12
48	Carlingford Parade	M15
27	Carlingford Road	K12
48	Carlisle Avenue	L17
54	Carlisle Court	JI8
39	Carlisle Street	K16
69	Carlisle Terrace	U21
	(Dun Laoghaire)	
7	Carlisle Tce (Malahide)	S3
38	*Carlisle Terrace	JI3
	(Off Nth Circular Rd)	
59	*Carlisle Terrace	U20
	(on Tivoli Road)	
40	Carlton Ct (Clontarf)	N12
3	Carlton Court (Swords)	N2
48	*Carlton Villas	M16
	(Shelbourne Ave)	
67	Carmanhall Court	P22
67	Carmanhall Road	P22
38	Carman's Hall	JI5
35	Carna Road	C15
18	Carndonagh Drive	S9
18	Carndonagh Lawn	S9
18	Carndonagh Park	S9
18	Carndonagh Road	S9
9	Carne Court	ZZ8
3	Carnegie Court	N1
38	Carnew Street	H13
25	Carnlough Road	H12
40	Caroline Row	N15
22	Carpenterstown Av	B11
23	Carpenterstown Manor	B12
22	Carpenterstown Pk East	B11
23	Carpenterstown Road	B12
14	*Carraig Close	J8
	(Barrow Court)	
71	Carraig Glen	T24
72	Carraig Grennane	V24
18	Carraroe Avenue	R9
8	Carrick Court	T5
66	Carrick Lawn	N21
46	Carrick Terrace	H15
20	Carrickbrack Heath	W10
20	Carrickbrack Hill	W10
20	Carrickbrack Lawn	W10
20	Carrickbrack Park	W10
21	Carrickbrack Road	X11
58	Carrickbrennan Lawn	T20
59	Carrickbrennan Road	T20
37	Carrickfoyle Terrace	G15
7	Carrickhill Close	U4
8	Carrickhill Drive	U5
8	Carrickhill Heights	U5
7	Carrickhill Rise	U4
8	Carrickhill Road	U5
8	Carrickhill Road Middle	U5
7	Carrickhill Road Upper	T4
8	Carrickhill Walk	U4
71	Carrickmines	S24
71	Carrickmines Avenue	S24
71	Carrickmines Chase	S24
71	Carrickmines Dale	S24
71	Carrickmines Garth	S24
70	Carrickmines Green	R25
70	Carrickmines Little	R24
70	Carrickmines Manor	R25
71	Carrickmines Oaks	S24
55	Carrickmount Avenue	L20
65	Carrickmount Drive	K21
14	Carrig Road	J8
25	Carrigallen Drive	H11
25	Carrigallen Park	H11
25	Carrigallen Road	H11
69	Carriglea Avenue	T22
	(Kill O'the Grange)	
62	Carriglea Ave (Tallaght)	E22
69	Carriglea Court	T21
	(Kill O'the Grange)	
62	Carriglea Ct (Tallaght)	E22
69	Carriglea Downs	T22
	(Kill O'the Grange)	
62	Carriglea Downs	E22
	(Tallaght)	
62	Carriglea Drive	E22
69	Carriglea Gardens	T21
62	Carriglea Grove	E22
62	Carriglea Rise	E22
62	Carriglea View	E22
62	Carriglea Walk	E22
61	Carrigmore Close	C23

Page		Grid Ref

(Oldbawn)
60 Carrigmore Court **ZZ22**
60 Carrigmore Crescent **ZZ21**
61 Carrigmore Drive **C23**
61 Carrigmore Park **C23**
61 Carrigmore Road **C22**
61 Carrigmore View **C23**
60 Carrigmore Way **ZZ22**
62 Carrigwood **F22**
45 Carrow Road **F16**
3 Carwell Court **P2**
58 Carysfort Avenue **R20**
67 Carysfort Downs **Q21**
67 Carysfort Downs **R21**
73 Carysfort Drive **W21**
68 Carysfort Grove **R21**
58 Carysfort Hall **R20**
57 Carysfort Park **R20**
73 Carysfort Road **W21**
67 Carysfort Woods **R21**
21 Casana View **Z10**
13 Casement Close **G9**
13 Casement Drive **G9**
13 Casement Green **G9**
13 Casement Grove **G9**
13 Casement Park **G9**
13 Casement Road **G9**
25 Casement Road **G10**
68 Casement Villas **S21**
46 Cashel Avenue **H18**
46 Cashel Road **G17**
47 Casimir Avenue **J17**
47 *Casimir Court **J17**
 (Casimir Avenue)
47 Casimir Road **J17**
28 Casino Park **N11**
28 Casino Road **M12**
25 *Cassian Court **G11**
 (Lockkeeper's Walk)
9 Castaheany **YY8**
29 Castilla Park **Q12**
43 Castle Ave (Clondalkin) **B17**
29 Castle Ave (Clontarf) **P12**
3 Castle Ave (Swords) **N2**
43 Castle Cl (Clondalkin) **B17**
73 Castle Cl (Dalkey) **W21**
57 Castle Cl (Booterstown) **Q18**
28 Castle Cl (Clontarf) **N12**
65 Castle Cl (Dundrum) **M21**
72 Castle Court **V25**
 (Loughlinstown)
53 *Castle Court **G20**
 (off Cypress Lawn)
55 Castle Ct (Rathfarnham) **K20**
54 *Castle Court **J20**
 (Main Street Rathfarnham)
73 Castle Cove (Dalkey) **W22**
6 Castle Cove (Malahide) **R2**
43 Castle Crescent **B17**
62 Castle Down Croft **Q2**
6 Castle Down Grove **Q2**
6 Castle Down Road **Q2**
43 Castle Dr (Clondalkin) **B17**
3 Castle Dr (Swords) **N2**
17 Castle Elms **P9**
31 Castle Farm **V27**
31 Castle Farm Wood **V27**
43 Castle Gro (Clondalkin) **B17**
28 Castle Grove (Clontarf) **P12**
3 Castle Grove (Swords) **N2**
6 Castle Lawns (Malahide) **Q2**
52 Castle Lawns (Tallaght) **E20**
39 *Castle Market **K15**
 (off Drury Street)
43 Castle Pk (Clondalkin) **B17**
59 Castle Park (Monkstown) **T20**
3 Castle Park (Swords) **N2**
52 Castle Park (Tallaght) **E20**
62 Castle Park Estate **E21**
 (Tallaght)
73 *Castle Place **V21**
 (on Breffni Road)
33 Castle Riada Avenue **YY15**
33 Castle Riada Crescent **YY14**
33 Castle Riada Drive **YY15**
33 Castle Riada Grove **YY14**
33 Castle Road **ZZ14**
41 Castle Road (Clontarf) **P12**
33 Castle Road (Lucan) **YY14**
19 Castle Rosse **T8**
39 Castle Steps **K15**
 (off Castle St)
39 Castle St **K15**
73 Castle Street (Dalkey) **W22**
7 Castle Tce (Malahide) **S3**
73 *Castle Terrace **W21**
 (off Ulverton Road)
38 Castle Terrace **J13**
 (Phibsborough Ave)
70 Castle View **R24**
 (Carrickmines)

43 Castle Vw (Clondalkin) **B17**
73 Castle Villas **W22**
66 Castlebrook **M21**
58 Castlebyrne Park **R20**
10 Castlecurragh Heath **A8**
10 Castlecurragh Park **B8**
10 Castlecurragh Vale **B8**
57 Castledawson Ave **Q19**
2 Castlefarm **M1**
63 Castlefield Avenue **F21**
9 Castlefield Court **ZZ10**
 (Clonsilla)
63 Castlefield Ct (Firhouse) **F21**
63 Castlefield Drive **F22**
63 Castlefield Green **F22**
63 Castlefield Grove **F22**
63 Castlefield Lawn **F21**
63 Castlefield Manor **F22**
 (Firhouse)
7 Castlefield Manor **S3**
 (Malahide)
63 Castlefield Orchard **F21**
63 Castlefield Pk (Firhouse) **F22**
9 Castlefield Pk **ZZ10**
 (Clonsilla)
63 Castlefield Way **F22**
22 Castlefield Woods **ZZ10**
40 Castleforbes Road **M14**
32 Castlegate (Lucan) **WW15**
69 *Castlegate (Monkstown) **T21**
 (Oliver Plunkett Road)
31 Castlegate (Shankill) **U27**
32 Castlegate Chase **WW15**
32 Castlegate Close **WW15**
32 Castlegate Crescent **WW15**
32 Castlegate Dene **WW15**
32 Castlegate Drive **WW15**
32 Castlegate Elms **WW15**
32 Castlegate Green **WW15**
32 Castlegate Grove **WW15**
32 Castlegate Park **WW16**
32 Castlegate Place **WW16**
32 Castlegate Square **WW16**
32 Castlegate Walk **WW15**
32 Castlegate Way **WW15**
9 Castlegate **YY9**
9 Castlegrange Avenue **YY9**
 (Clonsilla)
3 Castlegrange Avenue **N1**
 (Swords)
42 Castlegrange Close **YY17**
 (Clondalkin)
3 Castlegrange Close **N1**
 (Swords)
42 Castlegrange Court **YY17**
 (Clondalkin)
9 Castlegrange Court **YY9**
 (Clonsilla)
9 Castlegrange Dale **YY9**
42 Castlegrange Drive **YY17**
 (Clondalkin)
9 Castlegrange Drive **YY9**
 (Clonsilla)
9 Castlegrange Gardens **YY9**
42 Castlegrange Green **YY17**
 (Clondalkin)
9 Castlegrange Green **YY9**
 (Clonsilla)
3 Castlegrange Green **N1**
 (Swords)
9 Castlegrange Grove **YY8**
3 Castlegrange Heights **N1**
3 Castlegrange Hill **N1**
42 Castlegrange Lawn **YY17**
 (Clondalkin)
9 Castlegrange Lawn **YY9**
 (Clonsilla)
9 Castlegrange Park **YY9**
42 Castlegrange Road **YY17**
 (Clondalkin)
3 Castlegrange Rd **N1**
 (Swords)
9 Castlegrange Row **YY9**
42 Castlegrange Square **YY17**
 (Clondalkin)
9 Castlegrange Square **YY9**
 (Clonsilla)
9 Castlegrange Terrace **YY9**
3 Castlegrange Way **N1**
6 Castleheath **R3**
16 Castlekevin Road **N9**
23 Castleknock **C11**
23 Castleknock Avenue **C11**
23 Castleknock Brook **C11**
23 Castleknock Close **B11**
23 Castleknock Court **C11**
23 Castleknock Crescent **C11**
23 Castleknock Dale **C11**
23 Castleknock Downs **B11**
23 Castleknock Drive **C11**
23 Castleknock Elms **C11**

24 Castleknock Gate **E12**
23 Castleknock Glade **C11**
23 Castleknock Grange **C11**
24 Castleknock Green **C11**
23 Castleknock Grove **C11**
23 Castleknock Laurels **C11**
23 Castleknock Lodge **D12**
24 Castleknock Manor **D11**
23 Castleknock Meadows **C11**
23 Castleknock Oaks **C11**
23 Castleknock Park **D11**
23 Castleknock Rise **B11**
24 Castleknock Road **D12**
23 Castleknock Road **C11**
23 Castleknock Vale **C11**
23 Castleknock View **C11**
23 Castleknock Walk **B11**
23 Castleknock Way **C11**
23 Castleknock Wood **C11**
73 Castlelands **W21**
73 Castlelands Grove **W21**
18 Castlemoyne **R7**
73 Castlepark Court **V22**
73 Castlepark Road **V22**
19 Castlerosse Crescent **T8**
19 Castlerosse Drive **T8**
19 Castlerosse View **T8**
54 Castleside Drive **J19**
16 Castletimon Avenue **M9**
16 Castletimon Drive **M9**
15 Castletimon Gardens **M9**
16 Castletimon Green **M9**
16 Castletimon Park **M9**
16 Castletimon Road **M9**
52 Castletymon Court **E20**
52 Castletymon Gardens **E20**
52 Castletymon Road **E20**
41 Castleview **P12**
23 Castleview (Artane) **P10**
65 Castleview (Dundrum) **M21**
13 Castleview Park **R3**
7 Castlewood **ZZ9**
47 Castlewood Avenue **K17**
47 Castlewood Close **K17**
47 Castlewood Park **K17**
47 Castlewood Place **K17**
47 Castlewood Terrace **K17**
39 Cathal Brugha Street **K14**
47 Cathedral Lane **K15**
47 Cathedral Street **K14**
47 Cathedral View Court **K15**
47 Cathedral View Walk **K15**
39 *Catherine Court **L13**
 (off William Street Nth)
38 Catherine Lane **J14**
38 Catherine Street **J15**
 (Swift's Alley)
73 Cats Ladder **W22**
30 Causeway Road **S11**
39 Cavendish Row **K13**
21 Ceanchor Road **Y12**
38 *Ceannt Fort **H15**
 (off Mount Brown)
28 Cecil Avenue **N12**
39 *Cecilia Street **K14**
 (off Temple Bar)
51 Cedar Avenue **D19**
43 Cedar Brook **C16**
43 Cedar Brook Avenue **B15**
43 Cedar Brook Place **B15**
43 Cedar Brook Walk **B15**
72 Cedar Court **U25**
 (Loughlinstown)
46 Cedar Ct (Terenure) **J18**
35 Cedar Dr (Palmerstown) **C14**
22 Cedar Grove **ZZ10**
48 Cedar Hall **M17**
23 Cedar Lodge **D12**
64 Cedar Lodge Apts **H22**
18 Cedar Pk (Donaghmede) **R9**
57 Cedar Sq (Stillorgan) **Q20**
2 Cedar Sq (Swords) **L3**
30 Cedar Walk **S10**
24 Cedarhurst Green **E11**
24 Cedarhurst Road **E11**
56 Cedarmount Road **P20**
14 Cedarwood Ave **J9**
14 Cedarwood Close **J9**
14 Cedarwood Green **J9**
14 Cedarwood Grove **J9**
14 Cedarwood Park **J9**
14 Cedarwood Rise **J9**
14 Cedarwood Road **J9**
2 Ceder Park **L3**
2 Ceder View **L3**
32 Celbridge Rd (Lucan) **VV14**
40 *Celestine Avenue **N15**
 (off Dermot O'Hurley Ave)
28 Celtic Park Avenue **M10**
28 Celtic Park Road **M10**
72 Cenacle Grove **V25**

33 Chalet Gardens **YY13**
6 Chalfont Avenue **S2**
6 Chalfont Park **S2**
6 Chalfont Place **S2**
6 Chalfont Road **R2**
47 *Chamber Court **J15**
 (off Chamber St)
47 Chamber Street **J15**
6 Chamley Park **Q3**
39 Champions Avenue **L14**
25 Chancel Mews **G12**
39 Chancery Lane **K15**
39 Chancery Place **K14**
38 Chancery Street **K14**
29 Chanel Avenue **P10**
17 Chanel Grove **P9**
29 Chanel Road **P10**
40 *Chapel Ave **N15**
 (off Bath St)
25 Chapel Crescent **G11**
39 Chapel Lane (Parnell St) **K14**
3 Chapel Lane (Swords) **N2**
33 Chapel View Apts **XX13**
36 Chapelizod **E14**
36 Chapelizod Bypass **E14**
36 Chapelizod Court **E14**
36 Chapelizod Hill Road **E14**
36 Chapelizod Road **F14**
14 Charlemont **M14**
59 Charlemont Avenue **U20**
47 Charlemont Gardens **K16**
47 Charlemont Mall **K16**
39 Charlemont Parade **L13**
47 Charlemont Place **L16**
28 Charlemont Road **N12**
47 Charlemont Street **K16**
59 *Charlemont Terrace **U20**
 (Charlemont Avenue)
39 Charles Lane **L13**
39 Charles Street Great **L13**
38 *Charles Street West **K14**
 (off Ormond Quay Upper)
47 Charleston Avenue **L17**
47 Charleston Court Flats **L17**
47 Charleston Road **L17**
13 Charlestown Ave **G8**
13 Charlestown Court **H8**
13 Charlestown Drive **H8**
13 Charlestown Green **H8**
13 Charlestown Park **H8**
13 Charlestown Way **H8**
55 Charleville **L20**
39 Charleville Avenue **L13**
47 Charleville Close **K17**
39 Charleville Mall **L13**
38 Charleville Road **J13**
 (Phibsborough)
47 Charleville Road **K17**
 (Rathmines)
54 Charleville Square **H20**
47 *Charleville Terrace **K17**
 (on Charleville Rd)
44 Charlotte Quay **M15**
73 Charlotte Terrace **W22**
47 Charlotte Way **K16**
56 Charlton Lawn **N20**
9 Charnwood (Clonsilla) **ZZ10**
9 Charnwood Avenue **ZZ10**
9 Charnwood Court **ZZ10**
22 Charnwood Gardens **ZZ10**
22 Charnwood Green **ZZ10**
9 Charnwood Grove **ZZ10**
9 Charnwood Heath **ZZ10**
22 Charnwood Meadows **ZZ10**
9 Charnwood Park **ZZ10**
39 *Chatham Court **K15**
 (on Chatham Street)
39 *Chatham Lane **K15**
 (off Chatham Street)
39 Chatham Row **K15**
39 Chatham Street **K15**
38 *Chaworth Terrace **J15**
 (Hanbury Lane)
60 Cheeverstown Road **A21**
48 Chelmsford Avenue **L16**
48 Chelmsford Lane **L17**
48 Chelmsford Road **L17**
29 Chelsea Gardens **Q12**
42 Cheltenham Place **K16**
57 Cherbury Court **Q19**
57 Cherbury Gardens **Q19**
57 Cherbury Mews **Q19**
33 Cherbury Park Ave **XX14**
33 Cherbury Park Rd **XX14**
66 Cherries Road **N22**
31 Cherrington Close **V27**
31 Cherrington Drive **V27**
31 Cherrington Road **V27**
22 Cherry Avenue **B11**
 (Carpenterstown)

Page		Grid Ref
2	Cherry Avenue (Swords)	M3
72	Cherry Court	U25
	(Loughlinstown)	
47	Cherry Ct (Terenure)	J18
22	Cherry Drive	B11
57	Cherry Garth (Stillorgan)	P20
2	Cherry Garth (Swords)	L2
45	Cherry Grove (Crumlin)	F18
2	Cherry Grove (Swords)	L3
22	Cherry Lawn	B11
32	Cherry Lawns	WW14
23	Cherry Lodge	D12
43	Cherry Orchard Ave	C15
43	Cherry Orchard Court	C16
44	Cherry Orchard Cres	C16
44	Cherry Orchard Drive	C15
43	Cherry Orchard Green	C15
43	Cherry Orchard Grove	C16
44	Cherry Orchard Parade	C16
44	Cherry Orchard Way	C16
22	Cherry Park	B11
	(Carpenterstown)	
2	Cherry Park (Swords)	L3
72	Cherry Wood	U25
53	Cherryfield Avenue	F18
48	Cherryfield Ave Lwr	L17
48	Cherryfield Avenue Upr	L17
9	Cherryfield Close	ZZ9
9	Cherryfield Court	YY9
53	Cherryfield Drive	F18
9	Cherryfield Lawn	ZZ9
9	Cherryfield Park	ZZ9
45	Cherryfield Road	F18
9	Cherryfield View	YY9
9	Cherryfield Walk	ZZ9
53	Cherryfield Way	G20
28	Cherrymount Crescent	N11
28	Cherrymount Grove	N11
38	Cherrymount Park	J13
42	Cherrywood Avenue	A17
42	Cherrywood Crescent	ZZ17
42	Cherrywood Drive	Z17
42	Cherrywood Grove	A17
42	Cherrywood Lawn	Z18
42	Cherrywood Park	ZZ18
	(Clondalkin)	
72	Cherrywood Park	U25
	(Loughlinstown)	
72	Cherrywood Road	U26
42	Cherrywood Villas	ZZ17
43	Cherrywood Villas	A17
69	Chester Downs	U21
47	Chester Road	L17
73	Chester Square	V21
24	Chesterfield Avenue	E12
	(Phoenix Park)	
24	Chesterfield Avenue	E12
	(Phoenix Park)	
24	Chesterfield Close	E12
24	Chesterfield Copse	E11
24	Chesterfield Grove	E12
24	Chesterfield Park	E11
24	Chesterfield View	E11
28	Chestnut Court	M10
65	Chestnut Gro (Ballinteer)	L22
51	Chestnut Grove	C19
	(Clondalkin)	
68	Chestnut Park	R22
44	Chestnut Road	D17
	(Clondalkin)	
57	Chestnut Road	P19
	(Mount Merrion)	
38	Christchurch Place	K15
38	Christchurch Square	K15
23	Church Avenue	C10
	(Blanchardstown)	
27	Church Avenue	L11
	(Drumcondra)	
26	Church Ave (Glasnevin)	K11
49	Church Ave (Irishtown)	N15
72	Church Ave (Killiney)	V24
8	Church Avenue	T6
	(Portmarnock)	
47	Church Ave (Rathmines)	K17
46	Church Avenue South	H15
	(Dolphin's Barn)	
38	Church Avenue West	J14
	(Church Street)	
38	*Church Avenue	H15
	(off Irvine Street)	
23	Church Ct (Castleknock)	C11
40	Church Ct (East Wall)	M13
47	Church Gardens	K17
61	Church Grove	D22
39	Church Lane	K14
	(College Green)	
54	Church Lane	J19
	(Rathfarnham)	
47	*Church Lane South	K15
	(off Kevin Street)	
46	Church Park	J17
46	Church Park Avenue	J17
46	Church Park Court	J17
46	Church Park Drive	J17
46	Church Park Lawn	J17
46	Church Park Way	J17
40	*Church Place	M14
	(off Irvine Terrace)	
72	Church Rd (Ballybrack)	V24
73	Church Rd (Dalkey)	W21
40	Church Rd (East Wall)	M13
25	Church Rd (Finglas)	G10
69	Church Rd (Killiney)	U23
7	Church Rd (Malahide)	S3
10	Church Rd (Mulhuddart)	A8
20	Church Rd (Sutton)	W9
3	Church Rd (Swords)	N2
25	Church St (Finglas)	H10
38	Church St (Four Courts)	J14
21	Church St (Howth)	Y9
40	Church Street East	M14
38	Church Street New	J14
38	Church Street Upper	J14
25	Church Tce (Finglas)	H10
38	*Church Terrace	J14
	(off Church Street)	
50	Church Vw (Clondalkin)	A18
27	Church View	L11
	(Drumcondra)	
25	Church View (Finglas)	G10
71	Church Villas	T24
25	Church Walk	G12
55	Churchfields	M18
41	Churchgate Avenue	Q13
73	Churchill Mews	W21
49	Churchill Terrace	N16
66	Churchland's	N23
55	Churchtown	L20
55	Churchtown Avenue	L19
55	Churchtown Close	L19
55	Churchtown Drive	L19
55	Churchtown Rd Lower	L19
55	Churchtown Rd Upper	K20
55	Churchtown Rd Upper	L20
69	Churchview Ave	U23
69	Churchview Drive	U23
72	Churchview Park	U23
69	Churchview Road	U23
27	Cian Park	L12
2	Cianlea	L1
61	Cill Cais	C22
29	Cill Eanna	Q10
39	City Quay	L14
60	Citywest Avenue	ZZ21
60	Citywest Road	ZZ21
35	Claddagh Green	C15
35	Claddagh Road	C15
28	Clanawley Road	P11
28	Clanboy Road	P11
47	Clanbrassil Close	J16
47	Clanbrassil St Lower	J16
47	Clanbrassil St Upper	J16
28	Clancarthy Road	N11
13	Clancy Avenue	H9
14	Clancy Road	H9
28	Clandonagh Road	N11
57	Clanfadda Wood	Q19
28	Clanhugh Road	P11
28	Clanmahon Road	P11
28	Clanmaurice Road	N11
31	Clanmawr	V26
28	Clanmoyle Road	N11
28	Clanranald Road	N11
28	Clanree Road	N11
48	Clanwilliam Place	M15
38	Clanwilliam Square	M15
38	Clanwilliam Terrace	M15
18	Clare Hall	R8
14	Clare Lane	L15
27	Clare Park Villas	L11
42	Clare Road	L11
39	Clare Street	L14
26	Claremont Avenue	K11
26	Claremont Close	J12
26	Claremont Ct (Finglas)	J12
48	Claremont Court	N16
	(Sandymount)	
26	Claremont Crescent	J12
26	Claremont Drive	J10
73	Claremont Grove	V23
26	Claremont Lawn	J12
20	Claremont Mews	X9
49	Claremont Park	N15
71	Claremont Road	S24
	(Carrickmines)	
73	Claremont Rd (Killiney)	V23
49	Claremont Road	N15
	(Sandymount)	
20	Claremont Rd (Sutton)	W9
57	Claremont Terrace	M20
69	Claremont Villas	V21
31	Claremount	V27
71	Claremount Pines	S24
47	Clarence Mangan Rd	J15
38	*Clarence Mangan Sq	K15
	(off John Dillon St)	
39	Clarence Place Great	M15
39	Clarence St Great North	L13
59	Clarence Street	T20
39	*Clarendon Market	K15
	(off William St)	
39	*Clarendon Row	K15
	(off King St South)	
39	Clarendon Street	K15
39	Clareville Court	J12
26	Clareville Grove	J12
47	Clareville Road	J17
26	Clarinda Manor	U20
59	Clarinda Park East	U20
59	Clarinda Park North	U20
59	Clarinda Park West	U20
46	Clarke Terrace	H15
35	Clarkeville Terrace	C13
27	Claude Road	K12
36	Clayton Terrace	E14
25	*Clearwater Court	G11
	(Lockkeeper's Walk)	
59	Clearwater Cove	T20
35	Cleggan Avenue	C15
35	Cleggan Park	C15
35	Cleggan Road	C15
44	Clifden Drive	C15
35	Clifden Road	D15
73	Cliff Terrace	V21
3	Clifford's Lane	P2
58	Clifton Avenue	T20
58	Clifton Lane	T20
72	Clifton Park	V26
58	Clifton Terrace	T20
26	Cliftonville Road	K12
39	Clinch's Court	L13
46	Clogher Road	H16
4	Cloghran	M4
4	Cloghran Roundabout	M4
57	Cloister Avenue	R20
57	Cloister Close	R20
25	Cloister Court	G11
58	Cloister Gate	R20
57	Cloister Green	R20
58	Cloister Grove	R20
57	Cloister Square	R20
57	Cloister Way	R20
46	Clonallen	H18
66	Clonard Avenue	M22
66	Clonard Close	M22
66	Clonard Court	H18
66	Clonard Drive	M22
66	Clonard Grove	M22
66	Clonard Lawn	M22
66	Clonard Park	M22
46	Clonard Rd (Crumlin)	G17
66	Clonard Rd (Sandyford)	M22
31	Clonasleigh	V26
43	Clondalkin	A17
46	Clonfert Road	H17
18	Clongriffin	S8
68	Clonkeen Court	S23
68	Clonkeen Crescent	S22
68	Clonkeen Drive	S22
68	Clonkeen Grove	S22
68	Clonkeen Lawn	S23
68	Clonkeen Road	S22
68	Clonkeen Road	S23
40	Clonlara Rd (Ringsend)	N15
65	Clonlea	M22
65	Clonlea Wood	M22
39	Clonliffe Avenue	L13
39	Clonliffe Gardens	L12
39	Clonliffe Road	L12
46	Clonmacnoise Gro	H17
46	Clonmacnoise Rd	H17
26	Clonmel Road	K10
47	Clonmel Street	K15
18	Clonmellon Grove	R8
26	Clonmore Court	K11
39	Clonmore Road	L13
	(Ballybough)	
57	Clonmore Road	P20
	(Goatstown)	
39	Clonmore Terrace	L13
39	*Clonmore Villas	L13
	(Clonmore Road)	
17	Clonrosse Court	Q9
17	Clonrosse Drive	Q9
17	Clonrosse Park	Q9
16	Clonshaugh Avenue	P8
16	Clonshaugh Close	P8
16	Clonshaugh Court	N8
16	Clonshaugh Crescent	N8
16	Clonshaugh Drive	P8
16	Clonshaugh Glen	P8
16	Clonshaugh Green	P8
16	Clonshaugh Grove	P8
16	Clonshaugh Heights	N8
16	Clonshaugh Lawns	P8
16	Clonshaugh Meadow	N8
16	Clonshaugh Park	P8
16	Clonshaugh Rise	P8
16	Clonshaugh Road	N7
16	Clonshaugh Walk	P8
9	Clonsilla	ZZ10
23	Clonsilla Close	B10
23	Clonsilla Park	B10
9	Clonsilla Road	ZZ10
48	Clonskeagh	M18
56	Clonskeagh Drive	M18
56	Clonskeagh Road	M18
56	Clonskeagh Square	M18
41	Clontarf	Q13
29	Clontarf Park	Q13
30	Clontarf Road	R12
27	Clonturk Avenue	L11
27	Clonturk Court	L11
27	Clonturk Gardens	L12
27	Clonturk Park	L12
25	Cloonlara Crescent	H11
25	Cloonlara Drive	H11
25	Cloonlara Road	H11
60	Cloonmore Avenue	A22
60	Cloonmore Close	A22
60	Cloonmore Crescent	A22
60	Cloonmore Drive	A22
60	Cloonmore Gardens	A22
60	Cloonmore Green	A22
60	Cloonmore Grove	A22
60	Cloonmore Lawn	A22
60	Cloonmore Park	A22
60	Cloonmore Road	A22
44	Clover Hill Drive	D15
44	Clover Hill Road	A16
35	Cloverhill Road	B15
46	Cloyne Road	H17
59	Cluain Mhuire	U21
33	Cluain Ri	ZZ14
44	Club Road	D17
13	Clune Road	H9
69	Cluny Grove	U23
73	Cluny Park	V22
48	Clyde Court	M16
48	Clyde Lane	M16
48	Clyde Road	M16
32	Cnoc Aoibhean	VV14
19	Coast Road (Baldoyle)	U8
7	Coast Road (Malahide)	T2
39	Coburg Place	L13
39	*Coghill's Court	K15
	(off Dame Street)	
72	Cois Coillte	U25
47	*Cois Eala	N16
	(Grove Road)	
61	Cois Na hAbhann	C22
38	*Coke Lane	J14
	(Arran Quay)	
26	Coke Ovens Cottages	J12
51	Colbert's Fort	C20
34	Coldcut Road	A14
69	Coldwell Street	U21
36	Colepark Avenue	D15
36	Colepark Drive	D15
36	Colepark Green	D15
36	Colepark Road	D15
38	Coleraine Street	J14
73	Coliemore Road	W22
73	Coliemore Road	X22
73	Coliemore Villas	W22
53	College Crescent	G19
53	College Drive	G19
23	College Fort	C12
23	College Gate	C11
39	College Green	K14
23	College Grove	C12
39	College Lane	L15
	(Trinity College)	
27	College Manor	L12
39	College Mews	L12
23	College Park	D12
	(Castleknock)	
53	College Pk (Kimmage)	G19
66	College Park Avenue	M22
66	College Park Close	M22
66	College Park Court	M22
66	College Park Drive	M22
66	College Park Grove	M22
66	College Park Way	M22
23	College Park Ct	C12
	(Castleknock)	
64	College Road	J23
	(Whitechurch Road)	
19	College St (Baldoyle)	U8
39	College Street	L14
	(Trinity College)	
27	College View	L11
	(Drumcondra)	

Page		Grid Ref

62 College View (Tallaght) **D21**
23 College Wood **C12**
48 Collier's Avenue **L17**
27 Collindale **M10**
28 Collins Avenue **M10**
28 Collins Avenue East **N11**
27 Collins Ave Extension **K10**
27 Collins Avenue West **L10**
28 Collins Close **M11**
58 Collins Ct (Blackrock) **R19**
28 Collins Court **M11**
(Collins Avenue)
14 Collins Drive **H9**
14 Collins Green **H9**
28 Collins Park **N11**
14 Collins Place **H9**
26 Collins Row **H10**
43 Collinstown Crescent **A15**
43 Collinstown Grove **B15**
34 Collinstown Road **A15**
28 Collinswood **M10**
3 Colmcille Court **N2**
33 Colthurst Close **ZZ14**
33 Colthurst Crescent **ZZ14**
33 Colthurst Gardens **ZZ14**
33 Colthurst Green **ZZ14**
33 Colthurst Mews **ZZ14**
33 Colthurst Park **ZZ14**
33 Colthurst Rise **ZZ14**
33 Colthurst Road **ZZ14**
33 Colthurst Way **ZZ14**
45 Comeragh Road **F16**
3 Commons East **N3**
72 Commons Road **V26**
(Loughlinstown)
50 Commons Road **A18**
(St. John's Gate)
39 Commons Street **L13**
39 Compass Court **F11**
27 Comyn Place **K11**
37 Con Colbert Road **G15**
73 Congress Gardens **V21**
3 Connaught Parade **J12**
59 *Connaught Place **U20**
(Kelly's Avenue)
38 Connaught Street **J12**
45 Connolly Avenue **G15**
(Kilmainham)
6 Connolly Ave (Malahide) **R4**
45 Connolly Gardens **G15**
25 Conor Clune Road **F12**
41 Conquer Hill Ave **Q13**
41 Conquer Hill Road **Q13**
28 Constellation Road **M8**
38 Constitution Hill **K13**
27 Convent Ave (Marino) **L12**
67 Convent Close **P21**
48 Convent Court **L15**
8 Convent Lane **U4**
(Portmarnock)
54 Convent Lane **J20**
(Willbrook)
36 Convent Lawns **E15**
29 Convent Lodge **Q10**
47 Convent Place **L16**
58 Convent Rd (Blackrock) **R20**
28 Convent Rd (Clondalkin) **B17**
73 Convent Road (Dalkey) **W22**
59 Convent Road **U20**
(Dun Laoghaire)
25 Convent View Cottages **G12**
(Cabra)
50 Convent View Cottages **A18**
(St. John's Gate)
25 Convent View Cres **G12**
25 Convent Way **G12**
29 Conway Court **M15**
37 Conyngham Road **G14**
28 Cook Street **J14**
51 Cookstown Court **C20**
51 Cookstown Road **B20**
51 Cookstown Road **C20**
51 Cookstown Way **C21**
63 Coolamber Court **G21**
63 Coolamber Park **G21**
28 Coolatree Close **M10**
28 Coolatree Park **M10**
28 Coolatree Road **M10**
3 Cooldriona Court **N2**
16 Cooleen Avenue **M9**
72 Coolevin (Ballybrack) **U24**
47 Coolevin Road **K15**
45 Cooley Close **F16**
45 Cooley Road **F16**
28 Coolgariff Road **M10**
28 Coolgreena Close **M10**
28 Coolgreena Road **M10**
66 Coolkill **N23**
22 Coolmine Boulevard **B10**
22 Coolmine Close **A10**
10 Coolmine Cottages **A8**

22 Coolmine Court **B10**
22 Coolmine Green **A11**
22 Coolmine Lawn **A10**
22 Coolmine Mews **B10**
22 Coolmine Park **B10**
22 Coolmine Road **B11**
22 Coolmine Woods **B10**
67 Coolnevaun **P21**
17 Coolock **P9**
17 Coolock Drive **P9**
15 Coolock Lane (Santry) **L8**
29 Coolock Village **P10**
17 Coolock Village Close **P9**
38 Coolrua Drive **M9**
38 Coombe Court **J15**
39 Cope Street **K14**
28 Copeland Avenue **N12**
28 Copeland Grove **N12**
39 *Copper Alley **K15**
(Lord Edward Street)
57 Coppinger **R20**
57 Coppinger Close **Q20**
57 Coppinger Glade **Q20**
39 Coppinger Row **K15**
57 Coppinger Walk **Q20**
57 Coppinger Wood **Q20**
60 Corbally **ZZ23**
60 Corbally Avenue **ZZ22**
60 Corbally Close **ZZ22**
60 Corbally Downs **ZZ22**
60 Corbally Drive **ZZ22**
60 Corbally Glade **ZZ22**
60 Corbally Green **ZZ22**
60 Corbally Heath **ZZ22**
60 Corbally Lawn **ZZ22**
60 Corbally Park **ZZ22**
60 Corbally Rise **ZZ22**
60 Corbally Square **ZZ22**
60 Corbally Vale **ZZ22**
60 Corbally Way **ZZ22**
31 Corbawn Avenue **W26**
31 Corbawn Close **W26**
31 Corbawn Court **W26**
31 Corbawn Dale **V26**
31 Corbawn Drive **W26**
31 Corbawn Glade **V27**
31 Corbawn Grove **W26**
31 Corbawn Lane **V26**
31 Corbawn Lawn **V27**
31 Corbawn Wood **V26**
11 Corduff **C9**
11 Corduff Avenue **C9**
11 Corduff Close **C9**
11 Corduff Cottages **B9**
11 Corduff Crescent **C9**
11 Corduff Gardens **C9**
11 Corduff Green **C9**
11 Corduff Grove **B8**
11 Corduff Park **B8**
11 Corduff Place **C9**
11 Corduff Way **C9**
39 *Cork Hill (off Dame St) **K15**
36 Cork Street **J15**
43 Corkagh View **A18**
54 Cormac Terrace **J18**
39 Corn Exchange Place **L14**
68 Cornelscourt **S23**
68 Cornelscourt Hill Rd **S23**
38 Cornmarket **J15**
20 Corr Castle **W9**
20 Corr Castle Apts **W9**
20 Corrbridge Terrace **W9**
54 Corrib Road **H18**
54 Corrib Road **J18**
59 Corrig Avenue **U20**
52 Corrig Close **E19**
59 Corrig Park **U20**
73 Corrig Road (Dalkey) **W21**
69 Corrig Road **J14**
(Dun Laoghaire)
66 Corrig Rd (Stillorgan) **P22**
53 Corrybeg **G20**
47 Cosy Lodge **K17**
47 Coulson Avenue **J18**
15 Coultry Avenue **L9**
15 Coultry Close **K9**
15 Coultry Court **K8**
15 Coultry Crescent **K8**
15 Coultry Drive **K8**
15 Coultry Gardens **K8**
15 Coultry Green **K8**
15 Coultry Grove **L8**
15 Coultry Lawn **L8**
15 Coultry Park **L8**
15 Coultry Road **K8**
15 Coultry Terrace **K8**
15 Coultry Way **L9**
72 Coundon Court **V24**
69 Courtlands **T23**
39 Courtney Place **M13**
25 Courtview Apts **F11**

47 Cow Parlour **J15**
21 Cowbooter Lane **Z10**
39 Cowley Place Lower **K13**
38 Cowley Place Upper **K12**
47 Cowper Downs **K17**
48 Cowper Drive **L18**
48 Cowper Gardens **L18**
47 Cowper Mews **K18**
47 Cowper Road **K18**
38 Cowper Street **H13**
47 Cowper Village **K17**
43 Cows Lane **K14**
43 Crag Avenue **B16**
43 Crag Crescent **B16**
43 Crag Terrace **B16**
28 Craigford Avenue **P11**
28 Craigford Drive **P11**
73 Craiglands **W22**
58 Craigmore Gardens **R19**
48 Crampton Avenue **M16**
39 *Crampton Court **K14**
(off Dame St)
39 Crampton Quay **K14**
39 *Crane Lane **K14**
(off Dame Street)
38 Crane Street **J15**
49 Cranfield Place **N15**
54 Cranford Ct (Kimmage) **H18**
56 Cranford Court **N18**
(Stillorgan Road)
48 Cranmer Lane **M15**
48 Crannagh **M18**
54 Crannagh Castle **J19**
54 Crannagh Court **J19**
54 Crannagh Grove **K19**
55 Crannagh Hall **K19**
54 Crannagh Park **J19**
54 Crannagh Road **J19**
54 Crannagh Way **K19**
14 Crannogue Close **J8**
14 Crannogue Road **J8**
27 Cranford Avenue **K12**
39 *Crawford Terrace **L13**
(off Kings Avenue)
39 Creighton Street **L14**
44 Cremona Road **E15**
26 Cremore Avenue **J11**
26 Cremore Crescent **J11**
26 Cremore Drive **J11**
26 Cremore Heights **J10**
26 Cremore Lawn **J11**
26 Cremore Park **K11**
26 Cremore Road **J11**
26 Cremore Villas **J11**
63 Cremorne (Knocklyon) **G21**
54 Cremorne **J18**
(Terenure Road East)
40 Crescent Gardens **M13**
28 Crescent House **N12**
28 Crescent Place **N12**
27 Crescent Villas **K12**
27 Crestfield Avenue **L10**
27 Crestfield Close **L10**
27 Crestfield Drive **L10**
27 Crestfield Park **L10**
27 Crestfield Road **L10**
39 Crinan Strand **L14**
31 Crinken Glen **V27**
31 Crinken Lane **U28**
37 Croaghpatrick Road **G12**
59 Crofton Avenue **U20**
59 *Crofton Mansions **U20**
(Crofton Avenue)
59 Crofton Road **U20**
59 Crofton Terrace **U20**
44 Croftwood Crescent **C15**
44 Croftwood Drive **C15**
44 Croftwood Gardens **C15**
44 Croftwood Green **D15**
44 Croftwood Grove **C15**
44 Croftwood Park **D15**
39 Croke Villas **L13**
16 Cromcastle Avenue **N9**
16 Cromcastle Close **N9**
16 Cromcastle Court **N9**
16 Cromcastle Drive **N9**
16 Cromcastle Green **N9**
16 Cromcastle Park **N9**
16 Cromcastle Road **N9**
70 Cromlech Close **Q26**
14 Cromlech Court **J8**
72 Cromlech Fields **V25**
38 Cromwell's Quarters **H15**
45 Cromwellsfort Road **F18**
48 Crosbie House **L16**
57 Cross Ave (Booterstown) **Q19**
59 Cross Avenue **U20**
(Dun Laoghaire)
21 Crosstrees Court **Y10**
69 Crosthwaite Park East **U21**
69 Crosthwaite Park South **U21**

69 Crosthwaite Park West **U21**
59 Crosthwaite Terrace **U20**
38 *Crostick Alley **J15**
(off Meath St)
47 Crotty Avenue **F17**
39 *Crow St (off Dame St) **K14**
39 *Crown Alley **K14**
(Off Temple Bar)
27 Croydon Gardens **M12**
28 Croydon Green **M12**
28 Croydon Park Avenue **M12**
27 Croydon Terrace **M11**
45 Crumlin **G17**
45 Crumlin Park **G17**
(off Crumlin Road)
46 Crumlin Road **H16**
39 Cuala Road (Cabra) **J12**
21 *Cuan na Mara **Y9**
(Harbour Road)
47 Cuckoo Lane **K14**
47 Cuffe Lane **K15**
47 Cuffe Street **K15**
14 Cuilenn Park **J9**
61 Cul na Greine **C22**
28 Cullen's Cottages **B8**
48 *Cullen's Wood House **L16**
(Crosbie House)
47 *Cullenswood Court **L17**
(off Cullenswood Park)
48 Cullenswood Gardens **L17**
48 Cullenswood Park **L17**
47 *Cullenswood Road **L17**
(Charleston Road)
35 Culmore Park **C14**
35 Culmore Road **C14**
38 *Cumberland Pl Nth **J13**
(on North Circular Road)
48 Cumberland Road **L16**
59 Cumberland Street **T20**
39 Cumberland St Nth **L13**
39 Cumberland St Sth **L25**
73 Cunningham Drive **W22**
73 Cunningham Road **W22**
45 Curlew Road **F16**
18 Curracloe Drive **R9**
10 Curragh Hall **B7**
10 Curragh Hall Avenue **B7**
10 Curragh Hall Close **B7**
10 Curragh Hall Court **B7**
10 Curragh Hall Cres **B7**
10 Curragh Hall Drive **B7**
10 Curragh Hall Gate **B7**
10 Curragh Hall Green **B7**
10 Curragh Hall Grove **B7**
10 Curragh Hall Lane **B7**
10 Curragh Hall Lodge **B7**
10 Curragh Hall Road **B7**
10 Curragh Hall View **B7**
10 Curragh Hall Way **B7**
39 *Curved Street **K14**
(Eustace Street)
47 Curzon Street **K16**
61 Cushlawn Avenue **C23**
61 Cushlawn Close **C23**
61 Cushlawn Dale **C23**
61 Cushlawn Drive **C22**
61 Cushlawn Grove **C22**
61 Cushlawn Park **C22**
61 Cushlawn Walk **C23**
61 Cushlawn Way **C23**
39 Custom House Harbour **L14**
38 Custom House Quay **L14**
40 Cymric Road **N15**
64 *Cypress Avenue **H22**
(Brookwood)
72 Cypress Court **V25**
53 Cypress Drive **G19**
53 Cypress Garth **G20**
53 Cypress Grove North **G19**
53 Cypress Grove Road **G19**
53 Cypress Grove South **G20**
19 Cypress House **U9**
53 Cypress Lawn **G19**
53 Cypress Park **G20**
56 Cypress Road **P19**

39 *DAISY MARKET **K13**
(on Parnell Street)
15 Dakota Avenue **M8**
38 Dakota Court **K12**
7 Dal Riada **T4**
26 Dalcassian Downs **J12**
67 Dale Close **P21**
67 Dale Drive **P21**
66 Dale Road **P21**
72 Dale View **V24**
72 Dale View Park **V24**
62 Dalepark Road **D22**
64 Daletree Avenue **E22**
63 Daletree Close **E23**
63 Daletree Court **F23**

Page		Grid Ref	Page		Grid Ref	Page		Grid Ref	Page		Grid Ref
62	Daletree Crescent	F22	42	Deansrath Park	ZZ17	22	Diswellstown Road	A11		(Seafort Terrace)	
63	Daletree Drive	F22	42	Deansrath Road	ZZ17	69	Dixon Villas	V21	28	Dromawling Road	M10
62	Daletree Park	F23	25	Deanstown Avenue	G10	62	Dodder Avenue	E22	28	Drombawn Avenue	M10
63	Daletree Place	F27	25	Deanstown Drive	G10	55	Dodder Bank	L18	61	Dromcarra Avenue	B22
63	Daletree Road	F23	25	Deanstown Green	G10	62	Dodder Court	E22	61	Dromcarra Drive	B22
63	Daletree Terrace	F23	25	Deanstown Park	G10	62	Dodder Crescent	E22	60	Dromcarra Green	A22
62	Daletree View	E23	25	Deanstown Road	G10	54	Dodder Dale	J19	61	Dromcarra Grove	B22
2	Daleview Road	M1	36	Decies Road	E15	62	Dodder Green	E22	28	Dromeen Avenue	M10
73	Dalkey	W21	9	Deerhaven	ZZ8	54	Dodder Lawn	E22	10	Dromheath Avenue	B8
73	Dalkey Avenue	W22	9	Deerhaven Avenue	ZZ8	54	Dodder Park Drive	J19	10	Dromheath Drive	B8
73	Dalkey Court	W22	9	Deerhaven Close	ZZ8	54	Dodder Park Grove	J19	10	Dromheath Gardens	B8
73	Dalkey Grove	W22	9	Deerhaven Crescent	ZZ8	54	Dodder Park Road	J19	10	Dromheath Grove	B8
73	Dalkey Park	V22	9	Deerhaven Green	ZZ8	54	Dodder Road Lower	J19	10	Dromheath Park	B8
73	Dalkey Rock	W23	9	Deerhaven Park	ZZ8	40	Dodder Terrace	N15	28	Dromlee Crescent	M10
7	Dalton Mews	S3	9	Deerhaven View	ZZ8	55	Dodder Vale	K19	28	Drommanane Park	M10
38	Dalymount	J13	9	Deerhaven Walk	ZZ8	48	*Dodder View Cottages	M16	28	Drommanane Road	M10
10	Damastown Avenue	A7	61	Deerpark	C23		(Herbert Cottages)		45	Dromore Road	G16
10	Damastown Close	ZZ7	24	Deerpark Avenue	D12	32	Dodsboro Cottages	VV14	14	Druid Court	J8
10	Damastown Court	A7		(Castleknock)		32	Dodsboro Road	WW14	71	Druid Valley	T25
10	Damastown Way	A8	61	Deerpark Ave (Kiltipper)	C23	39	D'Olier Street	L14	66	Drumahill	N21
39	Dame Court	K15	24	Deerpark Close	D11	29	Dollymount Avenue	R12	38	Drumalee Avenue	H13
39	Dame Lane	K14		(Castleknock)		29	Dollymount Grove	Q12	38	Drumalee Court	H13
39	Dame Street	K15	61	Deerpark Cl (Kiltipper)	C23	29	Dollymount Park	R12	38	Drumalee Drive	H13
3	Damer House	P2	61	Deerpark Downs	C23	29	Dollymount Rise	R12	38	Drumalee Grove	H13
14	*Dane Close	J8	24	Deerpark Drive	D11	14	Dolmen Court	K8	38	Drumalee Park	H13
	(Dane Road)			(Castleknock)		46	Dolphin Avenue	J16	38	Drumalee Road	H13
14	Dane Road	J8	61	Deerpark Dr (Kiltipper)	C23	46	Dolphin Court	H16	60	Drumcairn Avenue	A21
29	Danes Court	R12	24	Deerpark Green	E11	46	Dolphin House	H16	60	Drumcairn Drive	A21
41	Danesfort	P13	24	Deerpark Lawn	E11	46	*Dolphin Market	H16	60	Drumcairn Gardens	A21
26	Daneswell Road	K12	61	Deerpark Lodge	C23		(off Dolphin's Barn St)		60	Drumcairn Green	A21
45	Dangan Avenue	G18	61	Deerpark Place	C23	46	Dolphin Park	H16	61	Drumcairn Park	B21
45	Dangan Drive	G18	61	Deerpark Rise	C23	46	Dolphin Road	H16	27	Drumcliffe Drive	H12
53	Dangan Park	G18	24	Deerpark Road	D11	46	Dolphin's Barn	H16	25	Drumcliffe Road	H12
47	Daniel Street	K16		(Castleknock Road)		46	Dolphin's Barn Street	H16	27	Drumcondra	K12
28	Danieli Drive	P10	61	Deerpark Rd (Kiltipper)	C23	39	Dominick Lane	K14	39	Drumcondra Park	L13
28	Danieli Road	P10	56	Deerpark Road	N20	39	Dominick Place	K14	27	Drumcondra Rd Lower	L12
63	Dargle Drive	K21		(Mount Merrion)		59	Dominick Street	U20	27	Drumcondra Rd Upper	L12
68	Dargle Road	R21	61	Deerpark Square	C23	38	Dominick Street Lower	K14	28	*Drumderg Court	M12
	(Dean's Grange)		61	Deerpark Terrace	C23	38	Dominick Street Upper	K13		(Fairview)	
27	Dargle Rd (Drumcondra)	K12	61	Deerpark Walk	C23	53	Domville Drive	G20	35	Drumfinn Avenue	C14
65	Dargle Valley	K21	61	Deerpark Way	C23	53	Domville Green	G20	35	Drumfinn Park	D15
65	Dargle View	K21	19	Del Val Avenue	T10	72	Domville Grove	V25	35	Drumfinn Road	D14
63	Dargle Wood	G21	19	Del Val Court	T10	53	Domville Road	G20	69	Drumkeen Manor	U23
47	Darley Street	K16	63	Delaford Avenue	F21	18	Donaghmede	S8	56	Drummartin Close	N20
46	Darley's Terrace	J15	63	Delaford Drive	F21	18	Donaghmede Avenue	S9	66	Drummartin Crescent	N21
24	Darling Estate	F11	63	Delaford Grove	F21	18	Donaghmede Drive	S9	56	Drummartin Park	N21
48	Dartmouth Lane	L16	63	Delaford Lawn	F21	18	Donaghmede Park	S9	56	Drummartin Road	N20
47	Dartmouth Place	L16	63	Delaford Park	F21	18	Donaghmede Road	S9	56	Drummartin Terrace	N20
47	Dartmouth Road	L16	66	Delbrook Manor	M22	45	Donard Road	F16	47	*Drummond Place	J16
47	Dartmouth Sq East	L16	66	Delbrook Park	M22	38	Donoellan Avenue	H15		(off Mount Drummond Ave)	
47	Dartmouth Sq North	L16	9	Delhurst Avenue	YY9	39	Dominick Place	K14	39	Drury Street	K15
47	Dartmouth Sq South	L16	9	Delhurst Close	YY9	48	Donnybrook Castle	M17	5	Drynam Avenue	P3
47	Dartmouth Sq West	L16	9	Delhurst Mews	YY9	48	Donnybrook Close	N18	5	Drynam Close	P4
47	Dartmouth Terrace	L16	9	Delhurst Terrace	YY9	48	Donnybrook Court	M18	5	Drynam Copse	P4
55	Dartry Cottages	L19	26	Delville Road	K10	56	Donnybrook Green	N18	3	Drynam Court	N2
55	Dartry Park	L18	22	Delvin Road	J12	48	Donnybrook Manor	M17	5	Drynam Crescent	P3
55	Dartry Road	K18	22	Delwood Close	B11	48	Donnybrook Mews	M17	5	Drynam Drive	P3
26	David Park	K12	22	Delwood Drive	B11	47	Donnybrook Road	M17	5	Drynam Glen	P3
26	David Road	K12	22	Delwood Grove	B11	28	Donnycarney	N11	5	Drynam Green	P3
38	*Davis Place	J15	22	Delwood Lawn	B11	28	Donnycarney Road	N11	5	Drynam Grove	P3
	(Francis Street)		22	Delwood Park	B11	61	Donomore Avenue	B22	5	Drynam Hall	P3
45	Davitt House	G16	22	Delwood Road	B11	61	Donomore Crescent	B22	5	Drynam Mews	P4
72	Davitt Park	U24	22	Delwood Walk	B11	61	Donomore Green	B22	5	Drynam Place	P4
35	Davitt Rd (Inchicore)	F16	29	Demesne	P11	61	Donomore Park	B22	5	Drynam Rise	P4
57	Dawson Court	Q19	39	Denmark Street Great	K13	46	Donore Avenue	J15	5	Drynam Road	N2
39	*Dawson Court	K15	72	Denville Court	U24	47	Donore Road	J15	5	Drynam Square	P2
	(off Stephen St Lower)		39	Denzille Lane	L15	47	Donore Terrace	J15	3	Drynam View	P3
39	Dawson Lane	L15	38	*Derby Square	K15	47	Donovan Lane	J16	3	Drynam Walk	P3
39	Dawson Street	L15		(off Werburgh St)		38	Doon Avenue	H13	5	Drynam Way	P3
54	*De Bret House	J20	40	Dermot O'Hurley Ave	M15	14	Doon Court	J8	62	Drysdale Close	D22
	(Stonepark Court)		54	Derravaragh Road	H18	72	Doonamana Road	U22	57	Dualla Court	P20
38	De Burgh Road	H14	46	Derry Drive	G17	69	Doonanore Park	U23	4	Dublin Airport	L5
26	De Courcy Square	K12	46	Derry Park	G17	71	Doonsalla Drive	U23	31	Dublin Road (Bray)	V28
60	De Selby	A22	46	Derry Road	G17	69	Doonsalla Park	U23	19	Dublin Rd (Kilbarrack)	T10
60	De Selby Close	A22	40	Derrynane Gardens	N15	40	Doris Street	M15	6	Dublin Rd (Malahide)	R3
60	De Selby Court	A22	39	Derrynane Parade	K13	57	Dornden Park	P18	31	Dublin Rd (Shankill)	V26
60	De Selby Crescent	A22	59	Desmond Avenue	U20	31	Dorney Court	V27	20	Dublin Rd (Sutton)	V9
60	De Selby Downs	A22	73	Desmond Cottages	W22	39	Dorset Lane	K13	2	Dublin Rd (Swords)	M3
60	De Selby Drive	A22	47	Desmond Street	K15	39	Dorset Place	K13	18	Dublin St (Baldoyle)	U8
60	De Selby Green	A22	46	Devenish Road	H17	39	Dorset Street Lower	K13	38	Duck Lane	J14
60	De Selby Lane	A22	14	Deverell Place	L14	39	Dorset Street Upper	K13	47	Dufferin Avenue	J16
60	De Selby Lawns	A22	38	Devery's Lane	K12	45	Dowland Road	G17	39	Duke Lane Lower	L15
60	De Selby Park	ZZ22	69	Devitt Villas	V21	39	Dowling's Court	L14	39	Duke Lane Upper	L15
60	De Selby Rise	A22	39	Devlin's Place	L15	16	Downpatrick Road	H16	39	*Duke Row	L13
39	*De Velara Place	K13	68	Devon Close	S21	38	Dowth Avenue	J12		(Bailey's Row)	
	(Synott Place)		46	Devoy Road	G15	26	Drapier Green	J10	39	Duke Street	K15
59	*De Vesci Court	T20	8	Dewberry Park	U14	26	Drapier Road	J10	61	Dun Aengus	C22
	(off Sloperton)		47	Dexter Terrace	L16	58	Drayton Close	S20	61	Dun an Oir	C22
59	De Vesci Terrace	T20	39	Digges Lane	K15	38	Drimnagh	F16	66	Dun Emer Drive	M21
38	Dean Street	K15	47	Digges Street Upper	K15	45	Drimnagh Road	F17	66	Dun Emer Park	M21
26	Dean Swift Green	K10	38	*Dillon Place South	K15	70	Drinagh Park	Q24	66	Dun Emer Road	M21
26	Dean Swift Road	K10		(off John Dillon St)		70	Drinaghmore	Q24	59	Dun Laoghaire	U20
38	Dean Swift Square	J15	25	Dingle Road	H12	70	Drinaghmore Avenue	Q24	37	Dunard Avenue	G13
58	Deans Court	S21	32	Dispensary Lane	XX13	70	Drinaghmore Close	Q24	37	Dunard Court	H13
68	Deans Grange	S22		(Lucan)		70	Drinaghmore Court	Q24	37	Dunard Drive	H13
8	Dean's Grange Road	S21	54	Dispensary Lane	J20	33	Droim na Coille Ave	ZZ14	37	Dunard Park	H13
42	Deansrath Avenue	ZZ16		(Willbrook)		33	Droim na Coille Court	ZZ14	37	Dunard Road	H13
42	Deansrath Crescent	ZZ17	36	*Distillery House Apts	E14	33	Droim na Coille Place	ZZ14	37	Dunard Walk	H13
42	Deansrath Green	ZZ17		(Hibernian Terace)		45	Dromard Road	F16	42	Dunawley Avenue	A17
42	Deansrath Grove	ZZ16	27	Distillery Road	L12	49	*Dromard Terrace	N16	43	Dunawley Drive	A17
42	Deansrath Lawn	ZZ16	23	Diswellstown Cottages	B12				42	Dunawley Grove	A17

Page		Grid Ref
43	Dunawley Way	A17
21	Dunbo Hill	Y9
21	Dunbo Terrace	Y9
70	Dunboy	R24
20	Duncarraig	W10
16	Dundaniel Road	N9
73	Dundela Avenue	V21
73	Dundela Crescent	V21
73	Dundela Haven	V21
73	Dundela Park	V21
65	Dundrum	L21
55	Dundrum By Pass	L20
65	Dundrum Gate Apts	M21
55	Dundrum Road	M19
65	Dundrum Wood	L21
69	Dunedin Court	T21
69	Dunedin Drive	T21
68	Dunedin Park	T21
69	Dunedin Terrace	T21
59	Dungar Terrace	U20
21	Dungriffan Road	Y10
21	Dungriffan Villas	Y10
59	Dunleary Hill	T20
59	Dunleary Road	T20
29	Dunluce Road	P11
25	Dunmanus Road	H12
51	Dunmore Grove	C18
51	Dunmore Lawn	C19
51	Dunmore Park	C18
39	Dunree Street	L13
17	Dunree Park	Q9
24	Dunsandle Court	D11
24	Dunsandle Grove	D11
29	Dunseverick Road	P12
25	Dunsink Avenue	G10
25	Dunsink Drive	G10
25	Dunsink Gardens	G10
25	Dunsink Green	G10
24	Dunsink Lane	F10
25	Dunsink Park	G10
25	Dunsink Road	G10
13	Dunsoghly	F9
13	Dunsoghly Avenue	F9
13	Dunsoghly Close	F9
13	Dunsoghly Court	F9
13	Dunsoghly Drive	F9
13	Dunsoghly Green	F9
13	Dunsoghly Grove	F9
13	Dunsoghly Park	F9
67	Dunstaffnage Hall Apts	Q21
47	Dunville Avenue	L17
69	Durham Place	U21
47	Durham Road	P16
46	Durrow Road	H17
11	Dursey Row	C9
58	**EAGLE HILL**	**R19**
54	Eagle Hill Avenue	J18
16	Eagle Park	N9
66	Eagle Tce (Dundrum)	M21
69	Eaglewood Apts	T22
69	Eaglewood House	T22
69	Eaglewood Mews	T22
39	Earl Place	K14
34	Earl Street North	K14
38	Earl Street South	J14
38	Earls Court (Cabra)	H13
54	Earls Court (Terenure)	J18
34	Earlsfort	ZZ15
34	Earlsfort Avenue	ZZ15
34	Earlsfort Close	ZZ14
34	Earlsfort Court	ZZ14
34	Earlsfort Drive	ZZ15
34	Earlsfort Gardens	ZZ14
34	Earlsfort Green	ZZ15
34	Earlsfort Grove	ZZ15
34	Earlsfort Lane	ZZ14
34	Earlsfort Lawn	ZZ14
34	Earlsfort Meadows	ZZ14
34	Earlsfort Park	ZZ14
34	Earlsfort Rise	ZZ15
47	Earlsfort Terrace	L16
34	Earlsfort Vale	ZZ15
34	Earlsfort View	ZZ15
34	Earlsfort Way	ZZ15
59	East Pier	V19
	(Dun Laoghaire)	
21	East Pier (Howth)	Y9
40	East Road	M14
40	East Wall	M13
40	East Wall Road	M13
48	Eastmoreland Lane	M16
48	Eastmoreland Place	M16
25	Eastwood	F10
55	Eaton Brae (Orwell Rd)	K19
31	Eaton Brae (Shankill)	V26
54	Eaton Close	J18
47	Eaton Court (Terenure)	J18
54	Eaton Hall	J18
58	Eaton Place	S20
54	Eaton Road	J18
58	Eaton Sq (Monkstown)	S20
54	Eaton Sq (Terenure)	J18
31	Eaton Wood Avenue	V26
31	Eaton Wood Court	V27
31	Eaton Wood Green	V27
31	Eaton Wood Grove	V26
31	Eaton Wood Square	V26
47	Ebenezer Terrace	J15
29	Eblana Avenue	U20
39	Eblana Villas	M15
	(Lwr Grand Canal St)	
38	*Eblana Villas	K13
	(off Arbour Hill)	
39	Eccles Court	K13
39	Eccles Place	K13
39	Eccles Street	K13
38	Echlin Street	J15
64	Eden Avenue	K21
65	Eden Court	K21
64	Eden Crescent	K21
64	Eden Grove	K21
59	Eden Park	U21
66	Eden Park Avenue	N21
56	Eden Park Drive	N20
66	Eden Park Road	N21
39	Eden Quay	L14
69	Eden Road Lower	U21
69	Eden Road Upper	U21
27	Eden Tce (Botanic Ave)	K12
69	Eden Terrace	U21
	(Dun Laoghaire)	
69	Eden Villas	U21
64	Edenbrook Court	H21
54	Edenbrook Drive	H20
54	Edenbrook Park	H20
29	Edenmore	Q10
29	Edenmore Avenue	Q10
29	Edenmore Crescent	R10
29	Edenmore Drive	Q10
29	Edenmore Gardens	Q10
29	Edenmore Green	R10
29	Edenmore Grove	Q10
29	Edenmore Park	Q10
65	Edenvale	K22
48	Edenvale Road	L17
56	Edenwood (Goatstown)	N20
27	Edgewood	L12
	(Richmond Road)	
11	Edgewood Lawns	B9
33	Edmondsbury Court	YY13
64	Edmondstown	H23
64	Edmondstown Green	H22
64	Edmondstown Road	H23
73	*Edward Terrace	X22
	(Off Nerano Rd)	
64	Edwards Court	H22
73	Edwin Court	V22
47	Effra Road	K17
48	Eglinton Court	M17
48	Eglinton Park	M17
	(Donnybrook)	
48	Eglinton Road	M17
48	Eglinton Square	M17
48	Eglinton Terrace	M17
	(Donnybrook)	
56	Eglinton Tce (Dundrum)	M20
38	*Églinton Terrace	K13
	(Royal Canal Bank)	
48	Eglinton Wood	M17
17	Eklad Close	Q8
17	Eklad Park	Q8
32	Elderberry	XX15
35	Elderwood Road	C14
46	*Elford Terrace	J15
	(off Donore Avenue)	
48	Elgin Road	M16
39	Elizabeth Street	L12
63	Elkwood	H21
27	Ellenfield Road	M10
61	Ellensborough	C23
61	Ellensborough Ave	C23
61	Ellensborough Close	C23
61	Ellensborough Copse	C23
61	Ellensborough Court	C23
61	Ellensborough Cres	C23
61	Ellensborough Dale	C23
61	Ellensborough Downs	C23
61	Ellensborough Grange	C23
61	Ellensborough Green	C23
61	Ellensborough Grove	C23
61	Ellensborough Lawn	C23
61	Ellensborough Mdws	C23
61	Ellensborough Park	C23
61	Ellensborough Rise	C23
61	Ellensborough View	C23
61	Ellensborough Walk	C23
61	Ellensborough Way	C23
67	Ellesmere	Q22
38	Ellesmere Avenue	H13
38	*Ellis Court	J14
	(Ellis Street)	
38	Ellis Quay	J14
38	Ellis Street	J14
33	Elm Close	YY15
60	Elm Court (Jobstown)	A22
33	Elm Court (Lucan)	YY15
33	Elm Dene	YY15
60	Elm Drive (Jobstown)	A22
33	Elm Drive (Lucan)	YY15
33	Elm Green	YY15
58	Elm Grove	R10
60	Elm Grove (Jobstown)	A22
33	Elm Grove (Lucan)	YY15
28	Elm Mount Avenue	N11
28	Elm Mount Close	M10
28	Elm Mount Close	N10
28	Elm Mount Court	N11
28	Elm Mount Crescent	N10
28	Elm Mount Drive	N10
28	Elm Mount Grove	N10
28	Elm Mount Heights	N10
28	Elm Mount Lawn	N10
28	Elm Mount Park	N10
28	Elm Mount Rise	N10
28	Elm Mount Road	N10
28	Elm Mount View	N10
49	Elm Park (Nutley Lane)	N17
54	Elm Park Terrace	J18
44	Elm Rd (Donnycarney)	N11
28	Elm Rd (Fox & Geese)	D17
33	Elm Vale	YY15
65	Elm Way (Grange Wood)	K22
33	Elm Way (Lucan)	YY15
33	Elm Wood	YY15
33	Elmbrook	YY14
33	Elmbrook Crescent	YY14
33	Elmbrook Lawn	YY14
33	Elmbrook Walk	YY14
52	Elmcastle Court	D19
52	Elmcastle Drive	D19
52	Elmcastle Green	D19
52	Elmcastle Park	D19
52	Elmcastle Walk	D19
43	Elmdale Crescent	C15
43	Elmdale Drive	C15
43	Elmdale Park	C15
18	Elmfield Avenue	R8
18	Elmfield Close	R8
18	Elmfield Court	R8
43	Elmfield Ct (Clondalkin)	B17
18	Elmfield Crescent	S8
18	Elmfield Drive	S8
18	Elmfield Green	R8
18	Elmfield Grove	R8
18	Elmfield Lawn	S8
18	Elmfield Park	R8
18	Elmfield Rise	R8
18	Elmfield Vale	S8
18	Elmfield Walk	R8
18	Elmfield Way	R8
72	Elmgrove	U24
49	Elmpark Apts	P18
48	Elmpark Avenue	L17
57	Elms	Q19
48	Elmwood Ave Lwr	L17
48	Elmwood Ave Upr	L27
2	Elmwood Close	Y9
2	Elmwood Court	M1
2	Elmwood Drive	M1
2	Elmwood Park	M1
2	Elmwood Road	M1
8	Elner Court	U4
17	Elton Court (Coolock)	Q9
49	Elton Court (Dalkey)	V21
27	*Elton Court (Marino)	M12
	(Philipsburgh Avenue)	
17	Elton Drive (Coolock)	R9
17	Elton Park (Coolock)	R9
73	Elton Park (Dalkey)	V21
17	Elton Walk	R9
62	Ely Close	E23
62	Ely Crescent	E23
62	Ely Drive	E23
62	Ely Green	D23
62	Ely Grove	E23
47	Ely Place	L15
47	Ely Place Upper	L15
62	Ely View	E23
56	Embassy Lawn	M18
48	Emerald Cottages	M15
39	Emerald Place	L14
46	Emerald Square	H15
39	Emerald Street	M14
46	Emerald Terrace	J15
45	Emmet Court	Q15
37	Emmet Road	G15
57	Emmet Square	J16
47	Emmet Street	J16
	(Harold's Cross)	
39	Emmet Street	L13
	(Nth Circular Rd)	
69	Emmet St (Sallynoggin)	U21
47	Emor Street	K16
47	Emorville Avenue	K16
72	Empress Place	L13
39	*Enaville Avenue	M13
	(off Annesley Place)	
39	Enaville Road	M13
38	*Engine Alley	J15
	(off Meath St)	
29	Ennafort Avenue	Q10
29	Ennafort Court	Q11
29	Ennafort Drive	Q10
29	Ennafort Grove	Q10
29	Ennafort Park	Q11
29	Ennafort Road	Q11
29	Ennel Avenue	Q10
72	Ennel Court	V25
29	Ennel Drive	Q10
29	Ennel Park	Q10
40	Ennis Grove	N15
38	Enniskerry Road	K12
	(Phibsborough)	
39	Erne Place	K15
39	Erne Place Little	L15
39	Erne Place Lower	L14
39	Erne Street Lower	L14
39	Erne Street Upper	L15
39	Erne Terrace Front	L15
39	Erne Terrace Rere	L15
45	Errigal Gardens	F17
45	Errigal Road	F16
45	Errigal Road	F17
38	Erris Road	H12
33	Esker Drive	XX14
33	Esker Glebe	XX14
33	Esker Lane	YY13
33	Esker Lane	YY13
33	Esker Lawns	XX13
33	Esker Lodge	YY14
33	Esker Lodge Avenue	YY14
33	Esker Lodge Close	YY14
33	Esker Lodge View	YY14
33	Esker Manor	YY14
33	Esker Meadow	YY14
33	Esker Meadow Close	YY14
33	Esker Meadow Court	YY14
33	Esker Meadow Green	YY14
33	Esker Meadow Grove	YY14
33	Esker Meadow Lawn	YY14
33	Esker Meadow Rise	YY14
33	Esker Meadow View	YY14
33	Esker Park	YY14
33	Esker Pines	YY13
33	Esker Road	XX15
33	Esker South	XX15
47	Esker Villas	K17
33	Esker Woods	YY14
33	Esker Woods Close	YY14
33	Esker Woods Court	YY14
33	Esker Woods Drive	YY14
33	Esker Woods Rise	YY14
33	Esker Woods View	YY14
33	Esker Woods Walk	YY14
44	Esmond Avenue	M12
45	Esposito Road	F17
39	*Essex Gate	K14
	(off Essex Quay)	
39	Essex Quay	K14
39	Essex Street East	K14
38	*Essex Street West	K14
	(off Fishamble St)	
49	Estate Avenue	P17
48	Estate Cottages	L15
	(Northumberland Rd)	
48	Estate Cottages	M16
	(Shelbourne Rd)	
3	Estuary Court	N1
6	Estuary Road	Q2
3	Estuary Road	P1
6	Estuary Row	S2
6	Estuary Walk	Q2
46	Eugene Street	J15
39	Eustace Street	K14
38	Everton Avenue	H13
21	Evora Crescent	Y9
21	Evora Park	Y9
21	Evora Terrace	Y9
38	Ewington Lane	H15
38	*Exchange St Lower	K14
	(off Wood Quay)	
39	*Exchange St Upper	K15
	(off Lord Edward St)	
39	Exchequer Street	K15
3	Eyre Court	P3
68	**FABER GROVE**	**S21**
39	Fade Street	K15
7	Fair Haven	S2

Page		Grid Ref	Page		Grid Ref	Page		Grid Ref	Page		Grid Ref
6	Fairacre	Q3	22	Fernleigh Vale	A11	48	Fitzwilliam Square West	L15	33	Foxborough Avenue	YY15
54	Fairbrook Lawn	J20	22	Fernleigh View	A12	40	Fitzwilliam Street	N15	33	Foxborough Close	ZZ15
40	Fairfield Avenue	M13	47	Fernley Court	K15		(Ringsend)		33	Foxborough Court	ZZ15
54	Fairfield House	J18	46	Ferns Road	H17	48	Fitzwilliam St Lower	L15	33	Foxborough Crescent	ZZ15
55	Fairfield Park	K18	45	Fernvale Drive	G17	48	Fitzwilliam St Upper	L15	33	Foxborough Downes	YY15
26	Fairfield Road	K12	61	Fernwood Avenue	B21	39	Fleet Street	K14	33	Foxborough Drive	YY15
26	Fairlawn Park	H10	61	Fernwood Close	B21	27	Fleming Road	K11	33	Foxborough Gardens	ZZ15
26	Fairlawn Road	H10	61	Fernwood Court	B21	48	Fleming's Place	L16	33	Foxborough Glade	ZZ15
73	Fairlawns	V22	61	Fernwood Lawn	B21	55	Flemingstown Park	L20	33	Foxborough Glen	ZZ15
28	Fairview	M12	61	Fernwood Park	B21	48	Flemming House	L16	33	Foxborough Green	ZZ15
28	Fairview Ave Lower	M12	61	Fernwood Way	B21	58	Fleurville	R20	33	Foxborough Hall	ZZ15
28	Fairview Ave Upper	M12	54	Ferrard Road	J18	43	Floraville Avenue	B17	33	Foxborough Heights	ZZ15
28	Fairview Court	M12	17	Ferrycarrig Avenue	P8	43	Floraville Drive	B18	33	Foxborough Hill	YY15
28	Fairview Green	M12	17	Ferrycarrig Drive	P8	43	Floraville Estate	B17	33	Foxborough Lane	YY15
72	Fairview Lawn	U25	17	Ferrycarrig Green	P8	43	Floraville Lawn	B17	33	Foxborough Lawn	ZZ15
40	Fairview Passage	M12	17	Ferrycarrig Park	P8	47	*Florence Street	K16	33	Foxborough Manor	ZZ15
40	Fairview Strand	M12	17	Ferrycarrig Road	P8		(Victoria Street)		33	Foxborough Meadows	YY15
28	Fairview Terrace	M12	39	Ferryman's Crossing	M14	48	*Florence Terrace	L16	33	Foxborough Park	YY15
54	Fairways	H20	38	Fertullagh Road	J12		(Leeson Park Avenue)		33	Foxborough Place	YY15
26	Fairway's Green	J10	51	Fettercairn	B20	69	Flower Grove	U22	33	Foxborough Rise	YY15
26	Fairway's Grove	J10	51	Fettercairn Road	B20	39	Foley Street	L14	33	Foxborough Road	YY15
26	Fairway's Park	J10	42	Fey Yerra	Q22	38	Fontenoy Street	K13	33	Foxborough Row	ZZ15
40	Fairyhill (Stillorgan)	R21	33	Fforester	YY14	64	Fonthill Abbey	J21	33	Foxborough Walk	ZZ15
40	Faith Avenue	M13	33	Fforester Close	YY14	64	Fonthill Park	J21	33	Foxborough Way	YY15
27	Falcarragh Road	L10	33	Fforester Court	YY14	34	Fonthill Rd (Clondalkin)	A14	42	Foxdene Avenue	ZZ15
31	Falls Road	U26	33	Fforester Drive	YY14	64	Fonthill Road	J21	42	Foxdene Drive	ZZ15
56	Farmhill Drive	M20	33	Fforester Lawn	YY14		(Rathfarnham)		42	Foxdene Gardens	ZZ15
56	Farmhill Park	M20	33	Fforester Park	YY14	34	Fonthill Road North	A15	42	Foxdene Green	ZZ15
56	Farmhill Road	M20	33	Fforester Walk	YY14	34	Fonthill Road South	B18	42	Foxdene Grove	ZZ15
23	Farmleigh Avenue	D12	33	Fforester Way	YY14	38	Forbes Lane	J15	42	Foxdene Park	ZZ15
	(Castleknock)		45	Field Avenue	F17	40	Forbes Street	M14	31	Foxes Grove	V27
67	Farmleigh Avenue	Q21	47	Field's Terrace	L17	2	Forest Avenue	D19	30	Foxe's Lane	S10
	(Stillorgan)		58	Fieldview Cottages	R20		(Kilnamanagh)		32	Foxfield	XX15
23	Farmleigh Close	D12	21	*Findlater Building Apts	Y9	2	Forest Avenue (Swords)	L3	30	Foxfield Avenue	S10
	(Castleknock)			(Harbour Road)		2	Forest Boulevard	L3	30	Foxfield Crescent	S10
67	Farmleigh Close	Q21	39	Findlater Place	K14	52	Forest Close	D19	30	Foxfield Drive	S10
	(Stillorgan)		69	Findlater Street	U21	2	Forest Court	L2	30	Foxfield Green	S10
23	Farmleigh Court	C12		(Dun Laoghaire)		2	Forest Crescent	L3	30	Foxfield Heights	S10
	(Castleknock)		38	Findlater Street	H14	2	Forest Dale	L3	30	Foxfield Lawn	S10
23	Farmleigh Park	D12		(Nth Circular Rd)		52	Forest Dr (Kilnamanagh)	D19	30	Foxfield Park	S10
	(Castleknock)		38	Fingal Place	J13	2	Forest Drive (Swords)	L3	30	Foxfield Road	S10
67	Farmleigh Park	Q21	46	Fingal Street	J15	52	Forest Green	D19	30	Foxfield St John	S10
	(Stillorgan)		13	Finglas	G9		(Kilnamanagh)		33	Foxford	ZZ14
23	Farmleigh View	D12	13	Finglas East	H9	2	Forest Green (Swords)	L3	17	Foxhill Avenue	R9
23	Farmleigh Woods	D12	14	Finglas Park	H9	2	Forest Grove	L2	17	Foxhill Close	R9
49	Farney Park	N16	25	Finglas Place	H10	2	Forest Hills (Swords)	M3	17	Foxhill Court	R9
23	Farnham Crescent	H10	25	Finglas Road	H10	52	Forest Lawn	D19	17	Foxhill Crescent	R9
23	Farnham Drive	H10	26	Finglas Road Old	J11	52	Forest Pk (Kilnamanagh)	D19	17	Foxhill Drive	R9
55	Farrenboley Cottages	L19	25	Finglas South	G10	2	Forest Park (Swords)	L2	18	Foxhill Green	R9
55	Farrenboley Park	L19	56	Finglas Square	N19	2	Forest Road	M3	17	Foxhill Grove	R9
45	Father Kitt Court	G17	13	Finglas West	G9	2	Forest View	L3	17	Foxhill Lawn	R9
54	Father Lemass Court	D15	22	Finglaswood Road	G9	2	Forest Walk	M3	18	Foxhill Way	R9
38	*Father Mathew Square	J14	38	Finn Street	H14	2	Forest Way	L3	32	Foxpark	XX15
	(Church Street)		25	Finneber Fort	H10	15	Forestfields Road	M3	68	Foxrock	R23
46	Fatima Mansions	H15	25	Finneber Fort Square	H10	15	Forestwood Avenue	K8	68	Foxrock Avenue	R22
	(off James's Walk)		32	Finnscourt	XX15	15	Forestwood Close	K8	68	Foxrock Close	S22
46	Faughart Road	H17	32	Finnsgreen	XX15	21	*Forge Court	Y10	68	Foxrock Court	R22
25	Faulkner's Terrace	H15	32	Finnsgrove	XX15		(Main Street)		68	Foxrock Crescent	S22
28	Faussagh Avenue	H12	32	Finnslawn	XX16	3	Forster Way	N2	68	Foxrock Green	R22
28	Faussagh Road	J12	32	Finnspark	XX15	46	Fort Ostman	H16	68	Foxrock Grove	S22
6	Feltrim	R4	32	Finnstown Fairways	XX15	47	Fortescue Lane	K16	68	Foxrock Manor	Q22
3	Feltrim Hall	N3	33	Finnstown Hall	XX15	53	Fortfield Avenue	H19	68	Foxrock Mount	R22
5	Feltrim Road	Q4	32	Finnsvale	XX15	54	Fortfield Court	H18	68	Foxrock Park	R22
39	Fenian Street	L15	32	Finnswalk	XX15	54	Fortfield Drive	H19	68	Foxrock Wood	S22
54	Fergus Road	J18	32	Finnswood	XX15	47	Fortfield Gardens	K18	32	Foxwood (Lucan)	XX15
27	Ferguson Road	K11	55	Finsbury Green	L20	54	Fortfield Grove	H19	3	Foxwood (Swords)	N2
66	Ferncarrig Avenue	N23	55	Finsbury Park	L20	54	Fortfield Park	H19	27	Foyle Road	M12
66	Ferncarrig Court	N23	63	Firgrove	V24	54	Fortfield Road	H18	54	*Frances Ball House	J20
66	Ferncarrig Rise	N23	63	Firhouse	F21	54	Fortfield Square	H19		(Stonepark Court)	
62	Ferncourt Avenue	E23	53	Firhouse Road	G20	47	Fortfield Terrace	K18	38	Francis Street	J15
62	Ferncourt Close	E23	62	Firhouse Road West	D22	40	Forth Road	M13	55	Frankfort	L20
62	Ferncourt Crescent	E23	51	First Avenue	C20	64	Forthill Court	J21	47	Frankfort Avenue	K18
62	Ferncourt Drive	E23		(Belgard Heights)		10	Fortlawn Avenue	A9	39	Frankfort Cottages	L13
62	Ferncourt Green	E23	36	First Avenue	F15	10	Fortlawn Drive	A9	54	Frankfort Court	J18
62	Ferncourt Park	E23		(Sarsfield Road)		10	Fortlawn Park	A9	54	Frankfort Flats	J18
62	Ferncourt View	E23	39	First Avenue	M14	73	Fortlawns	V22	55	Frankfort Mews	L20
9	Ferndale (Hartstown)	ZZ8		(Seville Place)		53	Fortrose Park	H20	55	Frankfort Park	L20
61	Ferndale (Tallaght)	D22	38	Fishamble Street	K14	60	Fortunestown	ZZ21	58	Frascati Court	R19
26	Ferndale Avenue	J10	40	*Fishermans Wharf	N14	60	Fortunestown Close	ZZ21	58	Frascati Hall	R19
31	Ferndale Glen	U27		(York Road)		60	Fortunestown Cres	ZZ21	58	Frascati Park	R19
31	Ferndale Hill	U28	69	Fitzgerald Park	T21	60	Fortunestown Lane	ZZ21	58	Frascati Road	R19
31	Ferndale Road (Bray)	U29	47	Fitzgerald Street	K16	60	Fortunestown Road	A22	39	Frederick Court	K13
26	Ferndale Rd (Glasnevin)	J10	39	Fitzgibbon Lane	L13	60	Fortunestown Way	A21	39	Frederick Lane Nth	K13
31	Ferndale Rd (Shankill)	U27	39	Fitzgibbon Street	L13	41	Fortview Avenue	Q13	39	Frederick Street Nth	K13
53	Fernhill Avenue	F19	26	Fitzmaurice Road	J10	57	Fortwilliam	P20	39	Frederick Street Sth	L15
53	Fernhill Park	F19		(Glasnevin)		39	*Foster Place North	L13	39	Frenchman's Lane	L14
53	Fernhill Road	F19	47	Fitzpatrick's Cottages	J17		(Charleville Avenue)		43	Friar's Walk	B17
22	Fernleigh	A11	39	Fitzroy Avenue	L12	39	Foster Place South	K14	56	Friarsland Avenue	M19
22	Fernleigh Close	A11	48	Fitzwilliam Court	L15		(College Green)		56	Friarsland Crescent	M19
22	Fernleigh Court	A11		(Fitzwilliam Square)		39	Foster Terrace	L13	56	Friarsland Road	M19
22	Fernleigh Crescent	A11	57	*Fitzwilliam Court	P19	39	Fosterbrook	P18	38	Friary Avenue	J14
22	Fernleigh Dale	A11		(Greygates)		56	Fosters Avenue	N19	38	Friary Grove	J14
22	Fernleigh Dene	A12	48	Fitzwilliam Lane	L15	18	Fountain Place	J14	44	Friary Road	D16
22	Fernleigh Drive	A11	48	Fitzwilliam Place	L15	37	Fountain Road	H14	47	Fumbally Lane	K15
22	Fernleigh Grange	A12	38	*Fitzwilliam Place North	J14	39	Fourth Ave (Seville Pl)	M14	29	Furry Park Court	P11
22	Fernleigh Green	A11		(Grangegorman)		51	Fourth Ave (Tallaght)	C20	29	Furry Park Road	Q11
22	Fernleigh Grove	A12	40	Fitzwilliam Quay	N15	39	*Fownes Street Lower	K14	36	Furze Rd (Phoenix Pk)	E13
22	Fernleigh Heath	A12	48	Fitzwilliam Square East	L15		(off Temple Bar)		66	Furze Rd (Sandyford)	P22
22	Fernleigh Lawn	A11	48	Fitzwilliam Square Nth	L15	39	Fownes Street Upper	K14			
22	Fernleigh Park	A11	48	Fitzwilliam Square Sth	L15	39	Fox and Geese	D17			
22	Fernleigh Place	A11									

Page		Grid Ref
18	**GABLES**	R9
39	Gaelic Street	M13
6	Gainsborough	Q3
6	Gainsborough Ave	Q3
6	Gainsborough Close	Q3
6	Gainsborough Court	Q3
6	Gainsborough Cres	Q3
6	Gainsborough Downs	Q3
6	Gainsborough Green	Q3
6	Gainsborough Lawn	Q3
6	Gainsborough Park	Q3
14	Gallaun Road	J8
39	Gallery Quay	M15
67	Galloping Green	R21
67	Galloping Green	Q21
2	Gallows Hill	M2
38	Galmoy Road	J21
45	Galtymore Close	F16
46	Galtymore Drive	G16
45	Galtymore Park	F16
45	Galtymore Road	F16
47	Gandon Close	J17
33	Gandon Mews	XX13
28	Garden Lane	J15
47	*Garden Terrace	J16
	(off Clanbrassil St Upper)	
47	Garden Lane	K16
39	Gardiner Lane	L13
39	Gardiner Place	K13
39	Gardiner Row	K13
39	Gardiner St Middle	L13
39	Gardiner Street Lower	L13
39	Gardiner Street Upper	K13
11	Garnish Square	C9
71	Garrison Mews	U25
51	Garrynisk Close	C19
51	Garrynisk Road	C19
48	Garrynure	L18
38	Garryowen Road	E15
27	Gartan Avenue	K12
3	Gartan Court	P1
3	Gartan Drive	P1
63	Garthy Wood Apts	G21
47	Garville Avenue	K18
47	Garville Avenue Upper	J18
47	Garville Court	K18
47	Garville Drive	K18
47	Garville Lane	K18
47	Garville Place	K18
47	Garville Road	K18
7	Gas Yard Lane	S2
14	Gateway Avenue	K9
14	Gateway Court	K9
14	Gateway Crescent	K9
14	Gateway Gardens	K9
14	Gateway Mews	K9
14	Gateway Place	K9
14	Gateway View	K9
6	Gaybrook Lawns	R3
47	*Geoffrey Keating Rd	J15
	(St Thomas Road)	
40	*George Reynolds Flats	N15
	(off Oliver Plunkett Ave)	
39	George's Ave (Blackrock)	R19
39	George's Dock	L14
38	George's Hill	K14
38	George's Lane	J14
59	George's Pl (Blackrock)	R19
59	George's Place	U20
	(Dun Laoghaire)	
39	George's Place	K13
	(Temple Street)	
39	George's Quay	L14
13	Georges Road	H9
39	George's St Great Nth	K13
39	George's St Great Sth	K15
59	George's St Lower	U20
59	George's St Upper	U20
17	Georgian Hamlet	U8
24	Georgian Village	D12
39	Gerald Street	M15
38	Geraldine Street	K13
15	Geraldstown Woods	K8
	Apartments	
47	Gilbert Road	J16
49	Gilford Avenue	P16
49	Gilford Court	N16
49	Gilford Drive	N16
49	Gilford Park	N16
39	*Gilford Place	L13
	(Shamrock Place)	
49	Gilford Road	N16
49	Gilford Terrace	P17
69	Glandore Park	T21
27	Glandore Road	M11
26	Glasanaon Court	H10
26	Glasanaon Park	H10
26	Glasanaon Road	H10
26	Glasaree Court	H10
26	Glasaree Road	H10
26	Glasilawn Avenue	J10
26	Glasilawn Road	J10
28	Glaslyn	N12
26	Glasmeen Road	J10
2	Glasmore Park	M1
26	Glasnamana Place	J10
26	Glasnamana Road	J10
27	Glasnevin	K11
14	Glasnevin Avenue	J9
26	Glasnevin Court	H11
26	Glasnevin Downs	J11
14	Glasnevin Drive	J9
26	Glasnevin Hill	K11
14	Glasnevin North	J9
26	Glasnevin Oaks	J11
14	Glasnevin Park	J9
26	Glasnevin Woods	H11
55	Glasson Court	L19
69	Glasthule Buildings	V21
73	Glasthule Road	V21
71	Gleann na Ri	T25
58	Gleann na Smol	S20
	(Monkstown)	
61	Gleann na Smol	C22
	(Tallaght)	
5	Glebe (Airport)	N5
68	Glebe Hall	S21
25	Glebe View (Finglas)	H10
56	Gledswood Avenue	M19
56	Gledswood Close	M19
56	Gledswood Drive	M19
56	Gledswood Park	M19
68	Glen Avenue	S23
53	Glen Close	S23
68	Glen Dale	S23
68	Glen Drive	S23
72	Glen Druid	V25
2	Glen Ellan Avenue	M1
2	Glen Ellan Close	M1
2	Glen Ellan Court	M1
2	Glen Ellan Crescent	M1
2	Glen Ellan Drive	M1
2	Glen Ellan Gardens	M1
2	Glen Ellan Green	M1
2	Glen Ellan Grove	M1
2	Glen Ellan Park	M1
2	Glen Ellan Pines	M1
2	Glen Ellan Walk	M1
68	Glen Garth	S23
68	Glen Grove	S23
68	Glen Lawn Drive	S23
59	Glen Terrace	V21
68	Glen Walk	S23
27	Glenaan Road	M10
56	Glenabbey Road	P20
69	Glenageary Avenue	U22
69	Glenageary Court	U22
69	Glenageary Hall	V22
69	Glenageary Lodge	U22
69	Glenageary Park	U22
69	Glenageary Road Lwr	U20
69	Glenageary Road Upr	U21
69	Glenageary Woods	U21
67	Glenalbyn Road	Q27
73	Glenalua Heights	V23
72	Glenalua Road	V23
73	Glenalua Terrace	V23
70	Glenamuck Cottages	R25
70	Glenamuck North	Q25
70	Glenamuck Park	Q26
70	Glenamuck Road	R25
70	Glenamuck Road	S24
54	Glenann	J20
54	Glenanne	H16
38	Glenard Ave	H13
56	Glenard Hall	M19
27	Glenarm Avenue	L12
25	Glenarriff Road	F11
57	Glenart Avenue	Q20
36	Glenaulin	D14
36	Glenaulin Drive	D14
36	Glenaulin Green	C14
36	Glenaulin Park	D14
35	Glenaulin Road	C14
72	Glenavon Park	U25
54	Glenavy Park	H18
17	Glenayle Road	Q9
54	Glenayr Road	J18
38	Glenbeigh Park	H18
38	Glenbeigh Road	H18
70	Glenbourne Ave	Q24
70	Glenbourne Close	Q24
70	Glenbourne Cres	Q24
70	*Glenbourne Drive	Q24
70	Glenbourne Green	Q24
70	Glenbourne Grove	Q24
70	Glenbourne Park	Q24
70	Glenbourne Road	Q24
70	Glenbourne View	Q24
70	Glenbourne Walk	Q24
70	Glenbourne Way	Q24
55	Glenbower Park	L20
31	Glenbrae	V26
28	*Glenbrian Hall	N12
	(Castle Court)	
54	Glenbrook Park	J20
25	Glenbrook Road	F11
67	Glencairn	P23
67	Glencairn Avenue	P23
67	Glencairn Chase	P23
67	Glencairn Drive	Q23
67	Glencairn Garth	P23
67	Glencairn Heath	P23
67	Glencairn Park	P23
67	Glencairn Road	P23
70	Glencairn Thicket	Q23
67	Glencairn View	P23
67	Glencairn Way	P23
38	Glencar Road	H13
72	Glencarr Court	V25
72	Glencarr Lawn	V25
20	Glencarraig	W9
62	Glencarrig Court	E22
62	Glencarrig Drive	E22
62	Glencarrig Green	E22
28	Glencarthy Court Apts	N11
27	Glencloy Road	M10
27	Glencorp Road	M10
27	Glendale Park	G19
27	Glendalough Road	K12
39	*Glendenning Lane	K15
	(off Wicklow Street)	
25	Glendhu Park	F11
25	Glendhu Road	F11
64	Glendoher Avenue	J21
64	Glendoher Close	H21
64	Glendoher Drive	J21
64	Glendoher Park	H21
64	Glendoher Road	H21
52	Glendoo Close	H19
53	Glendown Avenue	G19
53	Glendown Close	G19
53	Glendown Court	G19
53	Glendown Crescent	F19
53	Glendown Drive	G19
53	Glendown Green	G19
53	Glendown Grove	G19
53	Glendown Lawn	G19
53	Glendown Park	G19
53	Glendown Road	G19
27	Glendun Road	L10
9	Glenealy Downs	ZZ8
46	Glenealy Road	H16
17	Glenfarne Road	Q9
34	Glenfield Avenue	A14
34	Glenfield Close	A14
34	Glenfield Drive	A14
34	Glenfield Park	A14
69	Glengara Close	U21
39	Glengariff Parade	K13
39	Glengarriff Crescent	K13
39	Glengarriff Parade	K13
26	Glenhill Avenue	H10
26	Glenhill Court	H10
26	Glenhill Drive	H10
26	Glenhill Grove	H10
26	Glenhill Road	H10
26	Glenhill Villas	H10
63	Glenlyon Crescent	F22
63	Glenlyon Grove	F22
63	Glenlyon Park	F22
46	Glenmalure Park	H15
48	Glenmalure Square	L18
35	Glenmaroon Park	C14
35	Glenmaroon Road	C14
64	Glenmore Court	J22
64	Glenmore Park	J22
38	Glenmore Road	H13
53	Glenmurry Park	F19
57	Glenomena Grove	P18
56	Glenomena Park	P18
35	Glenpark Close	B13
35	Glenpark Drive	B13
35	Glenpark Road	B13
60	Glenshane Close	A21
60	Glenshane Crescent	A21
60	Glenshane Drive	A21
60	Glenshane Gardens	A21
60	Glenshane Green	A21
60	Glenshane Grove	A21
60	Glenshane Lawns	A21
60	Glenshane Park	A21
27	Glenshesk Road	M10
35	Glenside Villas	C13
25	Glenties Drive	G10
25	Glenties Park	G10
27	Glentow Road	L10
17	Glentworth Park	R9
33	Glenvale	YY15
57	Glenvar Park	Q19
63	Glenvara Park	F22
69	Glenview	U23
	(Rochestown Avenue)	
62	Glenview Drive	E21
62	Glenview Lawns	E21
62	Glenview Park	E21
22	Glenville Avenue	B10
22	Glenville Court	B11
22	Glenville Drive	B11
22	Glenville Garth	B11
22	Glenville Green	B10
22	Glenville Grove	B10
22	Glenville Lawn	B10
22	Glenville Road	B11
55	Glenville Terrace	M20
22	Glenville Way	B10
17	Glenwood Road	Q9
16	Glin Avenue	P8
17	Glin Crescent	P8
16	Glin Drive	P8
17	Glin Grove	P8
16	Glin Park	P8
16	Glin Road	P8
39	Gloucester Diamond	L13
39	*Gloucester Lane	L13
	(off Sean McDermott St Lwr)	
39	Gloucester Place Lwr	L13
39	Gloucester Place Upr	L13
39	Gloucester Street Sth	L14
47	Glovers Alley	K15
47	*Glovers Court	K15
	(off York Street)	
56	Goatstown	N20
56	Goatstown Avenue	M20
56	Goatstown Road	M20
38	*Godfrey Place	J14
	(off Oxmanstown Road)	
13	Gofton Hall	H9
70	Golden Ball	Q26
39	Golden Lane	K15
46	Goldenbridge Avenue	G15
46	Goldenbridge Gardens	G15
46	Goldenbridge Terrace	G15
45	Goldenbridge Walk	F16
38	Goldsmith Street	K13
8	Golf Links Road	U6
68	Gordon Avenue	R23
47	Gordon Place	K16
29	Gordon Street	M15
29	Gorsefield Court	Q10
18	Gort na Mona Drive	S23
25	Gortbeg Avenue	H11
25	Gortbeg Drive	H11
25	Gortbeg Park	H11
25	Gortbeg Road	H11
25	Gortmore Avenue	H10
25	Gortmore Drive	H10
25	Gortmore Park	H10
25	Gortmore Road	H11
73	Gosworth Park	V21
69	Gowrie Park	U21
21	Grace O'Malley Drive	Y10
21	Grace O'Malley Road	Y10
27	Grace Park Avenue	L12
27	Grace Park Court	M10
27	Grace Park Gardens	L12
28	Grace Park Heights	M11
27	Grace Park Manor	L11
28	Grace Park Meadows	M11
27	Grace Park Road	M11
27	Grace Park Terrace	M11
29	Gracefield Avenue	Q10
29	Gracefield Road	P10
39	Grafton Street	K15
39	Graham Court	K13
39	Graham's Row	K13
14	Graigue Court	J8
39	Granby Lane	K13
39	Granby Place	K14
39	Granby Row	K13
40	Grand Canal Docks	M14
38	Grand Canal Place	J15
39	Grand Canal Quay	M15
39	Grand Canal Street Lwr	M15
48	Grand Canal Street Upr	M15
46	Grand Canal View	G15
48	Grand Parade	L18
18	Grange Abbey Crescent	S8
18	Grange Abbey Drive	S8
18	Grange Abbey Grove	S8
18	Grange Abbey Road	S8
18	Grange Avenue	T8
64	Grange Brook	J22
18	Grange Cl (Kilbarrack)	T9
69	Grange Clo (Pottery Rd)	T23
67	Grange Cottages	Q21
65	Grange Court	K22
68	Grange Crescent	S22
65	Grange Downs	K21
18	Grange Drive	T9
68	Grange Grove	S21
65	Grange Hall	L23

Page		Grid Ref

29 Grange Hall Apts **R10**
18 Grange Lodge Ave **S8**
18 Grange Lodge Cot **S8**
33 Grange Manor **XX15**
65 Grange Manor Ave **K21**
65 Grange Manor Close **K21**
65 Grange Manor Drive **K21**
65 Grange Manor Grove **K21**
65 Grange Manor Road **K21**
18 Grange Parade **T9**
19 Grange Pk (Baldoyle) **T8**
68 Grange Park **S22**
    (Cornelscourt)
54 Grange Pk (Willbrook) **J21**
18 Grange Park Avenue **R10**
18 Grange Park Close **S10**
18 Grange Park Cres **S10**
18 Grange Park Drive **R10**
18 Grange Park Green **S10**
18 Grange Park Grove **R10**
18 Grange Park Rise **S9**
18 Grange Park Road **R10**
18 Grange Park View **S9**
18 Grange Park Walk **R10**
18 Grange Rise **T8**
19 Grange Rd (Baldoyle) **T8**
65 Grange Road (Marley Pk) **K22**
54 Grange Road **J20**
    (Rathfarnham)
64 Grange Rd (The Priory) **J21**
68 Grange Terrace **S8**
42 Grange View Close **YY17**
42 Grange View Court **YY17**
42 Grange View Green **YY17**
42 Grange View Grove **YY17**
42 Grange View Lawn **YY17**
42 Grange View Park **YY17**
42 Grange View Road **YY17**
42 Grange View Walk **YY17**
42 Grange View Way **YY17**
42 Grange View Wood **YY17**
18 Grange Way **T9**
65 Grange Wood **K22**
    (Ballinteer)
64 Grangebrook Ave **J22**
64 Grangebrook Close **J22**
64 Grangebrook Park **J22**
64 Grangebrook Vale **J22**
65 Grangefield **L23**
38 Grangegorman Lwr **J14**
38 Grangegorman Upr **J13**
38 *Grangegorman Villas **J13**
    (Grangegorman Upper)
18 Grangemore **R8**
18 Grangemore Avenue **R8**
18 Grangemore Court **R8**
18 Grangemore Crescent **R8**
18 Grangemore Drive **S8**
18 Grangemore Grove **S8**
18 Grangemore Lawn **S8**
18 Grangemore Park **S9**
18 Grangemore Rise **R8**
18 Grangemore Road **R8**
68 Grangewood **T21**
69 Granite Hall **U21**
48 Granite Place **M16**
45 Granite Terrace **F15**
69 Granitefield **T23**
69 Granitefield **U23**
69 Granitefield Manor **T23**
47 Grantham Place **K16**
47 Grantham Street **K16**
39 Grant's Row **L15**
72 Granville Close **U23**
44 Granville Crescent **U23**
68 Granville Park **R21**
69 Granville Rd (Cabinteely) **T23**
68 Granville Road **R22**
    (Deans Grange)
39 Grattan Court East **M15**
45 Grattan Crescent **F15**
18 Grattan Hall **S8**
18 Grattan Lodge **S8**
42 Grattan Parade **K12**
39 Grattan Place **M15**
39 Grattan Row **M15**
39 Grattan Street **M15**
38 *Gray Square **J15**
    (Gray Street)
38 *Gray St (off Meath St) **J15**
38 Great Western Ave **J13**
38 Great Western Square **J13**
38 Great Western Villas **J15**
39 *Greeg Court **K14**
    (Moore Street)
38 Greek Street **K14**
63 Green Acre Court **G21**
50 Green Isle Court **A18**
50 Green Isle Road **ZZ19**
55 Green Park (Rathgar) **L19**
57 Green Road (Blackrock) **Q19**

38 Green Street **K14**
40 Green Street East **M14**
38 Green Street Little **K14**
17 Greencastle Avenue **P9**
17 Greencastle Crescent **P9**
17 Greencastle Drive **P8**
17 Greencastle Parade **Q9**
17 Greencastle Park **P8**
17 Greencastle Road **P9**
18 Greendale Avenue **T10**
18 Greendale Court **S10**
18 Greendale Road **S10**
56 Greenfield Crescent **N18**
56 Greenfield Manor **N18**
63 Greenfield Park **F22**
    (Ballycullen Road)
56 Greenfield Park **N18**
    (Stillorgan Road)
47 *Greenfield Place **J16**
    (off Mount Drummond Ave)
57 Greenfield Road **P20**
    (Mount Merrion)
20 Greenfield Rd (Sutton) **W9**
34 Greenfort Avenue **A14**
34 Greenfort Close **A14**
34 Greenfort Crescent **A14**
34 Greenfort Drive **A14**
34 Greenfort Gardens **A14**
34 Greenfort Lawns **A14**
34 Greenfort Park **A14**
34 Greenfort Walk **A14**
52 Greenhills **E19**
62 Greenhills Court **D21**
52 Greenhills Road **E18**
66 Greenlands **N22**
17 Greenlawns **P8**
54 Greenlea Avenue **H18**
54 Greenlea Drive **H18**
54 Greenlea Grove **H18**
54 Greenlea Place **J18**
54 Greenlea Road **H19**
47 Greenmount Avenue **J16**
47 Greenmount Court **J16**
47 Greenmount Lane **J16**
54 Greenmount Lawns **J18**
70 Greenmount Lodge **Q26**
54 Greenmount Road **J18**
47 Greenmount Square **J16**
39 *Greenmore Terrace **M15**
    (Conway Court)
32 Greenpark Road **WW14**
11 Greenridge Court **B9**
53 Greentrees Drive **F18**
53 Greentrees Park **F18**
53 Greentrees Road **F18**
8 Greenview **S6**
47 Greenville Avenue **J16**
47 *Greenville Parade **J15**
    (Blackpitts)
47 Greenville Place **J16**
58 Greenville Road **S20**
47 Greenville Terrace **J16**
5 Greenwood **Q5**
18 Greenwood Avenue **R8**
17 Greenwood Close **R8**
18 Greenwood Court **R8**
17 Greenwood Drive **R8**
17 Greenwood Park **R8**
17 Greenwood Walk **R8**
17 Greenwood Way **R8**
39 Grenville Lane **K13**
39 Grenville Street **K13**
57 Greygates **P19**
57 Greygates **P20**
    (Sycamore Crescent)
21 Grey's Lane **Y10**
33 Greythorn Park **U21**
33 Griffeen **YY15**
33 Griffeen Avenue **YY15**
33 Griffeen Glen Avenue **YY15**
33 Griffeen Glen **YY15**
    Boulevard
33 Griffeen Glen Chase **YY15**
33 Griffeen Glen Close **YY15**
33 Griffeen Glen Court **YY15**
33 Griffeen Glen Ct Yard **YY15**
33 Griffeen Glen Crescent **YY15**
33 *Griffeen Glen Dale **YY15**
33 Griffeen Glen Dene **YY15**
33 Griffeen Glen Drive **YY15**
33 Griffeen Glen Green **YY15**
33 Griffeen Glen Grove **YY15**
33 Griffeen Glen Lawn **YY15**
33 Griffeen Glen Place **YY15**
33 Griffeen Glen Road **YY15**
33 Griffeen Glen Vale **YY15**
33 Griffeen Glen View **YY15**
33 Griffeen Glen Way **YY15**
33 Griffeen Glen Wood **XX15**

33 Griffeen Road **YY15**
33 Griffeen Way **YY14**
28 Griffith Avenue **M11**
26 Griffith Close **J10**
27 Griffith Court **M12**
26 Griffith Crescent **J10**
26 Griffith Drive **J10**
28 Griffith Hall **M11**
26 Griffith Heights **J10**
27 Griffith Lawns **K11**
27 Griffith Parade **J10**
26 Griffith Road **J10**
47 Griffith Square **J16**
29 Grosvenor Ct (Clontarf) **P12**
53 Grosvenor Court **G19**
    (Templeville Road)
47 Grosvenor Lane **K17**
47 Grosvenor Lodge **K17**
47 Grosvenor Park **K17**
47 Grosvenor Place **K17**
47 Grosvenor Road **K17**
47 Grosvenor Square **K17**
73 Grosvenor Tce (Dalkey) **X22**
59 Grosvenor Terrace **T20**
    (Dun Laoghaire)
73 *Grosvenor Villas **W22**
    (Off Sorrento Rd)
47 Grosvenor Villas **K17**
    (Rathmines)
57 Grotto Avenue **Q18**
57 Grotto Place **Q13**
14 Grove Ave (Finglas) **H9**
67 Grove Avenue **K16**
    (Harold's Cross)
7 Grove Ave (Malahide) **T3**
57 Grove Avenue **Q20**
    (Mount Merrion)
45 Grove Court (Bluebell) **F16**
57 Grove House Gardens **Q20**
17 Grove Lane **Q8**
57 Grove Lawn (Stillorgan) **Q20**
7 Grove Lawns (Malahide) **T3**
57 Grove Paddock **Q20**
17 Grove Park (Coolock) **Q8**
47 Grove Park (Rathmines) **K16**
14 Grove Park Avenue **J9**
14 Grove Park Crescent **J9**
14 Grove Park Drive **J9**
14 Grove Park Road **H9**
22 Grove Road **A10**
    (Blanchardstown)
14 Grove Road (Finglas) **J9**
7 Grove Rd (Malahide) **S3**
47 Grove Rd (Rathmines) **K16**
14 Grove Wood (Finglas) **H9**
68 Grove Wood (Foxrock) **R23**
39 Guild Street **M14**
31 Guilford Terrace **V22**
47 Gulistan Cottages **K17**
47 Gulistan Place **K17**
47 Gulistan Terrace **K17**
63 Gunny Hill **F23**
35 Gurteen Avenue **D15**
35 Gurteen Park **D15**
35 Gurteen Road **D14**

72 **HACKETSLAND V25**
69 Haddington Lawns **V22**
73 Haddington Park **V22**
48 Haddington Place **M15**
48 Haddington Road **M15**
59 Haddington Terrace **U20**
40 Haddon Court **P12**
40 Haddon Park **N12**
40 Haddon Road **P12**
23 Hadleigh Court **D11**
23 Hadleigh Green **D11**
23 Hadleigh Park **D11**
48 Hagan's Court **L15**
59 Haigh Terrace **U20**
68 Hainault Drive **S23**
68 Hainault Grove **S23**
68 Hainault Lawn **S23**
68 Hainault Park **R23**
68 Hainault Road **R23**
38 Halliday Road **J14**
38 Halliday Square **J14**
38 Halston Street **K14**
47 *Hamilton Court **K14**
    (off Strand St Little)
47 Hamilton Street **J16**
38 Hammond Lane **J14**
47 Hammond Street **J16**
27 Hampstead Avenue **K10**
17 Hampstead Court **K10**
17 Hampstead Park **K11**
29 Hampton Ct (Clontarf) **Q12**
45 Hampton Court **F15**
    (Tyrconnell Road)
57 Hampton Crescent **P19**

37 Hampton Green **G13**
57 Hampton Park **P19**
37 Hampton Square **H13**
14 Hampton Wood **H8**
14 Hampton Wood Ave **H8**
14 Hampton Wood Ct **J8**
14 Hampton Wood Cres **H8**
14 Hampton Wood Drive **H8**
14 Hampton Wood Green **H8**
14 Hampton Wood Lawn **J8**
14 Hampton Wood Park **H8**
14 Hampton Wood Road **H8**
14 Hampton Wood Square **J8**
14 Hampton Wood Way **H8**
32 Hanbury Lane (Lucan) **XX13**
38 Hanbury Lane **J15**
    (The Coombe)
54 Hannaville Park **J18**
38 Hanover Lane **K15**
14 Hanover Quay **M14**
38 Hanover Square **K15**
39 Hanover Street East **L14**
38 *Hanover Street West **J15**
    (Carman's Hall)
9 Hansfield **YY8**
32 Hanstead Close **XX16**
32 Hanstead Dale **XX16**
32 Hanstead Drive **XX16**
32 Hanstead Place **XX16**
32 Hanstead Way **XX16**
32 Hansted Crescent **XX16**
32 Hansted Park **XX16**
32 Hansted Road **XX16**
39 Harbour Court **L14**
73 Harbour Crescent **W21**
39 Harbour Master Place **L14**
73 Harbour Road (Dalkey) **W21**
59 Harbour Road **U20**
    (Dun Laoghaire)
21 Harbour Road (Howth) **Y9**
59 *Harbour Square **T20**
    (Crofton Road)
59 Harbour Terrace **T20**
59 *Harbour View **T20**
    (Crofton Road)
21 Harbour View (Howth) **Y9**
47 Harcourt Lane **K16**
46 Harcourt Lodge **G15**
47 Harcourt Road **K16**
47 Harcourt Street **K16**
47 Harcourt Terrace **L16**
55 *Harcourt Villas **M19**
    (off Dundrum Rd)
45 Hardebeck Avenue **F17**
73 Hardiman Road **K11**
39 *Hardwicke Arch **K13**
    (off Hardwicke St)
39 Hardwicke Lane **K13**
39 Hardwicke Place **K13**
39 Hardwicke Street **K13**
34 Harelawn Avenue **A15**
34 Harelawn Crescent **A15**
34 Harelawn Drive **A14**
34 *Harelawn Green **A14**
34 Harelawn Grove **A14**
34 Harelawn Park **A14**
56 Harlech Crescent **N19**
56 Harlech Downs **N16**
56 Harlech Grove **N16**
56 Harlech Villas **M19**
47 *Harmac Court **J18**
    (Rathgar Villas)
47 Harman Street **J15**
29 Harmonstown Road **Q10**
48 Harmony Avenue **M17**
47 Harmony Court **M17**
39 Harmony Row **L15**
47 Harold Bridge Court **J16**
69 *Harold Crescent **U21**
    (off Eden Rd Lower)
38 Harold Road **J14**
40 Harold Ville Ave **H16**
47 *Harold's Cross **J17**
47 *Harold's Cross Cottages **J16**
    (Armstrong Street)
47 *Harold's Cross Cotts **K16**
    (Darley Street)
47 Harold's Cross Road **J17**
65 Harold's Grange Road **L23**
47 Harrington Street **K16**
54 Harrison Row **J18**
39 Harry Street **K15**
9 Hartstown Road **ZZ9**
45 Harty Avenue **F17**
45 Harty Court **F17**
47 *Harty Court **K16**
    (off Daniel Street)
47 Harty Place **K15**
56 Harvard **N19**
40 Hastings Street **M15**
73 Hastings Terrace **V21**

Page		Grid Ref
47	Hatch Lane	L16
47	Hatch Place	L16
47	Hatch Street Lower	L16
47	Hatch Street Upper	K16
47	Hatter's Lane	J11
48	Havelock Square	M15
48	Havelock Terrace	N15
6	Haven View	S2
28	Haverty Road	M12
39	Hawkins Street	L14
40	Hawthorn Avenue	M13
65	Hawthorn Drive	L21
23	Hawthorn Lawn	C11
23	Hawthorn Lodge	C11
23	Hawthorn Lodge	D12
58	Hawthorn Manor	R20
2	Hawthorn Park	M2
44	Hawthorn Road	C17
	(Fox and Geese)	
40	Hawthorn Terrace	M13
66	Hawthorns Road	N22
56	Hayden Square	N19
32	Hayden's Lane	XX15
33	Haydens Park	XX15
33	Haydens Park Ave	XX15
33	Haydens Park Close	XX15
33	Haydens Park Dale	XX15
33	Haydens Park Glade	XX15
33	Haydens Park Green	XX15
33	Haydens Park Grove	XX15
33	Haydens Park Lawn	XX15
33	Haydens Park View	XX15
33	Haydens Park Walk	XX15
33	Haydens Park Way	XX15
38	Haymarket	J14
38	*Haymarket House	J14
	(Haymarket)	
9	Hayworth Close	XX9
9	Hayworth Court	YY9
9	Hayworth Drive	YY9
9	Hayworth Mews	XX9
9	Hayworth Place	XX9
9	Hayworth Rise	XX9
9	Hayworth Terrace	XX9
66	Hazel Avenue	N21
8	Hazel Court	T6
8	Hazel Grove	T6
23	Hazel Lawn	B10
	(Blanchardstown)	
69	Hazel Lawn	T22
	(Kill O'the Grange)	
46	Hazel Park	H18
28	Hazel Road	N11
66	Hazel Villas	N21
66	Hazelbrook (Kilmacud)	N21
52	Hazelbrook (Tymon Nth)	E20
54	Hazelbrook Apts	H18
54	Hazelbrook Court	H18
54	Hazelbrook Drive	H18
54	Hazelbrook Road	H18
9	Hazelbury Green	YY8
9	Hazelbury Park	YY8
25	Hazelcroft Gardens	H11
25	Hazelcroft Park	H11
25	Hazelcroft Road	H11
48	Hazeldene	M17
62	Hazelgrove	A22
60	Hazelgrove Court	A22
31	Hazelwood (Shankill)	V26
9	Hazelwood Avenue	ZZ9
50	Hazelwood Bank	A18
50	Hazelwood Close	A18
16	Hazelwood Ct (Beaumont)	N9
9	Hazelwood Court	ZZ9
	(Hartstown)	
50	Hazelwood Crescent	A18
	(Clondalkin)	
9	Hazelwood Crescent	ZZ9
	(Hartstown)	
28	Hazelwood Drive	N10
9	Hazelwood Green	ZZ9
16	Hazelwood Grove	P9
47	Hazelwood House	K16
	(Atlumney Villas)	
50	Hazelwood Lane	A18
16	Hazelwood Park	P9
50	Hazelwood View	A18
35	Headford Grove	L20
54	Healthfield Road	J18
39	*Healy Street	L13
	(off Rutland Place North)	
44	Heaney Avenue	C16
73	Heany Avenue	W22
13	Heath Square	H9
65	Heather Close	K22
65	Heather Drive	K22
8	Heather Gardens	U4
65	Heather Gro (Ballinteer)	K22
35	Heather Gro (Palmerston)	B14
65	Heather Lawn	K22

Page		Grid Ref
65	Heather Park	L22
65	Heather Rd (Ballinteer)	K22
67	Heather Rd (Burton Hall)	P22
61	Heather View Avenue	C22
61	Heather View Close	C22
61	Heather View Drive	C22
61	Heather View Lawn	C22
61	Heather View Park	C22
61	Heather View Road	C22
8	Heather Walk	U4
58	Heathfield	S20
69	*Heatley Villas	T22
	(on Pearse Road)	
56	Heidelberg	N19
49	Hempenstal Terrace	M13
38	Hendrick Place	J14
38	Hendrick Street	J14
55	Henley Court	L20
55	Henley Park	L20
55	Henley Villas	L20
38	Henrietta Lane	K13
38	Henrietta Place	K14
38	Henrietta Street	K14
39	Henry Place	K14
44	Henry Road	D16
39	Henry Street	K14
49	Herbert Avenue	P17
48	Herbert Cottages	M16
23	Herbert Crescent	C10
48	Herbert Lane	L15
48	Herbert Pk (Ballsbridge)	M16
48	Herbert Park Lane	M16
48	Herbert Park Mews	M17
48	Herbert Place	M15
	(Baggot Street Lower)	
40	*Herbert Place	N15
	(off Bath St)	
23	Herbert Road	C10
	(Blanchardstown)	
48	Herbert Road	M15
	(Sandymount)	
48	Herbert Street	L15
46	Herberton Drive	H16
46	Herberton Park	H15
46	Herberton Road	H16
64	Hermitage Avenue	J21
64	Hermitage Close	J21
64	Hermitage Court	K21
33	Hermitage Crescent	K21
64	Hermitage Downs	K21
64	Hermitage Drive	J21
33	Hermitage Garden	J21
33	Hermitage Green	ZZ13
33	Hermitage Grove	J21
33	Hermitage Lawn	J21
33	Hermitage Manor	ZZ13
64	Hermitage Park	J21
	(Grange Road)	
33	Hermitage Pk (Lucan)	ZZ13
33	Hermitage Place	ZZ13
33	Hermitage Road	ZZ13
33	Hermitage Valley	ZZ13
33	Hermitage View	J21
33	Hermitage Way	ZZ13
71	Heronford Lane	T26
37	Heuston Square	G15
39	*Hewardine Terrace	L13
	(off Killarney Street)	
48	Heytesbury Lane	M16
47	Heytesbury Street	L16
39	Hibernian Avenue	M13
38	Hibernian Terrace	E14
27	High Park	M10
38	High St (Christ Church)	K15
61	High Street (Tallaght)	D21
65	Highfield Avenue	K22
	(Rathfarnham)	
2	Highfield Close	M2
55	Highfield Ct (Rathgar)	K18
65	Highfield Court	K22
	(Rathfarnham)	
2	Highfield Crescent	M2
2	Highfield Downs	M2
65	Highfield Drive	K22
2	Highfield Green	M2
55	Highfield Grove	K18
2	Highfield Lawn	M2
55	Highfield Manor	K18
55	Highfield Park	L19
	(Churchtown)	
55	Highfield Road	K18
71	Highland Avenue	S23
71	Highland Grove	S23
71	Highland Lawn	S23
71	Highland View	S23
67	Highridge Green	P21
69	Highthorn Park	T21
69	Highthorn Woods	T21
72	Hill Cottages	V23
8	Hill Court	T5
7	Hill Crest	T4

Page		Grid Ref
7	Hill Drive	S3
39	Hill Street	K13
65	Hill View	L21
10	Hillbrook Woods	A9
55	Hillcourt	K18
69	Hillcourt Park	U22
69	Hillcourt Road	U22
32	Hillcrest (Lucan)	XX14
6	Hillcrest (Malahide)	R2
54	Hillcrest (Rathgar)	K18
53	Hillcrest (Templeogue)	G20
32	Hillcrest Avenue	WW14
32	Hillcrest Close	WW14
66	Hillcrest Downs	N23
32	Hillcrest Court	XX14
32	Hillcrest Drive	WW14
32	Hillcrest Green	WW14
32	Hillcrest Grove	XX14
32	Hillcrest Heights	WW14
32	Hillcrest Lawns	WW14
53	Hillcrest Manor	G20
26	Hillcrest Pk (Glasnevin)	J10
32	Hillcrest Park (Lucan)	WW14
32	Hillcrest Rd (Lucan)	XX14
66	Hillcrest Rd (Sandyford)	N23
32	Hillcrest View	WW14
32	Hillcrest Walk	WW14
32	Hillcrest Way	WW14
53	Hillsbrook Avenue	G18
53	Hillsbrook Crescent	G18
53	Hillsbrook Drive	G18
53	Hillsbrook Grove	G18
73	Hillside	V22
55	Hillside Drive	K19
64	Hillside Park	H21
21	Hillside Terrace	Y10
31	Hilltop Lawn	V27
2	Hilltown	L3
2	Hilltown Close	M2
2	Hilltown Court	M2
2	Hilltown Green	M2
2	Hilltown Grove	M2
2	Hilltown Lawn	M2
2	Hilltown Park	M2
2	Hilltown Road	M2
2	Hilltown Way	M2
69	Hillview Cottages	T22
69	Hillview Court	L21
69	Hillview Drive	T22
69	Hillview Glade	L21
69	Hillview Grove	L21
69	Hillview Lawns	T22
18	Hilton Gardens	M22
18	Hoey Close	S8
18	Hoey Court	S8
18	Hoey Place	S8
38	Hoeys Court	K15
	(off Werburgh Street)	
39	Hogan Avenue	M15
54	Hogan House	J20
	(Stonepark Court)	
39	Hogan Place	L15
39	Holles Place	L15
39	Holles Row	L15
66	Holly Avenue	N21
72	Holly Court	U25
31	Holly Park	V26
68	Holly Park Avenue	R21
28	Holly Rd (Donnycarney)	N11
44	Holly Road	C17
	(Fox and Geese)	
14	*Holly Tree Square	J8
	(Balbutcher Lane)	
14	*Holly Tree Terrace	J8
	(Balbutcher Lane)	
48	Hollybank Avenue Lwr	L17
48	Hollybank Avenue Upr	L17
27	Hollybank Road	K12
28	Hollybrook Court	N12
28	Hollybrook Court Drive	N12
28	Hollybrook Grove	N12
28	Hollybrook Manor	N12
28	Hollybrook Pk (Clontarf)	N12
28	Hollybrook Road	N12
28	Hollybrook Wood	N12
45	Hollyville	E16
35	Hollyville Lawn	C13
14	Hollywell	J8
56	Hollywood Drive	N20
56	Hollywood Park	N20
47	Holme's Cottages	K17
	(on Church Ave Rathmines)	
69	Holmston Avenue	U21
71	Holmwood	S24
39	Holycross Avenue	L12
39	*Holycross Cottages	L12
	(off Holycross Avenue)	
49	Holyrood Park	N16
66	Holywell	N21
18	Holywell Avenue	S9

Page		Grid Ref
18	Holywell Crescent	S9
18	Holywell Road	S9
27	Home Farm Park	L11
27	Home Farm Road	K11
48	Home Villas	M17
62	Homelawn Avenue	E21
62	Homelawn Drive	D21
62	Homelawn Gardens	E21
62	Homelawn Road	D21
62	Homelawn Villas	D21
49	Homelee	N16
22	Homeleigh	A12
63	Homeville	F21
63	Homeville Court	F21
69	Honey Park	U22
40	Hope Avenue	M13
40	*Hope Street	M15
	(off Gordon Street)	
56	Hopkins Square	P19
61	*Horan Hall	C21
	(Belgard Square)	
54	Horton Court	J18
37	Hospital Lane	G14
39	Hotel Yard	K14
38	Houghton Terrace	J14
40	*Howard Street	M15
	(off Gordon Street)	
21	Howth	Y10
21	*Howth House Apts	Y9
	(Harbour Road)	
18	Howth Junction Cottages	S9
9	Howth Lodge Apts	X9
21	Howth Peninsula Apts	Y9
20	Howth Road (Howth)	X9
29	Howth Road (Killester)	P11
28	Howth Road (Marino)	N12
29	Howth Road (Raheny)	Q11
30	Howth Road (Raheny)	S10
20	Howth Road (Sutton)	W9
28	Howth Road Apts	P11
21	Howth Terrace	Y9
18	Howth View Park	S9
45	Huband Road	F16
69	Hudson Road	V21
45	Hughes Road East	F17
45	Hughes Road North	F17
45	Hughes Road South	F17
44	Hume Avenue	D16
47	Hume Street	L15
63	Hunters Avenue	F23
63	Hunters Court	F23
63	Hunters Crescent	F23
63	Hunters Green	F23
63	Hunters Grove	F23
63	*Hunters Hall	F23
	(Hunters Road)	
63	Hunters Hill	F23
63	Hunters Lane	F23
63	Hunters Meadow	F23
63	Hunters Parade	F23
63	Hunters Place	F23
63	Hunters Road	F23
9	Hunters Run	ZZ8
9	Hunters Run The Close	ZZ8
9	Hunters Run The Drive	ZZ8
9	Hunters Run The Glade	ZZ8
9	Hunters Run The Grove	YY8
9	Hunters Run The Park	YY8
9	Hunters Run The Rise	ZZ8
9	Hunters Run The View	ZZ8
9	Hunters Run The Way	ZZ8
63	Hunters Walk	F23
63	Hunters Way	F23
10	Huntstown Avenue	ZZ9
10	Huntstown Close	ZZ9
10	Huntstown Court	ZZ8
10	Huntstown Drive	ZZ8
10	Huntstown Glen	ZZ9
10	Huntstown Green	ZZ9
10	Huntstown Grove	ZZ8
10	Huntstown Lawn	A9
10	Huntstown Park	ZZ8
10	Huntstown Rise	A8
10	Huntstown Road	ZZ9
9	Huntstown Way	ZZ9
9	Huntstown Wood	ZZ9
3	Hutchinson's Strand	P1
46	Huxley Crescent	J15
39	Hyacinth Street	M13
46	Hybreasal	G15
72	Hyde Park (Dalkey)	V21
54	Hyde Park (Templeogue)	H19
57	Hyde Park Avenue	Q19
57	Hyde Park Gardens	Q19
73	Hyde Road	W21
56	Hyde Square	N19
63	**IDRONE AVENUE**	G21
63	Idrone Close	G21
63	Idrone Drive	G21
58	Idrone Mews	R19

Page		Grid Ref

63 Idrone Park **G21**
58 Idrone Terrace **R19**
38 Imaal Road **JI3**
72 Inagh Court **V25**
44 Inagh Road **D15**
6 Inbhir Ide **R2**
6 Inbhir Ide Close **R2**
6 Inbhir Ide Drive **R2**
45 Inchicore **F14**
37 Inchicore Road **G15**
37 Inchicore Square **F15**
37 Inchicore Terrace North **F15**
37 Inchicore Terrace South **F15**
38 Infirmary Road **H14**
38 Inglewood Close **ZZ10**
9 Inglewood Crescent **ZZ10**
22 Inglewood Drive **ZZ10**
22 Inglewood Road **ZZ10**
47 Ingram Road **J16**
61 Inis Fail **C22**
61 Inis Thiar **C22**
39 *Inkerman Cottages **L14**
(off Amiens Street)
39 Innisfallen Parade **K13**
22 Innishmaan Road **L10**
45 *Innishmore Terrace **G17**
(St Mary's Road)
45 Innismore **G17**
38 *Inns Court **K14**
(on Winetavern Street)
38 Inns Quay **J14**
18 Inver Road **H12**
18 Invermore Grove **R9**
22 Inverness Road **M12**
27 Iona Avenue **K12**
27 Iona Crescent **K12**
26 Iona Drive **K12**
26 Iona Park **K12**
26 Iona Road **K12**
27 Iona Villas **K12**
51 Iris Grove **P19**
49 Irishtown (Ringsend) **N15**
40 Irishtown Road **N15**
40 *Irvine Cottages **M14**
(Irvine Terrace)
40 Irvine Terrace **M14**
11 Irwin Court **H15**
38 Irwin Street **H15**
38 Island Street **J14**
19 Island View (Kilbarrack) **T10**
7 Island View (Malahide) **T3**
21 *Island View Apts **Y9**
(Harbour Road)
19 Island View Court Apts **T10**
39 Island Villa **M15**
37 Islandbridge **G14**
37 Islandbridge Court **G14**
59 Islington Avenue **V20**
40 Isolda Road **N15**
16 Isolde Gardens **E14**
36 *Isolde House Apts **E14**
(Hibernian Tce)
38 Ivar Street **J14**
45 Iveagh Buildings **K15**
46 Iveagh Gardens **G16**
22 Iveleary Road **L10**
16 Iveragh Court **M16**
27 Iveragh Road **L10**
16 Ivy Court **M9**
46 Ivy Terrace **J15**

43 **JAMES CONNOLLY A16 PARK**
39 James Joyce St **L14**
30 James Larkin Road **S10**
19 James McCormack Gdns **U9**
45 James Plunkett House **F15**
48 James's Place East **L15**
31 James's Street **H15**
48 James's Street East **L15**
40 James's Street North **M13**
7 James's Terrace **S2**
46 James's Walk **H15**
70 Jamestown **Q25**
45 Jamestown Avenue **F16**
45 Jamestown Court **F16**
13 Jamestown Rd (Finglas) **H9**
45 Jamestown Road **E16**
(Inchicore)
59 *Jane-Ville **U20**
(Off Tivoli Road)
39 Jervis Lane Lower **K14**
39 Jervis Lane Upper **K14**
39 Jervis Street **K14**
60 Jobstown **A22**
60 Jobstown Road **A22**
60 Jobstown Village Sq **A21**
38 John Dillon Street **K15**
44 John F Kennedy Avenue **D17**
44 John F Kennedy Drive **D17**
44 John F Kennedy Park **D16**

44 John F Kennedy Road **D16**
39 John Field Road **K15**
45 John MacCormack Ave **F17**
38 *John Street North **J14**
(off Ellis Quay)
38 John Street South **J15**
38 John Street West **J15**
38 John's Lane East **K15**
38 John's Lane West **J15**
33 Johnsbridge **XX15**
33 Johnsbridge Avenue **XX15**
33 Johnsbridge Close **XX15**
33 Johnsbridge Green **XX15**
33 Johnsbridge Grove **XX15**
33 Johnsbridge Meadows **XX15**
33 Johnsbridge Park **XX15**
33 Johnsbridge Walk **XX15**
39 *Johnson Place **K15**
(Clarendon Street)
39 Johnson's Court **K15**
69 Johnstown Avenue **T23**
69 Johnstown Court **T22**
26 Johnstown Gardens **H10**
26 Johnstown Grove **T23**
26 Johnstown House **J10**
69 Johnstown Park **T23**
(Cornelscourt)
26 Johnstown Pk (Glasnevin) **J10**
69 Johnstown Road **T23**
(Cornelscourt)
39 Jones's Road **L13**
13 Josephine Avenue **K13**
40 *Joy Street **M15**
(off Gordon Street)
68 Joyce Avenue **R23**
71 Joyce Hall **S24**
27 Joyce Road **K11**
43 Joyce Way **C15**
2 Jugback Close **M1**
2 Jugback Court **M1**
2 Jugback Crescent **M1**
2 Jugback Lane **M1**

44 **KAVANAGH AVE D16**
52 Keadeen Avenue **E19**
22 Kearn's Place **G15**
49 *Keegan's Cottages **P17**
(off Merrion Rd)
46 Keeper Road **H16**
46 Kells Road **H17**
59 Kelly's Avenue **U20**
38 *Kelly's Lane **K13**
(Phibsborough)
39 Kelly's Row **K13**
39 *Kelly's Square **K13**
(Kelly's Row)
67 Kelston Avenue **R22**
67 Kelston Drive **R22**
67 Kelston Hall **R22**
67 Kelston Park **R22**
67 Kelston View **R22**
8 Kelvin Close **U4**
24 Kempton **F11**
24 Kempton Avenue **F11**
24 Kempton Court **F11**
24 Kempton Green **F11**
24 Kempton Grove **F11**
24 Kempton Heath **F11**
25 Kempton Lawn **F11**
24 Kempton Park **F11**
24 Kempton Rise **F11**
24 Kempton View **F11**
24 Kempton Way **F11**
72 Kenah Court **V23**
47 Kengar Mews **J17**
47 Kenilworth Lane **J17**
47 *Kenilworth Lodge **J17**
(Laundry Lane)
47 Kenilworth Manor **J17**
47 Kenilworth Park **J17**
47 Kenilworth Road **J17**
47 Kenilworth Square **J17**
47 Kenilworth Square East **K17**
47 Kenilworth Square North **J17**
47 Kenilworth Square South **J17**
47 Kenilworth Square West **J17**
39 Kenmare Parade **K13**
49 *Kennedy Court **N15**
(Irishtown Road)
35 Kennelsfort Green **B14**
35 Kennelsfort Road Lower **C13**
35 Kennelsfort Road Upper **C14**
53 Kennington Close **F20**
53 Kennington Crescent **F20**
53 Kennington Lawn **F20**
53 Kennington Road **F19**
73 *Kent Terrace **V22**
(on Barnhill Road)
31 Kentfield **V26**
40 Kerlogue Road **N15**

47 *Kerrygold House **J17**
(Tivoli Avenue)
70 Kerrymount Avenue **R24**
68 Kerrymount Close **S23**
68 Kerrymount Green **S23**
68 Kerrymount Mall **S23**
68 Kerrymount Rise **S23**
5 Kettles Drive **P4**
5 Kettles Lane **P4**
5 Kettles Place **P4**
38 *Kevin Barry **J14**
(off Church Street Upper)
47 *Kevin Street Cross **K15**
(on Bride St New)
47 Kevin Street Lower **K15**
47 Kevin Street Upper **K15**
32 Kew Park **WW13**
32 Kew Park Avenue **WW14**
32 Kew Park Crescent **VV13**
46 Kickham Road **G15**
52 Kilakee Close **E19**
52 Kilakee Drive **E19**
18 Kilbarrack **T9**
18 Kilbarrack Avenue **T10**
18 Kilbarrack Gardens **T10**
18 Kilbarrack Grove **T10**
18 Kilbarrack Parade **S9**
18 Kilbarrack Road **S9**
18 Kilbarrack Way **S9**
16 Kilbarron Avenue **N9**
16 Kilbarron Court **N9**
16 Kilbarron Drive **N9**
16 Kilbarron Park **N9**
16 Kilbarron Road **N9**
73 Kilbegnet Close **W22**
71 Kilbogget Grove **T24**
71 Kilbogget Villas **T24**
28 Kilbride Road **P11**
42 Kilcarberry Ave **ZZ18**
42 Kilcarberry Close **ZZ18**
42 Kilcarberry Lawn **ZZ18**
51 Kilcarrig Avenue **B20**
51 Kilcarrig Close **B20**
51 Kilcarrig Crescent **B20**
51 Kilcarrig Green **B20**
61 Kildare Avenue **B22**
61 Kildare Crescent **B22**
61 Kildare Drive **B22**
61 Kildare Gardens **B22**
69 Kilcolman Court **V22**
42 Kilcronan Avenue **YY16**
42 Kilcronan Close **YY16**
42 Kilcronan Court **YY16**
42 Kilcronan Crescent **YY16**
42 Kilcronan Grove **YY16**
42 Kilcronan Lawns **YY16**
42 Kilcronan View **YY16**
66 Kilcross Avenue **N23**
66 Kilcross Close **N23**
66 Kilcross Court **M23**
66 Kilcross Crescent **M23**
66 Kilcross Drive **M23**
66 Kilcross Grove **M23**
66 Kilcross Lawn **N23**
66 Kilcross Park **M23**
66 Kilcross Square **M23**
66 Kilcross Way **M23**
45 Kildare Park **G17**
39 Kildare Place **L15**
46 Kildare Road **G17**
39 Kildare Street **L15**
13 Kildonan Avenue **G9**
13 Kildonan Court **G9**
13 Kildonan Drive **G9**
13 Kildonan Road **G9**
18 Kilfenora Drive **R9**
46 Kilfenora Road **H17**
66 Kilgobbin Road **P23**
25 Kilkieran Court **H12**
25 Kilkieran Road **H12**
68 Kill Abbey **S21**
68 Kill Avenue **S21**
69 Kill Lane **T21**
68 Kill Lane **S21**
68 Kill O' the Grange **T21**
62 Killakee Avenue **E22**
62 Killakee Court **E22**
62 Killakee Gardens **E22**
62 Killakee Green **E22**
62 Killakee Lawns **E22**
62 Killakee Park **E22**
62 Killakee Rise **E22**
62 Killakee View **E22**
62 Killakee Walk **E22**
62 Killakee Way **E22**
25 Killala Road **H12**
40 Killan Road **M14**
39 Killarney Avenue **L13**

39 Killarney Parade **K13**
39 Killarney Street **L13**
18 Killary Grove **S9**
6 Killeen **Q3**
6 Killeen Avenue **Q3**
6 Killeen Court **Q3**
6 Killeen Crescent **Q3**
7 Killeen Mews **S3**
6 Killeen Park **Q3**
44 Killeen Rd (Bluebell) **D16**
44 Killeen Road **D17**
(Fox and Geese)
47 Killeen Rd (Rathmines) **L17**
7 Killeen Terrace **S2**
29 Killester **P11**
28 Killester Avenue **P11**
28 Killester Court **P11**
28 Killester Park **P11**
61 Killinardan **B23**
61 Killinarden Estate **B22**
61 Killinarden Heights **B23**
61 Killinarden Road **B23**
73 Killiney **V23**
72 Killiney Avenue **V24**
72 Killiney Court **V25**
72 Killiney Gate **V24**
72 Killiney Grove **V24**
72 Killiney Heath **V24**
72 Killiney Hill Road **V24**
72 Killiney Hill Road **V25**
72 Killiney Oaks **V25**
73 Killiney Road **V22**
73 Killiney Terrace **V21**
73 Killiney Towers **V22**
73 Killiney View **V21**
62 Killininny Cottages **E22**
62 *Killininny Court Apts **E22**
(Killakee Grove)
62 Killininny Road **E22**
66 Kilmacud **N21**
66 Kilmacud Avenue **P21**
67 Kilmacud Park **P21**
66 Kilmacud Road Upper **N21**
42 Kilmahuddrick Ave **YY17**
42 Kilmahuddrick Clo **YY17**
42 Kilmahuddrick Ct **YY17**
42 Kilmahuddrick Cres **YY17**
42 Kilmahuddrick Drive **YY17**
42 Kilmahuddrick Green **YY17**
42 Kilmahuddrick Grove **YY17**
42 Kilmahuddrick Lawn **YY17**
42 Kilmahuddrick Place **YY17**
42 Kilmahuddrick Road **YY17**
42 Kilmahuddrick Walk **YY17**
42 Kilmahuddrick Way **YY17**
37 Kilmainham **G15**
37 Kilmainham Lane **H15**
60 Kilmartin Avenue **A21**
50 Kilmartin Crescent **A20**
50 Kilmartin Drive **A21**
50 Kilmartin Gardens **A20**
50 Kilmartin Green **A21**
50 Kilmartin Park **A20**
52 Kilmashogue Close **E19**
52 Kilmashogue Drive **E19**
52 Kilmashogue Grove **E19**
64 Kilmashogue Lane **J23**
16 Kilmore **N9**
16 Kilmore Ave (Coolock) **P9**
72 Kilmore Ave (Killiney) **V24**
16 Kilmore Close **P9**
16 Kilmore Court **N9**
16 Kilmore Crescent **P9**
16 Kilmore Drive **P9**
16 Kilmore Place Apts **N9**
28 Kilmore Road **N10**
16 Kilmorony Close **R9**
52 Kilnamanagh **D19**
45 Kilnamanagh Court **F17**
52 Kilnamanagh Estate **D19**
45 Kilnamanagh Road **F17**
21 Kilrock Road **Z10**
28 Kironan Court **N10**
12 Kilshane Rd (North Rd) **E7**
25 Kilshane Road **F10**
(Rathoath Road)
11 Kilshane Way **D7**
60 Kiltalown **A23**
60 Kiltalown Avenue **A22**
60 Kiltalown Close **A22**
60 Kiltalown Cottages **A22**
60 Kiltalown Court **A22**
60 Kiltalown Crescent **A22**
60 Kiltalown Drive **A22**
60 Kiltalown Green **A22**
60 Kiltalown Grove **A22**
60 Kiltalown Heights **A22**
60 Kiltalown Hill **A22**
60 Kiltalown Park **A22**
60 Kiltalown Road **A22**
60 Kiltalown View **A22**

Page		Grid Ref
60	Kiltalown Walk	**A22**
60	Kiltalown Way	**A22**
68	Kilteragh Drive	**R23**
68	Kilteragh Pines	**R23**
68	Kilteragh Road	**R23**
61	Kiltipper	**C23**
62	Kiltipper Avenue	**D22**
62	Kiltipper Close	**D22**
62	Kiltipper Drive	**D22**
61	Kiltipper Gate	**C23**
61	Kiltipper Rise	**C23**
61	Kiltipper Road	**C23**
61	Kiltipper View	**C23**
61	Kiltipper Way	**C23**
31	Kiltuck Park	**V28**
53	Kilvere	**H20**
45	Kilworth Road	**F16**
53	Kimmage	**G18**
46	Kimmage Court	**H18**
46	Kimmage Grove	**H18**
53	*Kimmage Manor Way	**G18**
	(Whitehall Road)	
46	Kimmage Road Lower	**H18**
46	Kimmage Road West	**G18**
38	Kinahan Street	**H14**
28	Kincora Avenue	**P12**
41	Kincora Court	**Q13**
28	Kincora Drive	**P12**
28	Kincora Grove	**P12**
41	Kincora Park	**P12**
29	Kincora Road	**P12**
38	King Street North	**J14**
39	King Street South	**K15**
48	Kingram Place	**L16**
13	King's Avenue	**L13**
38	King's Court	**J13**
3	King's Hall	**P2**
38	Kings Inns	**K14**
39	King's Inns Street	**K14**
47	Kingsland Parade	**K16**
47	Kingsland Park Avenue	**K16**
65	Kingston	**L23**
65	Kingston Avenue	**L23**
65	Kingston Close	**L23**
64	Kingston Court	**J22**
65	Kingston Crescent	**L23**
65	Kingston Drive	**L23**
65	Kingston Green	**L23**
65	Kingston Grove	**L23**
65	Kingston Hall	**L23**
65	Kingston Heights	**L23**
65	Kingston Lawn	**L23**
39	Kingston Lodge	**L12**
65	Kingston Park	**L23**
65	Kingston Rise	**L23**
65	Kingston View	**L23**
65	Kingston Walk	**L23**
50	Kingswood	**ZZ20**
50	Kingswood Avenue	**ZZ20**
	(Citywest)	
51	Kingswood Avenue	**C19**
	(Kilnamanagh)	
52	Kingswood Castle	**D18**
50	Kingswood Drive	**ZZ20**
	(Citywest)	
51	Kingswood Drive	**C19**
	(Kilnamanagh)	
51	Kingswood Heights	**C19**
50	Kingswood Road	**ZZ20**
51	Kingswood View	**C19**
6	Kinsaley Lane	**R4**
3	Kinsealy Court	**P3**
3	Kinsealy Downs	**P3**
6	Kinsealy Lane	**R4**
25	Kinvara Avenue	**G12**
25	Kinvara Drive	**F12**
25	Kinvara Grove	**F12**
25	Kinvara Park	**F12**
25	Kinvara Road	**F12**
52	Kippure Avenue	**E19**
25	Kippure Park	**G12**
22	Kirkfield	**A10**
22	Kirkpatrick Avenue	**A11**
22	Kirkpatrick Drive	**A11**
18	Kirkwood	**N16**
38	Kirwan Street	**J14**
38	Kirwan Street Cottages	**J13**
21	Kitestown Road	**Z11**
59	Knapton Court	**T20**
59	Knapton Lawn	**T20**
59	Knapton Road	**T20**
59	Knapton Terrace	**T20**
59	*Knapton Villas	**T20**
	(on Knapton Road)	
28	Knights Bridge	**P12**
15	Knights Wood	**M8**
36	Knock Riada	**D14**
63	Knockaire	**G21**
63	Knockcullen	**G21**
63	Knockcullen Drive	**G21**
63	Knockcullen Lawn	**G21**

Page		Grid Ref
63	Knockcullen Park	**G21**
63	Knockcullen Rise	**G21**
7	Knockdara	**T3**
63	Knockfield Manor	**F21**
63	Knocklyon	**G21**
63	Knocklyon Avenue	**F21**
63	Knocklyon Close	**G21**
63	Knocklyon Court	**G21**
63	Knocklyon Drive	**G21**
63	*Knocklyon Gate Apts	**F22**
	(Woodstown Avenue)	
63	Knocklyon Green	**G21**
63	Knocklyon Grove	**G21**
63	Knocklyon Heights	**F21**
63	Knocklyon Mews	**F21**
63	Knocklyon Park	**F21**
53	Knocklyon Road	**G20**
36	Knockmarce Apartments	**E14**
36	Knockmaroon Hill	**D13**
36	Knockmaroon Road	**D13**
43	Knockmeenagh Lane	**B18**
43	Knockmeenagh Road	**B18**
44	Knockmitten Close	**C17**
44	Knockmitten Lane	**D17**
44	Knockmitten Lane Nth	**C17**
61	Knockmore Avenue	**B22**
61	Knockmore Crescent	**B22**
61	Knockmore Drive	**B22**
61	Knockmore Gardens	**B22**
61	Knockmore Green	**B22**
61	Knockmore Grove	**B22**
61	Knockmore Park	**B22**
73	Knock-na-Cree Grove	**W22**
73	Knock-na-Cree Park	**W22**
73	Knock-na-Cree Road	**W22**
58	Knocknagow	**S20**
45	Knocknarea Avenue	**G16**
45	Knocknarea Road	**G16**
37	Knocknarrow Terrace	**H15**
56	Knocknashee	**M20**
56	Knocknashee	**N20**
68	Knocksinna	**R22**
68	Knocksinna Court	**R22**
68	Knocksinna Crescent	**R22**
68	Knocksinna Grove	**R22**
68	Knocksinna Park	**R22**
14	Knowth Court	**J8**
37	Kyber Road	**F14**
40	Kyle-Clare Road	**N15**
44	Kylemore Avenue	**D15**
44	Kylemore Drive	**D15**
44	Kylemore Park North	**D16**
44	Kylemore Park South	**D16**
44	Kylemore Park West	**D16**
36	Kylemore Road	**D14**
65	**LA TOUCHE COURT K22**	
	(Ballinteer)	
45	La Touche Court	**F16**
	(Bluebell)	
45	La Touche Drive	**E16**
45	La Touche Road	**F16**
20	La Vista Avenue	**W10**
44	Labre Park	**E16**
56	Laburnum Road	**M18**
35	Laburnum Walk	**C14**
48	Lad Lane	**L15**
48	Lad Lane Upper	**L16**
37	Lady's Lane	**G15**
10	Lady's Well Road	**A8**
25	Lagan Road	**H11**
50	Lake Drive	**ZZ20**
66	Lakelands Avenue	**N21**
66	Lakelands Close	**N21**
66	Lakelands Crescent	**P21**
66	Lakelands Drive	**P21**
66	Lakelands Grove	**N21**
66	Lakelands Lawn	**N21**
54	Lakelands Park	**H19**
66	Lakelands Road	**N21**
3	Lakeshore Drive	**N3**
3	Lakeview Drive	**N3**
36	Lally Road	**E15**
38	Lamb Alley	**J15**
72	Lambay Close	**V25**
7	Lambay Court	**T3**
72	Lambay Drive	**V25**
27	Lambay Road	**K11**
9	Lambourne Avenue	**ZZ10**
9	Lambourne Court	**ZZ10**
9	Lambourne Drive	**ZZ10**
9	Lambourne Park	**ZZ10**
9	Lambourne Road	**ZZ10**
28	Lambourne Village	**P12**
71	Lambourne Wood	**T24**
66	Lamb's Brook	**N23**
38	*Lamb's Court	**H15**
	(off James's Street)	
36	Landen Road	**F15**
55	Landore	**K19**
55	Landscape Avenue	**K19**

Page		Grid Ref
55	Landscape Crescent	**K20**
55	Landscape Gardens	**L19**
55	Landscape Park	**K20**
55	Landscape Road	**K19**
45	Landsdown Valley Place	**F17**
45	Landsdowne Valley	**F17**
45	Landsdowne Valley Park	**F16**
13	Lanesborough Avenue	**H8**
13	Lanesborough Court	**H8**
14	Lanesborough Drive	**H8**
13	Lanesborough Gardens	**H8**
14	Lanesborough Grove	**H8**
13	Lanesborough Mews	**H8**
13	Lanesborough Park	**H8**
13	Lanesborough Road	**H8**
13	Lanesborough Square	**H8**
13	Lanesborough Terrace	**H8**
14	Lanesborough View	**H8**
68	Lanesville	**S21**
68	Lanesville Terrace	**S21**
39	Langrishe Place	**L13**
61	Lanndale Lawns	**B21**
48	Lansdowne Crescent	**M15**
48	Lansdowne Gardens	**M16**
49	Lansdowne Hall	**N15**
48	Lansdowne Lane	**M15**
48	Lansdowne Park	**M15**
	(Ballsbridge)	
63	Lansdowne Park	**G21**
	(Templeogue)	
48	Lansdowne Road	**M16**
49	Lansdowne Square	**N16**
48	Lansdowne Terrace	**M15**
49	Lansdowne Village	**N16**
48	Lansdowne Villas	**M15**
18	Lapwing Apts	**P19**
18	Laracor Gardens	**R9**
72	Laragh	**V24**
18	Laragh Close	**R9**
27	Laragh Flats	**M10**
18	Laragh Grove	**R9**
64	Larch Drive	**H22**
9	Larch Grove	**ZZ10**
48	Larch Grove	**L17**
16	Larch Hill	**M8**
56	Larchfield	**M20**
56	Larchfield	**M20**
56	Larchfield Park	**M20**
56	Larchfield Road	**M20**
33	Larkfield	**ZZ14**
46	Larkfield Avenue	**J17**
	(Harold's Cross)	
33	Larkfield Avenue	**ZZ14**
	(Liffey Valley)	
33	Larkfield Close	**ZZ14**
33	Larkfield Court	**ZZ14**
46	Larkfield Gardens	**J17**
33	Larkfield Green	**ZZ14**
46	Larkfield Grove	**J17**
	(Harold's Cross)	
34	Larkfield Grove	**ZZ14**
	(Liffey Valley)	
46	Larkfield Park	**J17**
34	Larkfield Place	**ZZ14**
33	Larkfield Rise	**ZZ14**
34	Larkfield Square	**ZZ14**
33	Larkfield View	**ZZ14**
33	Larkfield Way	**ZZ14**
27	Larkhill Road	**L10**
46	Larrisa Court	**H17**
9	Latchford	**YY9**
9	Latchford Close	**YY9**
9	Latchford Court	**YY9**
9	Latchford Green	**YY9**
9	Latchford Park	**YY9**
9	Latchford Row	**YY9**
9	Latchford Square	**YY9**
9	Latchford Terrace	**YY9**
33	Latouka Apts	**ZZ13**
47	*Lauderdale Terrace	**J17**
	(on New Row South)	
20	Lauder's Lane	**V9**
14	Laundry Lane	**J17**
72	Laurel Ave (Ballybrack)	**V25**
65	Laurel Ave (Dundrum)	**L21**
68	Laurel Bank	**T21**
23	Laurel Court	**B11**
65	Laurel Drive	**L21**
69	Laurel Hill	**U21**
23	Laurel Lodge Road	**C11**
43	Laurel Park	**B17**
54	Laurel Place	**J18**
65	Laurel Road	**L21**
2	Laurelton	**M1**
	(Rathbeale Road)	
54	Laurelton (Terenure)	**J19**
36	Laurence Brook	**E14**
47	Laurence Court	**J17**
39	Laurence Place East	**M14**
67	Laurleen	**Q21**
54	Lavarna Grove	**H18**

Page		Grid Ref
54	Lavarna Road	**H18**
23	Laverna Avenue	**B11**
23	Laverna Dale	**B11**
23	Laverna Grove	**B11**
23	Laverna Way	**B11**
44	Lavery Avenue	**C16**
28	Lavista Avenue	**P11**
67	Lawnswood Park	**Q21**
29	Lawrence Grove	**N12**
5	Lawson Spinney	**R3**
73	Lawson Terrace	**V21**
47	Le Bas Terrace	**K16**
54	Le Brett Terrace	**J19**
44	Le Brocquy Avenue	**D16**
36	Le Fanu Drive	**D15**
36	Le Fanu Road	**D15**
47	*Le Vere Terrace	**J16**
	(Armstrong Street)	
49	Lea Crescent	**P16**
49	Lea Road	**P16**
23	Leahy's Terrace	**N15**
42	Lealand Avenue	**ZZ17**
42	Lealand Close	**ZZ17**
42	Lealand Crescent	**ZZ17**
42	Lealand Drive	**ZZ17**
42	Lealand Gardens	**ZZ17**
42	Lealand Grove	**ZZ17**
42	Lealand Road	**ZZ17**
42	Lealand Walk	**ZZ17**
71	Leamann	**T24**
26	Lee Road	**H11**
47	Leeson Close	**L16**
47	Leeson Lane	**L15**
48	Leeson Park	**L16**
48	Leeson Park Avenue	**L16**
47	Leeson Place	**L16**
47	Leeson Street Lower	**L15**
48	Leeson Street Upper	**L16**
48	Leeson Village	**L16**
47	Leeson Walk	**L16**
71	Lehaunstown Road	**T25**
47	Leicester Avenue	**K17**
46	Leighlin Road	**H17**
29	Lein Gardens	**Q10**
29	Lein Park	**Q10**
29	Lein Road	**Q10**
40	Leinster Avenue	**M13**
39	Leinster Lane	**L15**
56	Leinster Lawn	**M19**
39	*Leinster Market	**L14**
	(D'Olier Street)	
47	Leinster Park	**J17**
	(Harold's Cross)	
47	Leinster Place	**J17**
47	Leinster Road	**K17**
47	Leinster Road West	**J17**
47	Leinster Square	**K17**
40	Leinster Street East	**M13**
26	Leinster Street North	**J12**
39	Leinster Street South	**L15**
43	Leinster Terrace	**A17**
48	Leitrim Place	**M15**
38	Leix Road	**J13**
32	Leixlip Road	**WW13**
39	Lemon Street	**K15**
47	Lennox Place	**K16**
47	Lennox Street	**K16**
47	*Lennox Terrace	**K16**
	(Lennox Street)	
18	Lentisk Lawn	**R9**
39	*Leo Avenue	**K13**
	(Leo Street)	
39	Leo Street	**K13**
47	Leonard's Court	**J16**
67	Leopardstown	**Q23**
70	Leopardstown Abbey	**Q24**
67	Leopardstown Avenue	**Q22**
67	Leopardstown Court	**Q22**
67	Leopardstown Drive	**Q22**
67	Leopardstown Gardens	**Q22**
67	Leopardstown Grove	**Q22**
66	Leopardstown Heights	**P23**
67	Leopardstown Lawn	**Q22**
67	Leopardstown Oaks	**Q22**
67	Leopardstown Park	**Q22**
66	Leopardstown Rise	**P23**
66	Leopardstown Road	**N23**
67	Leopardstown Road	**Q22**
70	Leopardstown Valley	**Q24**
73	Leslie Avenue	**W21**
38	Leslie's Buildings	**J13**
40	Leukos Road	**N15**
39	Liberty House	**L13**
47	Liberty Lane	**K15**
59	Library Road	**U20**
	(Dun Laoghaire)	
31	Library Road (Shankill)	**V26**
38	*Library View Villas	**K12**
	(St Peter's Square)	
34	Liffey Ave	**ZZ14**
34	Liffey Close	**ZZ14**

Page		Grid Ref
34	Liffey Court	ZZ14
34	Liffey Crescent	ZZ14
34	Liffey Dale	ZZ14
34	Liffey Downs	ZZ14
34	Liffey Drive	ZZ14
34	Liffey Gardens	ZZ14
34	Liffey Glen	ZZ14
34	Liffey Green	ZZ14
34	Liffey Hall	ZZ14
34	Liffey Junction	ZZ14
34	Liffey Lawn	ZZ14
34	Liffey Park	ZZ14
34	Liffey Place	ZZ14
34	Liffey Rise	ZZ14
34	Liffey Road	ZZ14
34	Liffey Row	ZZ14
39	Liffey Street Lower	K14
36	Liffey Street South	F16
39	Liffey Street Upper	K14
38	Liffey Street West	J14
36	Liffey Terrace	E14
34	Liffey Vale	ZZ14
34	Liffey Valley Park	ZZ14
34	Liffey View	ZZ14
34	Liffey Villas	ZZ14
34	Liffey Walk	ZZ14
34	Liffey Way	ZZ14
34	Liffey Wood	ZZ14
9	Lilys Way	XX9
39	Lime Street	M14
52	Limekiln Avenue	E18
53	Limekiln Close	F19
53	Limekiln Drive	F19
52	Limekiln Green	E19
53	Limekiln Grove	F18
47	Limekiln Lane	J16
	(Harold's Cross)	
53	Limekiln Lane	F18
	(Kimmage)	
53	Limekiln Park	F19
52	Limekiln Road	E19
22	Limelawn Green	A10
22	Limelawn Park	A10
66	Limes Road	N22
7	Limetree Avenue	T4
8	Limetree Avenue	U4
17	Limewood Avenue	Q9
17	Limewood Park	Q9
17	Limewood Road	Q9
38	*Lincoln House	J14
	(Hammond Lane)	
38	*Lincoln Lane	J14
	(Hammond Lane)	
39	Lincoln Place	L15
57	Linden Court	Q20
67	Linden Lea Park	Q21
57	Linden Square	Q20
58	Lindenvale	R20
42	Lindisfarne Avenue	ZZ17
42	Lindisfarne Drive	ZZ17
42	Lindisfarne Green	ZZ17
42	Lindisfarne Grove	ZZ17
42	Lindisfarne Lawns	ZZ17
42	Lindisfarne Park	ZZ16
42	Lindisfarne Vale	ZZ17
42	Lindisfarne Walk	ZZ17
26	Lindsay Road	K12
38	Linenhall Parade	K14
38	*Linenhall Street	J14
	(off King Street North)	
38	Linenhall Terrace	K14
59	Link Road	V21
59	Link Road	T20
	(Off Monkstown Crescent)	
15	*Limbhla	K8
	(Ballymun Main Street)	
9	Linnetfields Avenue	YY8
9	Linnetfields Close	YY8
9	Linnetfields Drive	YY8
9	Linnetfields Park	XX9
9	Linnetfields Rise	YY8
9	Linnetfields Square	YY8
9	Linnetfields View	YY8
9	Linnetfields Walk	YY9
61	Lios na Sidhe	C22
2	Lioscian	L1
57	Lisalea	R19
38	Lisburn Street	K14
22	Liscannor Road	H12
73	Liscanor	W21
34	Liscarne Court	A15
34	Liscarne Dale	A15
34	Liscarne Gardens	A15
45	Lisle Road	G17
17	Lismeen Grove	P9
46	Lismore Road	H17
46	Lissadel Avenue	G16
46	Lissadel Court	G16
6	Lissadel Crescent	Q2
45	Lissadel Drive	G16

Page		Grid Ref
45	Lissadel Green	G16
6	Lissadel Grove	Q2
6	Lissadel Park	Q2
45	Lissadel Road	G16
6	Lissadel Wood	Q2
3	Lissen Hall	P1
47	Lissenfield	K16
3	Lissenhall Avenue	N1
3	Lissenhall Court	N1
3	Lissenhall Drive	N1
3	Lissenhall Park	N1
9	Little Britain Street	K14
48	Little Fitzwilliam Place	L15
69	Little Meadow	T23
9	Littlepace Close	YY8
9	Littlepace Court	YY8
9	Littlepace Crescent	YY8
9	Littlepace Drive	YY8
9	Littlepace Gallops	YY8
9	Littlepace Meadow	YY8
9	Littlepace Park	YY8
9	Littlepace Road	YY8
9	Littlepace View	YY8
9	Littlepace Walk	YY8
9	Littlepace Way	YY8
9	Littlepace Woods	YY8
39	Litton Lane	K14
65	Llewellyn Close	K21
65	Llewellyn Court	K21
65	Llewellyn Grove	K21
65	Llewellyn Lawn	K21
65	Llewellyn Park	K21
65	Llewellyn Way	K21
32	Lock Road	XX15
39	Lockkeeper's Walk	G11
39	Loftus Lane	K14
54	Loftus Square	J20
22	Lohunda Close	A10
22	Lohunda Court	A10
22	Lohunda Crescent	ZZ10
22	Lohunda Dale	A10
22	Lohunda Downs	A10
22	Lohunda Drive	A10
22	Lohunda Green	A10
22	Lohunda Grove	A10
22	Lohunda Park	ZZ10
22	Lohunda Park View	A10
22	Lohunda Road	ZZ10
39	Lombard Court	L14
47	Lombard Street East	L14
47	Lombard Street West	K16
22	Lomond Avenue	M12
48	Londonbridge Drive	N15
48	Londonbridge Road	N15
47	Long Lane	K15
47	*Long Lane Close	K15
	(off Long Lane)	
44	Long Mile Road	E17
15	Longdale Terrace	K9
15	Longdale Way	K9
39	Longford Lane	K15
59	Longford Place	T20
39	Longford Street Great	K15
39	Longford Street Little	K15
59	Longford Terrace	T20
3	Longlands	N2
68	Longmeadow	T23
69	Longmeadow Grove	T23
38	Long's Place	J15
47	Longwood Avenue	K16
54	Longwood Park	J20
15	Lorcan Avenue	M9
15	Lorcan Crescent	M9
15	Lorcan Drive	L9
16	Lorcan Green	M9
15	Lorcan Grove	M9
46	Lorcan O'Toole Court	G18
46	Lorcan O'Toole Park	G18
15	Lorcan Park	M9
15	Lorcan Road	L9
16	Lorcan Villas	M9
39	Lord Edward Street	K15
31	Lordello Road	U27
37	Lords Walk	G14
54	Loreto Abbey	K20
73	Loreto Avenue (Dalkey)	W21
54	Loreto Avenue	K20
	(Nutgrove Avenue)	
55	Loreto Court	K20
55	Loreto Crescent	K20
55	Loreto Park	K20
46	Loreto Road	G16
55	Loreto Row	K20
54	Loreto Terrace	J20
37	*Lorne Terrace	H15
	(off Almeida Avenue)	
61	*Losset Hall	C21
	(Belgard Square)	
39	Lotts	K14
35	Lough Conn Avenue	D14
36	Lough Conn Drive	D14

Page		Grid Ref
36	Lough Conn Road	D14
36	Lough Conn Terrace	D14
29	Lough Derg Road	R10
72	Loughlinstown	U25
72	Loughlinstown Drive	U25
72	Loughlinstown Park	U25
72	Loughlinstown Wood	U25
54	*Loughmorne House	J18
	(Olney Grove)	
21	Loughoreen Hills	Y11
47	Louis Lane	K17
39	Lourdes House	L13
46	Lourdes Road	H15
22	Louvain	N19
56	Louvain Glade	N20
36	Lower Glen Road	D13
56	Lower Kilmacud Road	N20
	(Goatstown)	
67	Lower Kilmacud Road	P21
	(Stillorgan)	
22	Lower Lucan Road	ZZ12
31	Lower Road (Shankill)	V27
34	Lower Road	A13
	(Strawberry Beds)	
37	Luby Road	G15
32	Lucan	XX14
32	Lucan Bypass	WW14
33	Lucan Heights	XX13
33	Lucan Newlands Road	XX13
36	Lucan Rd (Chapelizod)	D14
34	Lucan Road (Lucan)	ZZ14
34	Lucan Road	A13
	(near Quarryvale)	
35	Lucan Rd (Palmerston)	C13
34	Lucan-Newlands Rd	ZZ15
65	Ludford Drive	L21
65	Ludford Park	L21
65	Ludford Road	L22
52	Lugnaquilla Avenue	E19
39	Luke Street	L14
38	Lurgan Street	K14
22	Luttrell Park	A11
22	Luttrell Park Close	B11
22	Luttrell Park Court	A11
22	Luttrell Park Crescent	B11
22	Luttrell Park Drive	B11
22	Luttrell Park Green	B11
22	Luttrell Park Grove	A11
22	Luttrell Park Heath	B11
22	Luttrell Park Lawn	A11
22	Luttrell Park View	B11
22	Luttrellstown Avenue	B12
22	Luttrellstown Chase	A12
22	Luttrellstown Close	B12
22	Luttrellstown Court	A12
22	Luttrellstown Dale	A12
22	Luttrellstown Drive	A12
22	Luttrellstown Glade	A12
22	Luttrellstown Green	A12
22	Luttrellstown Grove	A12
22	Luttrellstown Heath	A12
22	Luttrellstown Heights	A12
22	Luttrellstown Lawn	A12
22	Luttrellstown Oaks	A12
22	Luttrellstown Park	A12
22	Luttrellstown Place	A11
22	Luttrellstown Rise	A11
22	Luttrellstown Thicket	A11
22	Luttrellstown View	B12
22	Luttrellstown Walk	A12
22	Luttrellstown Way	A11
22	Luttrellstown Wood	B12
46	Lyllymore Terrace	J16
15	Lymewood Mews	L8
33	Lynches Lane	ZZ16
38	Lynch's Lane	E15
33	Lynch's Place	K13
37	Lyndon Gate	G12
49	Lynton Court	N16
65	Lynwood	M21
56	Ma Tuire Apts	N20
39	Mabbot Lane	L14
39	Mabel Street	L12
39	Macken Street	M15
39	Macken Villa	M15
45	Mackies Place	L15
68	Mackintosh Park	T22
17	Macroom Avenue	P8
17	Macroom Road	P8
47	Madden Road	J15
38	*Madden's Court	J15
	(off Thomas Street)	
72	Madden's Lane	U24
55	Madison House	K18
46	Madison Road	H15
40	*Magdalen Terrace	N15
	(off Oliver Plunket Ave)	
39	Magennis Place	L14
39	Magennis Square	L14

Page		Grid Ref
15	Magenta Crescent	L9
15	Magenta Hall	L9
69	Magenta Place	U21
60	Magna Drive	ZZ22
55	*Maher's Terrace	M20
	(on Main Street Dundrum)	
36	Maidens Row	E14
19	Main Street (Baldoyle)	U8
58	Main Street (Blackrock)	R19
23	Main Street	B10
	(Blanchardstown)	
43	Main Street (Clondalkin)	B17
18	Main Street (Clongriffin)	S8
55	Main Street (Dundrum)	M20
25	Main Street (Finglas)	H10
21	Main Street (Howth)	Y10
32	Main Street (Lucan)	XX13
7	Main Street (Malahide)	S2
29	Main Street (Raheny)	R10
54	Main St (Rathfarnham)	J20
3	Main Street (Swords)	N2
62	Main Street (Tallaght)	D21
40	Malachi Place	M13
38	Malachi Road	J14
8	Malahide	R2
29	Malahide Road (Artane)	P10
17	Malahide Rd (Balgriffin)	R7
29	Malahide Rd (Coolock)	Q9
28	Malahide Rd (Marino)	P12
3	Malahide Rd (Swords)	N2
69	Malborough Court	V22
11	Malin House	C9
46	Mallin Avenue	H15
48	Malone Gardens	M15
47	Malpas Court	K15
47	*Malpas Place	K15
	(off Malpas Street)	
47	Malpas Street	K15
47	Malpas Terrace	K15
47	Mander's Terrace	L16
52	Mangerton Road	F16
22	Mannix Road	K12
53	Manor Avenue	H19
65	Manor Close	K22
22	Manor Court (Clonsilla)	A10
9	Manor Crescent	YY9
18	Manor Drive	R8
65	Manor Green	K22
53	Manor Grove	G18
65	Manor Heath	K21
38	*Manor Mews	J14
	(off Norseman Place)	
65	Manor Park (Ballinteer)	K22
35	Manor Park (Palmerston)	C14
22	Manor Place (Clonsilla)	XX9
38	Manor Pl (Stoneybatter)	J14
65	Manor Rise	K22
35	Manor Road	C14
9	Manor Square	XX9
38	Manor Street	J14
46	Manor Villas	J17
9	Manrfields	YY9
3	Mantua Park	N1
26	Maolbuille Road	K10
73	Mapas Avenue	V22
73	Mapas Road	V22
23	Maple Avenue	B11
	(Carpenterstown)	
66	Maple Avenue	N22
23	Maple Close	B11
23	Maple Drive	B11
	(Carpenterstown)	
46	Maple Drive	J18
	(Harold's Cross)	
22	Maple Glen	B11
23	Maple Green	B11
23	Maple Grove	B11
	(Carpenterstown)	
23	Maple Lawn	B11
23	Maple Lodge	D12
71	Maple Manor	T23
55	Maple Road	M18
66	Maples Road	N22
61	Maplewood Avenue	B21
61	Maplewood Close	B21
61	Maplewood Court	B21
61	Maplewood Drive	B21
61	Maplewood Green	B21
61	Maplewood Lawn	B21
61	Maplewood Park	B21
61	Maplewood Road	B21
61	Maplewood Way	B21
58	Maretimo Gdns East	S19
58	Maretimo Gdns West	R19
58	Maretimo Place	R19
58	Maretimo Road	R19
58	Maretimo Terrace	R19
58	Maretimo Villas	R19
14	Marewood Crescent	J9
14	Marewood Drive	J8
14	Marewood Grove	J9

Page		Grid Ref
48	Margaret Place	N15
26	Marguerite Road	K12
54	Marian Crescent	H20
54	Marian Drive	H20
54	Marian Grove	H20
19	Marian Pk (Baldoyle)	T9
68	Marian Pk (Blackrock)	R21
54	Marian Pk (Templeogue)	H20
54	Marian Road	H20
17	Marigold Avenue	Q8
17	Marigold Court	Q8
17	Marigold Crescent	Q8
17	Marigold Drive	Q8
17	Marigold Grove	Q8
17	Marigold Park	Q8
59	*Marina House Apts	T20
	(Clarence Street)	
7	Marina Village	S2
73	Marine Avenue	V21
73	Marine Court (Dalkey)	V21
59	*Marine Court	U20
	(Crofton Avenue)	
19	Marine Cove	U9
49	Marine Drive	N16
73	Marine Parade	V21
59	Marine Road	U20
59	Marine Terrace	U20
	(Dun Laoghaire)	
57	Marine View	Q19
21	Marine Villas	Y9
19	Mariners Court	T10
21	Mariners Cove	Z10
39	Mariner's Port	M14
28	Marino	M12
28	Marino Avenue	N12
72	Marino Avenue East	V24
72	Marino Avenue West	V24
28	Marino Court	M12
28	Marino Crescent	M12
28	Marino Green	M12
28	Marino Mart	M12
28	Marino Park	M12
28	Marino Park Avenue	M12
46	Marion Villas	J15
39	Mark Street	L14
38	Market Street South	J15
38	Mark's Alley West	J15
39	Mark's Lane	L14
65	Marley View	L22
39	Marlborough Court	L14
48	Marlborough Lane	L17
38	Marlborough Mews	H13
69	Marlborough Park	U21
39	Marlborough Place	L14
48	Marlborough Road	M17
	(Donnybrook)	
69	Marlborough Road	V21
	(Glenageary)	
38	Marlborough Road	H13
	(Nth Circular Rd)	
39	Marlborough Street	L14
65	Marley Avenue	K21
65	Marley Close	K21
65	Marley Court North	K21
65	Marley Court South	K21
65	Marley Drive	K21
65	Marley Grange	K21
65	Marley Grove	K21
65	Marley Lawn	K21
65	Marley Rise	K21
65	Marley Villas	K21
65	Marley Walk	K21
61	Marlfield	C23
69	Marlfield	T23
61	Marlfield Close	C23
61	Marlfield Court	C23
61	Marlfield Crescent	C23
61	Marlfield Green	C23
61	Marlfield Grove	C23
61	Marlfield Lawn	C23
61	Marlfield Mall	C23
61	Marlfield Place	C23
38	*Marmion Court	J14
	(on Blackhall Street)	
38	Marne Villas	J13
38	Marrowbone Lane	J15
38	Marrowbone Lane	J15
38	*Marrowbone Lane Clo	J15
	(off Marrowbone Lane)	
38	*Marshal Court Apts	J14
	(Marshal Lane)	
38	Marshal Lane	J14
67	Marsham Court	T23
68	Mart Lane	S23
57	Martello Avenue	U20
7	Martello Court	U4
49	Martello Mews	P17
57	Martello Terrace	Q19
	(Booterstown)	
59	Martello Terrace	V20
	(Dun Laoghaire)	

Page		Grid Ref
20	Martello Tce (Sutton)	W11
49	Martello View	P16
49	Martello Wood	P16
25	Martin Grove	G12
24	Martin Savage Park	F11
47	Martin Street	K16
44	Martin White Chalets	N15
36	Martin's Row	E14
39	*Martin's Terrace	L14
	(off Hanover Street East)	
39	Mary Street	K14
38	Mary Street Little	K14
28	Maryfield Avenue	P10
28	Maryfield Crescent	P10
28	Maryfield Drive	N10
31	Maryland	V26
38	Mary's Abbey	K14
38	Mary's Lane	K14
29	Maryville Road	Q11
29	Mask Avenue	P10
29	Mask Crescent	P10
29	Mask Drive	P10
29	Mask Green	P10
29	Mask Road	P10
56	Mather Road North	N19
56	Mather Road South	N20
39	Matt Talbot Court	L13
39	Maunsell Place	K13
47	Maxwell Court	K17
47	Maxwell Lane	K18
47	Maxwell Road	K17
46	Maxwell Street	J15
38	May Lane	J14
28	May Park	N11
39	*May Street	L12
	(off Fitzroy Ave)	
52	Mayberry Park	D20
51	Mayberry Road	C20
14	Mayeston Boulevard	H7
14	Mayeston Close	H7
14	Mayeston Court	H7
14	Mayeston Crescent	H7
14	Mayeston Downs	H7
14	Mayeston Drive	H7
14	Mayeston Lawn	H7
14	Mayeston Rise	H7
14	Mayeston Square	H7
14	Mayeston Walk	H7
7	Mayfair	T2
55	Mayfield	K18
43	Mayfield Park	B17
46	Mayfield Road	H15
	(Kilmainham)	
54	Mayfield Rd (Terenure)	J18
65	Mayfield Tce (Ballinteer)	M22
55	Mayola Court	K18
39	Mayor Street Lower	M14
40	Mayor Street Upper	M14
73	Mayville Terrace	W21
30	Maywood Avenue	S10
30	Maywood Close	S10
30	Maywood Crescent	S11
30	Maywood Drive	S10
30	Maywood Grove	S10
30	Maywood Lawn	S11
30	Maywood Park	S10
30	Maywood Road	S10
29	McAuley Avenue	Q10
29	McAuley Drive	Q10
29	McAuley Park	Q10
29	McAuley Road	Q10
57	McCabe Villas	P19
46	McCarthy Terrace	H15
6	McCreadies Lane	R3
38	McDowell Avenue	H15
66	McGrane Court	M21
13	McKee Avenue	H9
37	McKee Park	H13
14	McKee Road	H9
13	McKelvey Avenue	G8
13	McKelvey Road	G8
47	McMahon Street	K16
54	McMorrough Road	J18
39	Meade's Terrace	L15
65	Meadow Avenue	K21
65	Meadow Clo (Dundrum)	K21
68	Meadow Close	R21
	(Newtown Park Ave)	
9	Meadow Copse	ZZ9
72	Meadow Court	U24
9	Meadow Dale	ZZ9
9	Meadow Downs	ZZ9
9	Meadow Drive	ZZ9
9	Meadow Green	ZZ9
65	Meadow Grove	L21
65	Meadow Mount	K21
9	Meadow Park	K21
9	Meadow Park Avenue	K20
68	Meadow Vale	R21
65	Meadow View	K21
65	Meadow Villas	K21

Page		Grid Ref
9	Meadow Way	ZZ9
54	Meadowbank	J19
19	Meadowbrook Avenue	U9
	(Sutton)	
19	Meadowbrook Lawn	U9
19	Meadowbrook Park	U9
69	Meadowlands	T21
32	Meadowview Grove	WW14
13	Meakstown Cottages	H7
38	*Meath Market	J15
	(Earl Street South)	
38	Meath Place	J15
38	*Meath Square	J14
	(The Coombe)	
38	Meath Street	J15
38	*Meath Terrace	J15
	(on Meath Place)	
47	*Meathville Terrace	K15
	(on Long Lane)	
56	Meenan Square	N19
39	Meetinghouse Lane	K14
42	Meile an Ri Crescent	ZZ15
42	Meile an Ri Drive	ZZ15
42	Meile an Ri Green	ZZ15
42	Meile an Ri Park	ZZ15
42	Meile an Ri Road	ZZ15
42	Meile an Ri View	ZZ15
59	Mellifont Avenue	U20
13	Mellows Avenue	G9
25	Mellows Court	G10
25	Mellows Crescent	G10
13	Mellows Park	G9
13	Mellows Road	G9
42	Melrose Avenue	ZZ17
	(Clondalkin)	
27	Melrose Ave (Fairview)	M12
27	Melrose Court	M12
42	Melrose Crescent	ZZ17
42	Melrose Green	ZZ17
42	Melrose Grove	ZZ17
42	Melrose Lawn	ZZ16
42	Melrose Park	ZZ17
	(Clondalkin)	
3	Melrose Pk (Swords)	P3
3	Melrose Pk The Avenue	P3
3	Melrose Pk The Close	P3
3	Metrose Pk The Crescent	P3
3	Melrose Pk The Drive	P3
3	Melrose Pk The Green	P3
3	Melrose Pk The Grove	P3
3	Melrose Pk The Heights	P3
3	Melrose Pk The Lawn	P3
3	Melrose Pk The Park	P3
3	Melrose Pk The Rise	P3
3	Melrose Pk The Villa	P3
3	Melrose Pk The Walk	P3
42	Melrose Road	ZZ16
14	Melville Close	H8
14	Melville Court	H8
13	Melville Cove	H8
14	Melville Crescent	H8
14	Melville Drive	H8
14	Melville Green	H8
14	Melville Lawn	H8
14	Melville Park	H8
13	Melville Rise	H8
14	Melville Terrace	H8
14	Melville View	H8
14	Melville Way	H8
54	Melvin Road	J18
37	Memorial Court	G14
39	Memorial Road	L14
	(Custom House Quay)	
37	Memorial Road	G15
	(Inchicore Road)	
39	Mercer Street Lower	K15
47	Mercer Street Upper	K15
29	Merchamp	Q12
39	*Merchants Arch	K14
	(off Temple Bar)	
38	Merchant's Quay	J14
40	Merchant's Road	N13
40	Merchant's Square	M14
49	Merlyn Drive	N17
49	Merlyn Park	N17
49	Merlyn Road	N17
49	Merrion	P17
39	Merrion Close	L15
49	Merrion Court	P17
57	Merrion Crescent	P18
49	Merrion Gates	P17
57	Merrion Grove	P19
57	Merrion Hall	P19
57	Merrion Park	P19
39	Merrion Place	L15
49	Merrion Road	P17
47	Merrion Row	L15
39	Merrion Square East	L15
39	Merrion Square North	L15

Page		Grid Ref
39	Merrion Square South	L15
39	Merrion Square West	L15
49	Merrion Strand	P17
39	Merrion Street Lower	L15
39	Merrion Street Upper	L15
49	Merrion View Avenue	N16
49	Merrion Village	P17
47	Merton Avenue	J16
48	Merton Drive	L17
47	Merton Park	J16
47	Merton Road	L18
28	Merville Ave (Fairview)	M12
67	Merville Ave (Stillorgan)	Q21
67	Merville Road	Q21
48	Mespil Estate	L16
48	Mespil Road	L16
43	Michael Collins Park	A17
29	Middle Third	P11
3	Milesian Avenue	P2
3	Milesian Court	P2
3	Milesian Grove	P2
3	Milesian Lawn	P2
6	Milford	R2
72	Military Rd (Killiney)	V24
38	Military Road	H15
	(Kilmainham)	
36	Military Road	F14
	(Phoenix Park)	
47	Military Rd (Rathmines)	K16
35	Mill Brook Apts	C13
42	Mill Court Avenue	ZZ17
42	Mill Court Drive	ZZ17
24	Mill Lane (Ashtown)	E11
72	Mill Lane	V26
	(Loughlinstown)	
45	Mill Lane (Newmarket)	J15
35	Mill Lane (Palmerston)	C13
43	Mill Park	A17
23	Mill Road	C10
	(Blanchardstown)	
59	Mill St (Dun Laoghaire)	U20
47	Mill St (The Coombe)	J15
8	Millbank	T6
27	Millbourne Avenue	K12
18	Millbrook Avenue	R9
37	Millbrook Court	H15
18	Millbrook Drive	R9
17	Millbrook Grove	R9
62	Millbrook Lawns	D21
17	Millbrook Road	R9
37	*Millbrook Terrace	G15
	(Lady's Lane)	
48	Millbrook Village	M18
8	Millfield (Portmarnock)	T6
53	Millgate Drive	F19
27	Millmount Avenue	K12
55	Millmount Grove	L19
27	Millmount Place	K12
27	Millmount Terrace	K12
27	Millmount Villas	K12
24	Millrace Road	E11
45	Millrose Estate	E16
23	Millstead	C10
8	Millstream	T6
32	Millstream Road	WW14
48	Milltown (Clonskeagh)	L18
55	Milltown Bridge Road	L18
55	*Milltown Collonade	L18
	(on Milltown Road)	
55	Milltown Drive	K19
55	Milltown Grove	K19
	(Churchtown)	
55	Milltown Grove	L18
	(Clonskeagh)	
55	Milltown Hill	L18
48	Milltown Park	L17
47	Milltown Path	L18
55	Milltown Road	L18
55	Milltown Tce (Dundrum)	L19
43	Millview	B17
6	Millview Close	R3
45	*Millview Cottages	G15
	(Connolly Avenue)	
6	Millview Court	R2
6	Millview Lawns	R3
6	Millview Road	R3
17	Millwood Court	R9
17	Millwood Park	R9
17	Millwood Villas	R9
2	Milton Hall	M2
3	Milton Terrace	N2
54	*Minnow Brook	J18
	(Olney Grove)	
39	Misery Hill	M14
29	Moatfield Avenue	Q10
29	Moatfield Park	Q10
29	Moatfield Road	Q10
17	Moatview Avenue	P8
17	Moatview Court	P8
17	Moatview Drive	P8
17	Moatview Gardens	P8

Page		Grid Ref
26	Mobhi Court	K11
45	Moeran Road	F17
38	*Moira Road	H13
	(off Oxmantown Road)	
39	Moland Place	L14
39	Molesworth Place	L15
39	Molesworth Street	L15
17	Mollison Avenue	R8
38	Molyneux Yard	J15
63	Monalea Grove	F21
63	Monalea Park	F21
63	Monalea Wood	F21
68	Monaloe Avenue	T23
68	Monaloe Court	S23
68	Monaloe Crescent	S23
69	Monaloe Drive	T23
68	Monaloe Park	T23
68	Monaloe Park Road	T23
69	Monaloe Way	T23
46	Monasterboice Road	H17
43	Monastery Crescent	B17
43	Monastery Drive	B17
43	Monastery Gate	C17
43	Monastery Gate Avenue	C17
43	Monastery Gate Close	C17
43	Monastery Gate Copse	C17
43	Monastery Gate Green	C17
43	Monastery Gate Lawn	C17
43	Monastery Gate Villas	C17
43	Monastery Heath	B17
43	Monastery Heath Avenue	B17
43	Monastery Heath Court	B17
43	Monastery Heath Green	B17
43	Monastery Heath Square	B17
43	Monastery Heights	B17
43	Monastery Park	B17
43	Monastery Rise	B17
43	Monastery Road	B17
43	Monastery Walk	B17
38	Monck Place	J13
8	Monks Meadow	U4
43	Monksfield	C17
43	Monksfield Court	C17
43	Monksfield Downs	C17
43	Monksfield Grove	C17
43	Monksfield Heights	C17
43	Monksfield Lawn	C17
43	Monksfield Meadows	C17
43	Monksfield Walk	C17
58	Monkstown	S20
58	Monkstown Avenue	T20
59	Monkstown Crescent	T20
68	Monkstown Farm	S21
59	Monkstown Gate	T20
68	Monkstown Grove	T21
58	Monkstown Road	S20
58	Monkstown Square	S21
58	Monkstown Valley	S20
47	Montague Court	K15
47	Montague Lane	K15
47	Montague Place	K15
47	Montague Street	K15
73	Monte Vella	W22
38	Montpelier Court	H14
38	Montpelier Drive	H14
38	Montpelier Gardens	H14
38	Montpelier Hill	H14
58	Montpelier Manor	S20
58	Montpelier Parade	S20
38	Montpelier Park	H14
58	Montpelier Place	S20
60	Montpelier View	A22
28	Montrose Avenue	N10
28	Montrose Close	N10
28	Montrose Court	N10
16	Montrose Crescent	N9
16	Montrose Drive	N9
28	Montrose Grove	N10
28	Montrose Park	N10
39	Moore Lane	K14
39	Moore Street	K14
72	Moorefield	U24
58	*Moore's Cottages	R21
	(Annaville Avenue)	
2	Mooretown	L1
2	Mooretown Avenue	M1
2	Mooretown Grove	M1
2	Mooretown Park	M1
42	Moorfield	A16
43	Moorfield Avenue	A16
43	Moorfield Close	A16
43	Moorfield Drive	A16
43	Moorfield Green	A16
43	Moorfield Grove	A16
43	Moorfield Lawns	A16
43	Moorfield Parade	A16
43	Moorfield Walk	A16
46	Moracrete Cottages	H16
47	Moran's Cottages	L17
66	Moreen Avenue	N22
66	Moreen Close	N22

Page		Grid Ref
66	Moreen Lawn	N22
66	Moreen Park	N22
66	Moreen Road	N22
66	Moreen Walk	N22
48	Morehampton Lane	M16
48	Morehampton Mews	M16
48	Morehampton Road	M16
48	Morehampton Square	M16
48	Morehampton Terrace	M17
38	*Morgan Place	J14
	(Inns Quay)	
24	Morgans Place	D11
38	Moritz House	E22
39	Morning Star Avenue	J14
46	Morning Star Road	H15
73	Mornington Avenue	V20
28	Mornington Grove	P10
28	Mornington Park	P10
28	Mornington Road	L17
27	Morrogh Terrace	M11
39	Moss Street	L14
65	Mount Albany	R21
65	Mount Albion	L21
65	Mount Albion Road	L21
63	Mount Alton	F21
63	Mount Alton Court	G21
34	Mount Andrew	P21
34	Mount Andrew Ave	ZZ13
34	Mount Andrew Close	ZZ13
34	Mount Andrew Court	ZZ13
34	Mount Andrew Dale	ZZ13
34	Mount Andrew Grove	ZZ13
34	Mount Andrew Rise	ZZ13
56	Mount Annville Road	N20
56	Mount Annville Wood	N20
47	Mount Anthony Estate	K17
56	Mount Anville Lawn	N20
56	Mount Anville Park	N20
46	Mount Argus Avenue	J17
45	Mount Argus Close	J17
46	Mount Argus Court	J17
46	Mount Argus Crescent	J17
45	Mount Argus Green	J17
46	Mount Argus Grove	J17
46	Mount Argus Park	J17
47	Mount Argus Road	J17
46	Mount Argus Square	J17
46	Mount Argus Terrace	J17
46	Mount Argus View	J17
46	Mount Argus Way	J17
73	Mount Auburn	V23
33	Mount Bellew Cres	ZZ14
33	Mount Bellew Green	ZZ14
33	Mount Bellew Rise	YY14
33	Mount Bellew Way	YY14
38	Mount Brown	H15
56	Mount Carmel Avenue	M20
63	Mount Carmel Park	F21
56	Mount Carmel Road	M20
29	Mount Dillon Court	P10
3	Mount Drinan Avenue	P3
3	Mount Drinan Crescent	P3
3	Mount Drinan Grove	P3
3	Mount Drinan Lawn	P3
3	Mount Drinan Park	P3
3	Mount Drinan Walk	P3
47	Mount Drummond Ave	J16
47	Mount Drummond Ct	J16
47	Mount Drummond Sq	K16
67	Mount Eagle Court	P23
67	Mount Eagle Drive	P23
66	Mount Eagle Green	P23
67	Mount Eagle Grove	P23
67	Mount Eagle Lawn	P23
67	Mount Eagle Park	P23
66	Mount Eagle Rise	N23
66	Mount Eagle View	P23
66	Mount Eagle Way	P23
48	Mount Eden Road	M17
32	Mount Gandon	XX14
47	Mount Harold Terrace	J17
23	Mount Hybla Court	D12
23	Mount Hybla House	D12
56	Mount Merrion	N20
57	Mount Merrion Avenue	Q19
18	Mount Olive Grove	S9
18	Mount Olive Park	S9
18	Mount Olive Road	S9
29	Mount Prospect Ave	Q12
29	Mount Prospect Drive	Q12
29	Mount Prospect Grove	Q12
29	Mount Prospect Lawn	Q12
29	Mount Prospect Park	Q12
73	Mount Salus Road	W22
48	Mount Sandford	M17
48	Mount St Annes	L18
48	Mount Street Crescent	L15
38	Mount Street Lower	L15
48	Mount Street Upper	L15
9	Mount Symon Avenue	ZZ10
9	Mount Symon Close	ZZ10

Page		Grid Ref
9	Mount Symon Crescent	YY10
9	Mount Symon Dale	YY10
9	Mount Symon Drive	ZZ10
9	Mount Symon Estate	ZZ9
9	Mount Symon Green	YY10
9	Mount Symon Lawn	ZZ10
9	Mount Symon Park	ZZ10
9	Mount Symon Rise	YY10
46	Mount Tallant Avenue	J18
38	Mount Temple Road	J14
10	Mount View Road	A9
69	Mount Wood	T21
62	Mountain Park	D21
60	Mountain View	A21
47	Mountain View Avenue	J17
22	Mountain View Cottages	A12
	(Castleknock)	
48	Mountain View Cottages	L17
	(Ranelagh)	
47	*Mountain View Court	J17
	(Mountain View Ave)	
39	*Mountain View Court	L13
	(off Summerhill Place)	
65	Mountain View Drive	K21
55	Mountain View Park	K20
72	Mountain View Road	V24
	(Ballybrack)	
48	Mountain View Road	L17
	(Ranelagh)	
72	Mountain Villa	V24
57	Mountbrook	P19
53	Mountdown Avenue	F19
53	Mountdown Drive	F19
53	Mountdown Park	F19
53	Mountdown Road	F19
7	Mountfield	T3
3	Mountgorry Wood Apts	P2
39	Mountjoy Parade	L13
39	Mountjoy Place	L13
39	Mountjoy Square	L13
39	*Mountjoy Square Apts	L13
	(Mountjoy Place)	
39	Mountjoy Square East	L13
39	Mountjoy Square North	L13
39	Mountjoy Square South	L13
39	Mountjoy Square West	L13
39	Mountjoy Street	K13
38	Mountjoy St Middle	K13
47	Mountpleasant Ave Lwr	K16
47	Mountpleasant Ave Upr	K16
47	Mountpleasant Parade	K16
47	Mountpleasant Place	L16
47	Mountpleasant Square	K16
47	Mountpleasant Terrace	K16
47	*Mountpleasant Tce Upr	L16
	(off Mountpleasant Place)	
70	Mountsandel	S24
46	Mountshannon Road	H15
59	Mounttown Cottages	T20
69	Mounttown Park	T21
59	Mounttown Road Lower	T21
59	Mounttown Road Upper	T20
40	Mourne Road	F16
40	Moy Elta Road	M13
33	Moy Glas Chase	YY15
33	Moy Glas Close	YY15
33	Moy Glas Court	YY15
33	Moy Glas Dale	YY15
33	Moy Glas Dene	YY15
33	Moy Glas Drive	YY15
33	Moy Glas Glen	YY15
33	Moy Glas Green	YY15
33	Moy Glas Grove	YY15
33	Moy Glas Lawn	YY15
33	Moy Glas Park	YY15
33	Moy Glas Road	YY15
33	Moy Glas Vale	YY15
33	Moy Glas View	YY15
33	Moy Glas Way	YY15
33	Moy Glas Wood	YY15
19	Moyclare Avenue	U9
19	Moyclare Close	U9
19	Moyclare Drive	U9
19	Moyclare Gardens	U9
19	Moyclare Park	U9
19	Moyclare Road	U9
35	Moycullen Road	C15
43	Moyle Crescent	B17
25	Moyle Road	H11
48	Moyne Court	L18
19	Moyne Park	T9
18	Moyne Road (Balgriffin)	T7
48	Moyne Road (Ranelagh)	L17
62	Moynihan Court	E21
64	Moyville	H22
64	Moyville Lawns	H21
53	Muckross Avenue	G18
53	Muckross Crescent	G18
53	Muckross Drive	G18
53	Muckross Green	G18

Page		Grid Ref
53	Muckross Grove	G18
39	*Muckross Parade	K13
	(Killarney Parade)	
53	Muckross Park	G18
45	Muirfield Drive	F16
23	Mulberry Crescent	B12
23	Mulberry Drive	B12
23	Mulberry Park	B12
7	Muldowney Court	T3
59	Mulgrave Street	U20
59	Mulgrave Terrace	U20
10	Mulhuddart	A8
31	Mullinastill Road	U26
36	Mullingar Terrace	E14
26	Mulroy Road	H12
55	Mulvey Park	M19
32	Munster Street	J12
73	Munster Terrace	V21
37	Murphystown Road	P23
37	Murray's Cottages	F15
34	Murtagh Road	J14
36	Muskerry Road	E15
37	Myra Cottages	G15
6	Myra Manor	R4
69	Myrtle Avenue	U21
69	Myrtle Gro (Stillorgan)	Q21
69	Myrtle Park	U21
38	*Myrtle Street	K13
	(Auburn Street)	
44	NAAS ROAD	D17
	(Walkinstown)	
42	Nangor Crescent	A17
42	Nangor Place	ZZ17
42	Nangor Road	ZZ18
	(Clondalkin)	
44	Nangor Road	C17
	(Fox & Geese)	
29	Nanikin Avenue	R11
45	Nash Street	F15
21	Nashville Park	Z10
21	Nashville Road	Y10
35	Nassau Street	L15
4	Naul Road (Cloghran)	M4
24	Navan Road	D11
	(Blanchardstown)	
25	Navan Road (Cabra)	G12
9	Navan Rd (Mulhuddart)	ZZ8
54	Neagh Road	H18
43	Neilstown Avenue	A15
43	Neilstown Cottages	A16
43	Neilstown Crescent	A15
43	Neilstown Drive	A15
43	Neilstown Gardens	A15
43	Neilstown Park	A15
34	Neilstown Road	A15
43	Neilstown Village Court	A15
39	Nelson Street	K13
25	Nephin Road	G12
73	Neptune Terrace	V21
73	Nerano Road	X22
39	Nerney's Court	K13
3	Nethercross Court	N1
48	Neville Road	K18
2	Nevinstown Lane	M3
62	*New Bancroft Hall	D1
	(Main Street Tallaght)	
62	*New Bancroft Place	D1
	(Main Street Tallaght)	
62	*New Bancroft Square	D1
	(Main Street Tallaght)	
62	New Bawn Drive	D22
62	New Bawn Park	D22
47	New Bride Street	K15
68	New Grange Road	R21
18	New Grove Estate	S8
46	New Ireland Road	H15
34	New Lucan Road	B13
42	New Nangor Road	ZZ17
68	New Park Lodge	R22
68	New Park Road	R21
23	New River Road	D10
11	New Rd (Clondalkin)	B18
21	New Road (Howth)	Z11
45	New Road (Inchicore)	F15
3	New Road (Swords)	N2
36	New Row	E14
47	New Row South	J15
47	New Row Square	J15
7	New Street	S2
47	New Street Garden's	K15
38	*New Street North	J14
	(off Church Street)	
47	New Street South	K15
31	New Vale	V27
31	New Vale Cottages	U27
31	New Vale Crescent	U27
40	New Wapping Street	M14
49	Newbridge Avenue	N15
49	Newbridge Drive	N15

STREET INDEX

Page — Grid Ref

18 Newbrook Avenue **S9**
18 Newbrook Road **S9**
16 Newbury Avenue **N8**
16 Newbury Drive **N8**
16 Newbury Grove **N8**
16 Newbury Lawns **P8**
16 Newbury Park **N8**
16 Newbury Terrace **N8**
32 Newcastle Rd (Lucan) **XX14**
39 Newcomen Avenue **K13**
39 Newcomen Court **K13**
3 Newcourt Mews **N1**
38 Newgrange Road **J12**
49 Newgrove Avenue **P16**
60 Newhall Court **A22**
47 *Newington Terrace **K17**
  (Castlewood Avenue)
51 Newlands Avenue **B18**
51 Newlands Drive **B18**
50 Newlands Manor **A19**
50 Newlands Manor Court **A19**
50 Newlands Manor Drive **A19**
50 Newlands Manor Fairway **A19**
50 Newlands Manor Green **A19**
50 Newlands Manor Park **A18**
51 Newlands Park **B18**
51 Newlands Road **B18**
  (Clondalkin)
33 Newlands Road **ZZ15**
  (Ronanstown)
47 Newmarket **J15**
38 *Newmarket Street **J15**
  (St Luke's Avenue)
68 Newpark **R22**
38 Newport Street **J15**
64 Newrath (Rathfarnham) **H23**
58 Newtown Avenue **R19**
  (Blackrock)
17 Newtown Avenue **Q9**
  (Coolock)
17 Newtown Close **Q8**
17 Newtown Cottages **Q9**
  (Coolock)
17 Newtown Ct (Coolock) **Q8**
55 Newtown Ct (Rathgar) **K19**
17 Newtown Drive **Q9**
59 Newtown House **V25**
68 Newtown Pk (Blackrock) **R21**
17 Newtown Pk (Coolock) **Q9**
62 Newtown Pk (Tallaght) **E21**
17 Newtown Pk Court **R21**
17 Newtown Rd (Coolock) **Q8**
58 Newtown Villas **R19**
  (Blackrock)
55 Newtown Villas **K19**
  (Braemor Road)
17 Newtown Way **Q8**
58 Newtownpark Avenue **S20**
58 Newtownpark House **R21**
59 Newtownsmith **V20**
38 Niall Street **H14**
38 *Nicholas Avenue **J14**
  (Bow Street)
38 Nicholas Street **K15**
43 Ninth Lock Road **A17**
41 No2 Nth Road Extension **P13**
39 *Noel Purcell Park **K15**
  (Digges Lane)
25 Nore Road **H11**
38 Norfolk Road **J12**
38 *Norseman Court **J14**
  (off Noresman Place)
38 Norseman Place **J14**
57 North Avenue **P19**
30 North Bull Island **S12**
38 North Circular Road **J13**
  (Phibsborough)
38 North Circular Road **H13**
  (Phoenix Park)
39 North Clarence St Flats **L13**
39 North Great George's St **K13**
40 North Quay Extension **N14**
13 North Road (Finglas) **G8**
25 North Rd (Phoenix Park) **F12**
39 North Strand Road **L13**
3 North Street **N1**
40 North Wall **M14**
39 North Wall Quay **M14**
48 Northbrook Avenue **L16**
  (Ranelagh)
40 Northbrook Ave Lower **M13**
40 Northbrook Ave Upper **M13**
48 Northbrook Lane **L16**
48 Northbrook Road **L16**
40 Northbrook Terrace **M13**
48 *Northbrook Villas **L16**
  (on Northbrook Rd)
59 Northcote Avenue **T20**
59 Northcote Place **T20**
59 Northcote Terrace **T20**
17 Northern Close **P7**

12 Northern Cross Route **E9**
26 Northland Drive **J11**
26 Northland Grove **J11**
59 Northumberland Avenue **U20**
59 Northumberland Park **U20**
59 Northumberland Place **U20**
  (Dun Laoghaire)
48 Northumberland Place **M15**
  (Grand Canal St Upr)
48 Northumberland Road **M15**
39 Northumberland Square **L14**
13 Northway Estate **G8**
15 Northwood **L8**
38 Norton's Avenue **J13**
72 Norwood **V25**
48 Norwood Park **M17**
39 Nottingham Street **M13**
55 Nugent Road **K20**
36 Nunciature Road **F12**
72 Nun's Lane **P11**
18 Nurney Lawn **R8**
55 Nutgrove Avenue **L20**
55 Nutgrove Avenue **K20**
54 Nutgrove Court **K20**
65 Nutgrove Crescent **K21**
56 Nutgrove Park **M18**
  (Clonskeagh)
65 Nutgrove Way **K21**
49 Nutley Avenue **N17**
49 Nutley Lane **N18**
49 Nutley Park **N18**
49 Nutley Road **N17**
56 Nutley Square **N8**

55 **OAK APPLE GREEN K18**
15 Oak Avenue **M8**
44 Oak Close **C17**
15 Oak Court **M8**
15 Oak Crescent **M8**
69 Oak-Dene **V23**
50 Oak Downs **A18**
44 Oak Dr (Fox & Geese) **C17**
15 Oak Drive (Santry) **M8**
15 Oak Green **M8**
15 Oak Grove **M8**
7 Oak Hall **S3**
15 Oak Lawn (Castleknock) **C11**
15 Oak Lawn (Santry) **M8**
23 Oak Lodge **D12**
50 Oak Rise (Clondalkin) **A18**
15 Oak Rise (Santry) **M8**
28 Oak Rd (Donnycarney) **N11**
44 Oak Rd (Fox & Geese) **C17**
15 Oak View **L8**
15 Oak Way **A18**
35 Oakcourt Avenue **C14**
35 Oakcourt Close **C14**
35 Oakcourt Drive **C14**
35 Oakcourt Grove **C14**
35 Oakcourt Lawn **C14**
35 Oakcourt Park **C14**
62 Oakdale Close **E23**
62 Oakdale Crescent **E23**
62 Oakdale Dr (Firhouse) **E23**
69 Oakdale Drive **T22**
  (Sallynoggin)
62 Oakdale Grove **E23**
62 Oakdale Park **E23**
62 Oakdale Road **E23**
55 Oakdown Road **K20**
47 Oakfield Place **K16**
3 Oaklands Avenue **N2**
55 Oaklands Crescent **K18**
55 Oaklands Dr (Rathgar) **K18**
49 Oaklands Drive **N16**
  (Sandymount)
49 Oaklands Park **N16**
  (Sandymount)
3 Oaklands Pk (Swords) **N2**
54 Oaklands Terrace **J18**
57 Oakley Court **L17**
58 Oakley Grove **R20**
55 Oakley Park (Blackrock) **R20**
29 Oakley Park (Clontarf) **Q12**
48 Oakley Park (Ranelagh) **L17**
47 Oakley Road **L17**
47 Oakley Square **L17**
15 Oakpark Avenue **L9**
15 Oakpark Close **L9**
15 Oakpark Drive **L9**
15 Oakpark Grove **L9**
72 Oakton Court **U24**
72 Oakton Drive **U24**
72 Oakton Green **U24**
72 Oakton Park **U24**
72 Oakton Park **U25**
23 Oaktree Avenue **B11**
23 Oaktree Drive **B11**
23 Oaktree Green **B11**
23 Oaktree Grove **B11**
23 Oaktree Lawn **B11**

67 Oaktree Road **Q21**
9 Oakview Avenue **ZZ9**
9 Oakview Close **ZZ9**
9 Oakview Court **ZZ9**
9 Oakview Drive **ZZ9**
9 Oakview Grove **ZZ9**
9 Oakview Lawn **ZZ9**
9 Oakview Park **ZZ9**
9 Oakview Rise **ZZ9**
9 Oakview Walk **ZZ9**
9 Oakview Way **ZZ9**
59 Oakwood **T20**
14 Oakwood Ave (Glasnevin) **H9**
2 Oakwood Ave (Swords) **M2**
14 Oakwood Close **H9**
42 Oakwood Grove Estate **A16**
14 Oakwood Park **H9**
14 Oakwood Road **H9**
34 Oatfield Avenue **B15**
34 Oatfield Close **B15**
34 Oatfield Crescent **B15**
  (off Oatfield Drive)
34 Oatfield Drive **B15**
34 Oatfield Grove **B15**
34 Oatfield Lawn **B15**
34 Oatfield Park **B15**
57 Obelisk Avenue **R21**
67 Obelisk Ct (Stillorgan) **R21**
67 Obelisk Grove **R21**
67 Obelisk Rise **R21**
67 Obelisk Walk **R21**
45 Oblate Drive **F15**
67 O'Brien's Place North **K11**
26 O'Brien's Terrace **K12**
47 Observatory Lane **K17**
47 *O'Carolan Road **J15**
  (O'Curry Road)
44 O'Casey Avenue **C16**
38 O'Connell Avenue **K13**
48 O'Connell Gardens **N15**
39 O'Connell Street **K14**
47 O'Curry Avenue **J15**
47 O'Curry Road **J15**
27 O'Daly Road **K11**
37 Odd Lamp Road **F13**
38 O'Devany Gardens **H14**
69 O'Donnell Gardens **U21**
45 O'Donoghue Street **F15**
47 O'Donovan Road **J16**
47 O'Dwyer Road **F17**
38 Offaly Road **J12**
20 Offington Avenue **W10**
20 Offington Court **W10**
20 Offington Drive **W10**
20 Offington Lawn **W10**
20 Offington Manor Apts **W9**
20 Offington Park **W9**
7 O'Hanlon's Lane **S2**
47 O'Hara Avenue **K16**
36 O'Hogan Road **E15**
36 O'Hogan Road **E15**
66 Olaf Hall **N22**
38 Olaf Road **J14**
29 Olcovar **V28**
61 Old Bawn Avenue **C22**
62 Old Bawn Close **D22**
62 Old Bawn Court **D21**
62 Old Bawn Drive **D22**
62 Old Bawn Park **D22**
62 Old Bawn Road **D22**
62 Old Bawn Terrace **D22**
62 Old Bawn Way **D22**
51 Old Belgard Road **C20**
61 Old Blessington Road **C21**
53 Old Bridge Road **G20**
38 Old Cabra Road **H13**
37 *Old Camac Bridge **H15**
  (Old Kilmainham)
21 Old Carrickbrack Road **Y12**
11 Old Corduff Road **B9**
32 Old Cornmill Road **WW14**
46 Old County Glen **H16**
46 Old County Road **H16**
57 Old Dublin Road **P20**
  (Stillorgan)
59 Old Dunleary **T19**
37 Old Kilmainham **H15**
38 Old Kilmainham Village **H15**
47 *Old Mill Court **J15**
  (Blackpitts)
47 Old Mountpleasant **L16**
45 Old Naas Rd (Bluebell) **E16**
50 Old Naas Road **ZZ20**
  (Brownsbarn)
45 Old Naas Rd Cottages **E16**
73 Old Quarry (Dalkey) **W22**
20 Old Quay **W10**
20 Old Quay Mews **W10**
20 Old Quay Terrace **W10**
31 Old Rathmichael **U27**

33 Old Rectory **XX13**
55 Old Rectory Park **M20**
7 Old Street **S2**
6 Old Yellow Walls Road **Q2**
62 Oldbawn **D22**
33 Oldbridge **YY15**
33 Oldbridge Close **YY15**
33 Oldbridge Court **YY15**
33 Oldbridge Glen **YY15**
33 Oldbridge Green **YY15**
33 Oldbridge Grove **YY15**
33 Oldbridge Park **YY15**
33 Oldbridge View **YY15**
33 Oldbridge Walk **YY15**
33 Oldbridge Way **YY15**
20 Oldcastle Avenue **W10**
42 Oldcastle Drive **YY17**
42 Oldcastlepark **YY17**
42 Oldcastlepark Close **YY17**
42 Oldeastlepark Green **YY17**
42 Oldeastlepark Grove **YY17**
42 Oldcastlepark Lawn **YY17**
42 Oldcastlepark View **YY17**
42 Oldchurch Avenue **ZZ17**
42 Oldchurch Close **ZZ17**
42 Oldchurch Court **ZZ17**
42 Oldchurch Crescent **ZZ17**
42 Oldchurch Drive **ZZ17**
42 Oldchurch Grove **ZZ17**
42 Oldchurch Lawn **ZZ17**
42 Oldchurch Way **ZZ17**
42 Oldcourt Avenue **E22**
  (Bohernabreena)
62 Oldcourt Close **E22**
62 Oldcourt Cottages **E23**
62 Oldcourt Farm **E22**
62 Oldcourt Lawn **E22**
62 Oldcourt Lodge **E22**
62 Oldcourt Manor **E22**
62 Oldcourt Road **E23**
62 Oldcourt View **E22**
22 Oldfarm **B11**
34 Oldtower Crescent **A14**
15 Oldtown Avenue **K9**
15 Oldtown Park **K9**
15 Oldtown Road **K9**
46 O'Leary Road **G15**
55 Olivemount Grove **M19**
55 Olivemount Road **M19**
55 Olivemount Terrace **M19**
38 Oliver Bond Street **J15**
68 Oliver Plunkett Avenue **T21**
  (Dun Laoghaire)
40 Oliver Plunkett Avenue **N15**
  (Ringsend)
69 Oliver Plunkett Road **T21**
69 Oliver Plunkett Square **T21**
69 Oliver Plunkett Terrace **T21**
68 Oliver Plunkett Villas **S21**
54 Olney Crescent **J18**
54 Olney Grove **J18**
9 Omni Park **L9**
36 O'Moore Road **E15**
27 O'Neachtain Road **K11**
47 O'Neill's Buildings **K15**
9 Ongar Park Estate **YY9**
9 Ongar Road **YY10**
9 Ongar Village **XX9**
47 Ontario Terrace **K16**
4 Onward Close **T4**
7 Onward Walk **T4**
55 Ophaly Court **M20**
38 *O'Quinns Avenue **H15**
  (Burke Place)
40 O'Rahilly House Flats **M15**
39 O'Rahilly Parade **K14**
44 Oranmore Road **C15**
59 Oratory Mews Court **U20**
67 Orby Avenue **P23**
67 Orby Close **Q23**
67 Orby Court **Q23**
67 Orby Park **Q23**
67 Orby View **P23**
67 Orby Way **P23**
22 Orchard Ave (Clonsilla) **ZZ10**
22 Orchard Close **A10**
68 *Orchard Cottages **R21**
  (Orchard Lane)
22 Orchard Court **B10**
22 Orchard Green **A10**
22 Orchard Grove **B10**
  (Blanchardstown)
68 Orchard Lane **R21**
  (Blackrock)
43 Orchard Lane **B17**
  (Clondalkin)
47 Orchard Lane **L16**
  (Ranelagh)
44 Orchard Lawns **C15**
43 Orchard Lodge **B17**

Page		Grid Ref
39	Orchard Rd (Ballyhough)	**L12**
30	Orchard Road (Raheny)	**S10**
55	Orchard Road South	**L18**
56	Orchard Square	**M19**
38	*Orchard Terrace	**J13**
	(Grangegorman Upper)	
54	Orchardstown Avenue	**H20**
53	Orchardstown Drive	**H20**
54	Orchardstown Park	**H20**
54	Orchardstown Villas	**H20**
64	Orchardton	**H21**
28	Ordnance Survey Road	**E13**
37	O'Reilly Avenue	**H15**
39	Oriel Street Lower	**L14**
39	Oriel Street Upper	**M13**
63	Orlagh Avenue	**G22**
63	Orlagh Close	**G22**
63	Orlagh Court	**G22**
63	Orlagh Crescent	**G22**
63	Orlagh Downs	**G22**
63	Orlagh Grange	**G22**
63	Orlagh Green	**G22**
63	Orlagh Grove	**G22**
63	Orlagh Lawn	**G22**
63	Orlagh Lodge	**G22**
63	Orlagh Meadows	**G22**
63	Orlagh Park	**G22**
63	Orlagh Pines	**G22**
63	Orlagh Rise	**G22**
63	Orlagh View	**G22**
63	Orlagh Way	**G22**
63	Orlagh Wood	**G22**
73	Ormeau Drive	**W22**
40	Ormeau Street	**M15**
2	Ormond Avenue	**L1**
2	Ormond Close	**L1**
2	Ormond Crescent	**L1**
2	Ormond Drive	**L1**
2	Ormond Grove	**L1**
2	Ormond Lawn	**L1**
38	*Ormond Market	**K14**
	(off Ormond Quay Upper)	
38	*Ormond Place	**K14**
	(off Ormond Quay Upper)	
39	Ormond Quay Lower	**K14**
38	Ormond Quay Upper	**K14**
27	Ormond Road	**L12**
47	Ormond Road South	**L17**
38	Ormond Square	**K14**
47	Ormond Street	**J15**
73	*Ormond Terrace	**W22**
	(off Sorrento Road)	
2	Ormond View	**L1**
2	Ormond Way	**L1**
69	O'Rourke Park	**T22**
67	Orpen	**Q21**
57	Orpen Close	**Q20**
57	Orpen Dale	**Q20**
57	Orpen Green	**Q20**
67	Orpen Hill	**Q21**
67	Orpen Rise	**Q21**
55	Orwell Bank	**K19**
55	Orwell Court	**K19**
55	Orwell Gardens	**K19**
54	Orwell Mews	**K18**
55	Orwell Park (Rathgar)	**K18**
53	Orwell Pk (Templeogue)	**F21**
53	Orwell Park Avenue	**G19**
53	Orwell Park Close	**G19**
53	Orwell Park Crescent	**G19**
53	Orwell Park Dale	**G19**
53	Orwell Park Drive	**G19**
53	Orwell Park Glade	**F19**
53	Orwell Park Glen	**G19**
53	Orwell Park Green	**G19**
53	Orwell Park Grove	**F19**
53	Orwell Park Heights	**F20**
53	Orwell Park Lawns	**F19**
53	Orwell Park Rise	**F20**
53	Orwell Park View	**F20**
53	Orwell Park Way	**G19**
54	Orwell Road	**K18**
55	Orwell Walk	**K19**
55	Orwell Woods	**K18**
48	*Osborne Terrace	**L16**
	(Northbrook Road)	
47	Oscar Square	**J15**
16	Oscar Traynor Road	**N18**
71	O'Shea's Cottages	**T23**
53	Osprey Avenue	**F19**
53	Osprey Court	**V27**
53	Osprey Drive	**F19**
53	Osprey Lawn	**F19**
53	Osprey Park	**F19**
53	Osprey Road	**F19**
39	Ossory Road	**M13**
38	Ostman Place	**J14**
14	O'Sullivan Avenue	**L13**
49	Oswald Road	**N15**
73	Otranto Place	**V21**
54	Otterbrook	**J20**

Page		Grid Ref
2	Oulart	**M3**
41	Oulton Road	**P12**
46	*Our Lady's Close	**J15**
	(off Our Lady's Road)	
46	Our Lady's Road	**J15**
42	Outer Ring Road	**YY18**
23	Outfarm Lane	**B11**
2	Outlands	**L1**
66	Overend Way	**M21**
47	Ovoca Road	**K16**
69	Owendoher Lodge	**H21**
54	Owendore Avenue	**J20**
54	Owendore Crescent	**J20**
38	Owen's Avenue	**H15**
14	Owensilla	**J9**
56	Owenstown Park	**N19**
47	Oxford Lane	**L16**
47	Oxford Road	**L16**
40	*Oxford Terrace	**M13**
	(on Hawthorn Terrace)	
47	*Oxford Terrace	**M13**
	(off Church Road)	
38	Oxmantown Lane	**J14**
38	Oxmantown Road	**H13**
9	**PACE AVENUE**	**YY8**
9	Pace Crescent	**YY8**
9	Pace Road	**YY8**
9	Pace View	**YY8**
19	Pacelli Avenue	**T9**
22	Pairc Gleann Trasna	**D23**
59	Pakenham	**T20**
59	Pakenham Road	**T20**
39	*Palace Street	**K15**
	(off Dame Street)	
64	Palmer Park	**J22**
64	Palmer Park	**H22**
35	Palmers Avenue	**B14**
35	Palmers Close	**B14**
35	Palmers Copse	**B14**
35	Palmers Court	**B14**
35	Palmers Crescent	**B14**
35	Palmers Drive	**B14**
35	Palmers Glade	**B14**
35	Palmers Grove	**B14**
35	Palmers Lawn	**B14**
35	Palmers Park	**B14**
35	Palmers Road	**B14**
35	Palmers Walk	**B14**
35	Palmerston	**C13**
47	Palmerston Close	**L17**
47	*Palmerston Court	**L17**
	(rere of Palmerston Road)	
47	Palmerston Court	**K17**
47	Palmerston Gardens	**L18**
48	Palmerston Grove	**M18**
47	Palmerston Lane	**L18**
35	Palmerston Park	**B14**
	(Kennelsfort Road)	
55	Palmerston Pk (Rathgar)	**L18**
47	Palmerston Place	**K13**
47	Palmerston Road	**L17**
47	Palmerston Villas	**K18**
35	Palmerstown Avenue	**C14**
35	Palmerstown Close	**C14**
35	Palmerstown Court	**C14**
35	Palmerstown Drive	**C14**
35	Palmerstown Green	**C14**
35	Palmerstown Heights	**B14**
35	Palmerstown Lawn	**B14**
35	Palmerstown Manor	**B14**
43	Palmerstown Woods	**A16**
35	Paradise Place	**K13**
2	Park Avenue	**L2**
	(Brackenstown Road)	
23	Park Ave (Castleknock)	**C11**
68	Park Ave (Deans Grange)	**R21**
49	Park Ave (Sandymount)	**P16**
64	Park Ave (Willbrook)	**J22**
38	Park Avenue West	**H14**
69	Park Close (Sallynoggin)	**U22**
49	Park Ct (Sandymount)	**N10**
23	Park Court Apts	**D11**
37	Park Crescent	**G13**
	(Blackhorse Avenue)	
46	Park Cres (Kimmage)	**G18**
37	Park Crescent House	**G12**
68	Park Drive (Cabinteely)	**S23**
48	Park Drive (Ranelagh)	**L17**
23	Park Drive Avenue	**C11**
23	Park Drive Close	**C11**
23	Park Drive Court	**C11**
23	Park Drive Crescent	**C11**
23	Park Drive Green	**C11**
23	Park Drive Grove	**C11**
23	Park Drive Lawn	**C11**
36	Park Lane (Chapelizod)	**E14**
59	Park Lane	**U20**
	(Dun Laoghaire)	
49	Park Lane (Sandymount)	**N16**
29	Park Lawn	**R12**

Page		Grid Ref
23	Park Lodge	**C11**
23	Park Manor	**B11**
37	Park Place	**G14**
59	Park Rd (Dun Laoghaire)	**U20**
25	Park Rd (off Navan Rd)	**F11**
69	Park Rd (Sallynoggin)	**U22**
37	Park Spring's	**G12**
36	Park Street	**F16**
38	*Park Street	**J15**
	(Carman's Hall)	
38	Park Terrace (Coombe)	**J15**
24	Park View (Castleknock)	**E12**
42	Park View	**Q12**
	(Mount Prospect Lawns)	
8	Park View (Portmarnock)	**U5**
55	Park View (Rathgar)	**K19**
50	Park View Lawns	**A18**
24	Park Villas (Castleknock)	**D11**
57	Park Villas (Stillorgan)	**Q20**
43	Park West Avenue	**C16**
44	Park West Road	**C16**
44	Park West Road	**D16**
47	Parker Hill	**K17**
38	Parkgate Street	**H14**
51	Parkhill Avenue	**C19**
51	Parkhill Close	**C19**
51	Parkhill Court	**C19**
51	Parkhill Drive	**C19**
51	Parkhill Green	**C19**
51	Parkhill Heights	**D19**
51	Parkhill Lawn	**C19**
51	Parkhill Rise	**C19**
51	Parkhill Road	**C19**
51	Parkhill Way	**D19**
51	Parkhill West	**C19**
23	Parklands (Castleknock)	**C11**
15	Parklands (Santry)	**L8**
62	Parklands Avenue	**E22**
62	Parklands Court	**E22**
	(Scholarstown Link Road)	
62	Parklands Drive	**E22**
62	Parklands Road	**E22**
62	Parklands View	**E22**
23	Parkmore	**D11**
54	Parkmore Drive	**H18**
31	Parknasilla Avenue	**U26**
72	Parknasilla Close	**U26**
72	Parknasilla Lane	**U26**
31	Parknasilla Rise	**U26**
66	Parkvale (Dundrum)	**M21**
19	Parkvale (Sutton)	**U9**
52	Parkview (Kilnamanagh)	**D19**
2	Parkview (Swords)	**L2**
47	Parkview Avenue	**J17**
	(Harold's Cross)	
37	Parkview Court	**G13**
	(Blackhorse Avenue)	
47	Parkview Court	**J17**
	(Harold's Cross)	
40	Parkview Place	**N15**
62	Parkwood Avenue	**D22**
62	Parkwood Grove	**D22**
62	Parkwood Lawn	**D22**
62	Parkwood Road	**D22**
39	Parliament Street	**K14**
47	Parnell Avenue	**J16**
7	Parnell Cottages	**S3**
47	Parnell Court	**J16**
46	*Parnell Hall	**J16**
	(Parnell Road)	
39	Parnell Place	**K13**
46	Parnell Road	**J16**
	(Harold's Cross)	
39	Parnell Square East	**K13**
39	Parnell Square North	**K13**
39	Parnell Square West	**K13**
39	Parnell Street	**K13**
	(O'Connell Street)	
69	Parnell St (Sallynoggin)	**U21**
19	Parochial Avenue	**U8**
10	Parslickstown Avenue	**A8**
10	Parslickstown Close	**A8**
10	Parslickstown Court	**A8**
10	Parslickstown Drive	**A8**
10	Parslickstown Gardens	**A7**
10	Parslickstown Green	**A8**
45	Partridge Terrace	**F15**
69	Patrician Park	**T21**
57	Patrician Villas	**Q20**
59	Patrick Doyle Road	**L18**
59	Patrick Street	**U20**
	(Dun Laoghaire)	
38	Patrick Street	**K15**
	(Kevin Street Upr)	
58	Patrick's Row	**R19**
25	Patrickswell Court	**G10**
25	Patrickswell Place	**G10**
38	Paul Street	**J14**
70	Pavillion Gate	**R24**
57	Pea Field	**Q19**
69	Pear Tree Field	**Q21**

Page		Grid Ref
69	Pearse Avenue	**U22**
64	Pearse Brothers Park	**J22**
69	Pearse Close	**U22**
69	Pearse Drive	**U22**
69	Pearse Gardens	**T22**
69	Pearse Green	**U22**
39	Pearse Grove	**M15**
39	Pearse House	**L14**
69	Pearse Park	**T22**
69	Pearse Rd (Sallynoggin)	**T22**
39	Pearse Sq (Pearse St)	**M15**
69	Pearse St (Sallynoggin)	**U22**
39	Pearse Street	**L14**
	(Westland Row)	
69	Pearse Villas	**U22**
23	Peck's Lane	**D11**
25	Pelletstown Avenue	**F11**
57	Pembroke Cottages	**Q19**
	(Booterstown)	
48	Pembroke Cottages	**M17**
	(Donnybrook)	
55	Pembroke Cottages	**M20**
	(Dundrum)	
40	Pembroke Cottages	**N14**
	(Ringsend)	
48	Pembroke Gardens	**M16**
48	Pembroke Lane	**L15**
	(Lr Baggot Street)	
48	Pembroke Lane	**M16**
	(Pembroke Road)	
48	Pembroke Park	**M16**
48	Pembroke Place	**M16**
	(Ballsbridge)	
48	Pembroke Place	**L15**
	(Pembroke St Upr)	
48	Pembroke Road	**M16**
48	Pembroke Row	**L15**
40	Pembroke Street	**N15**
48	Pembroke Street Lower	**L15**
48	Pembroke Street Upper	**L16**
55	Pembroke Terrace	**M20**
40	Penrose Street	**M15**
45	Percy French Road	**F17**
48	Percy Lane	**M15**
48	Percy Place	**M15**
47	Peter Place	**K16**
64	Peter Row	**K15**
38	Peter Street	**K15**
38	Peter's Court	**K13**
3	Peterson's Court	**L14**
47	Petrie Road	**J16**
9	Pheasant Run	**ZZ8**
9	Pheasant Run The Drive	**ZZ8**
9	Pheasant Run The Green	**ZZ8**
9	Pheasant Run The Grove	**ZZ8**
9	Pheasant Run The Park	**ZZ8**
25	Phelan Avenue	**G11**
9	Phibblestown Avenue	**XX9**
9	Phibblestown House	**XX9**
38	Phibsborough	**K13**
38	Phibsborough Avenue	**J13**
38	Phibsborough Place	**K13**
38	Phibsborough Road	**K13**
27	Philipsburgh Avenue	**M12**
27	Philipsburgh Terrace	**M12**
40	*Philomena Terrace	**N15**
	(off Oliver Plunket Ave)	
24	Phoenix Avenue	**D11**
38	Phoenix Court	**H14**
	(Arbour Hill)	
24	Phoenix Court	**D11**
	(Castleknock)	
38	Phoenix Court	**H13**
	(North Circular Road)	
24	Phoenix Drive	**D11**
24	Phoenix Gardens	**D11**
38	Phoenix Manor	**H13**
24	Phoenix Park Way	**E11**
24	Phoenix Place	**D11**
36	Phoenix Street	**F15**
38	Phoenix Street West	**J14**
57	Phoenix Terrace	**Q19**
38	Phoenix View	**H15**
40	Pickford's Terrace	**M14**
39	Pig Lane	**L13**
40	Pigeon House Road	**N14**
	(Ringsend)	
41	Pigeon House Road	**P15**
	(Ringsend)	
39	*Pile's Terrace	**L15**
	(Sandwith St Upper)	
73	Pilot View	**W21**
38	Pim Street	**J15**
38	Pimlico	**J15**
38	Pimlico Cottages	**J15**
65	Pine Avenue	**R22**
65	Pine Copse Road	**L21**
68	Pine Court	**R21**
	(Deans Grange)	
8	Pine Ct (Portmarnock)	**U5**
63	Pine Grove	**G21**

Page		Grid Ref

2 Pine Grove Park **M1**
2 Pine Grove Road **M1**
57 Pine Haven **Q19**
37 Pine Hurst **H12**
68 Pine Lawn **R21**
(Deans Grange)
62 Pine Lawn (Tallaght) **D22**
40 Pine Road **N15**
65 Pine Valley Avenue **L22**
65 Pine Valley Drive **L23**
65 Pine Valley Grove **L23**
65 Pine Valley Park **L23**
65 Pine Valley Way **L23**
28 Pinebrook Avenue **N10**
9 Pinebrook Close **ZZ9**
28 Pinebrook Crescent **N10**
10 Pinebrook Downs **ZZ9**
28 Pinebrook Drive **P10**
10 Pinebrook Glen **ZZ9**
28 Pinebrook Grove **P10**
9 Pinebrook Heights **ZZ9**
10 Pinebrook Lawn **ZZ9**
28 Pinebrook Rise **N10**
28 Pinebrook Road **P10**
10 Pinebrook Vale **ZZ9**
9 Pinebrook View **ZZ9**
10 Pinebrook Way **ZZ9**
70 Pinecroft **Q25**
51 Pinetree Crescent **C20**
51 Pinetree Grove **C19**
62 Pineview Avenue **D22**
61 Pineview Drive **D22**
62 Pineview Grove **D22**
61 Pineview Lawn **D22**
62 Pineview Park **D22**
62 Pineview Rise **D22**
62 Pineview Road **D22**
72 Pinewood **U24**
14 Pinewood Avenue **J9**
10 Pinewood Court **ZZ8**
14 Pinewood Crescent **J9**
14 Pinewood Drive **J9**
14 Pinewood Green **J9**
14 Pinewood Grove **K9**
54 Pinewood Park **H20**
14 Pinewood Villas **J9**
50 Pinewoods **A18**
2 Pinnock Roundabout **M3**
9 Pipe Hill **M2**
47 Pleasants Lane **K15**
47 Pleasants Place **K15**
47 Pleasants Street **K15**
8 Plums Road **N21**
3 Plunket Hall **P2**
13 Plunkett Ave (Finglas) **G9**
68 Plunkett Ave (Foxrock) **R23**
13 Plunkett Crescent **G8**
13 Plunkett Drive **G9**
13 Plunkett Green **G9**
13 Plunkett Grove **G9**
13 Plunkett Road **G9**
46 Poddle Close **H17**
46 Poddle Green **H17**
46 Poddle Park **H18**
37 Polo Road **G13**
46 Poolbeg Quay **N15**
39 Poolbeg Street **L14**
39 Poole Street **J15**
40 Poplar Row **M13**
40 Poppintree **H8**
14 *Poppintree Lane **J8**
(Balbutcher Lane)
14 *Poppintree Parade **J8**
(Balbutcher Lane)
14 *Poppintree Pk Lane West **H8**
14 *Poppintree Terrace **J8**
(Carrig Road)
40 Port Tunnel (East Wall) **M13**
15 Port Tunnel (Santry) **M9**
14 Port View House **N14**
22 Porters Avenue **A10**
9 Porters Gate **YY10**
22 Porters Gate Avenue **ZZ10**
9 Porters Gate Close **ZZ10**
9 Porters Gate Court **ZZ10**
9 Porters Gate Crescent **YY10**
9 Porters Gate Drive **YY10**
9 Porters Gate Green **YY10**
9 Porters Gate Grove **YY10**
9 Porters Gate Heights **ZZ10**
9 Porters Gate Rise **ZZ10**
9 Porters Gate View **YY10**
9 Porters Gate Way **YY10**
22 Porters Road **A10**
22 Portersfield Apts **A10**
22 Porterstown Road **A11**
39 Portland Place **L13**
39 *Portland Court **K13**
(off Portland Place)
39 *Portland Lock **K13**
(Portland Place)

39 Portland Place **K13**
39 Portland Row **L13**
39 Portland Square **K13**
39 Portland Street North **L13**
38 Portland Street West **J15**
46 Portmahon Drive **H15**
8 Portmarnock **U5**
8 Portmarnock Avenue **U4**
8 Portmarnock Crescent **U4**
7 Portmarnock Drive **U4**
8 Portmarnock Grove **U4**
8 Portmarnock Park **U4**
8 Portmarnock Rise **U5**
7 Portmarnock Walk **U4**
47 Portobello Harbour **K16**
47 Portobello Harbour Apts **K16**
47 Portobello Place **K16**
47 Portobello Road **K16**
40 Portside Court **M13**
68 Pottery Road **S22**
8 Power's Court **M15**
38 *Power's Square **K15**
(off John Dillon Street)
38 Prebend Street **J13**
26 Premier Square **H10**
39 Preston Street **L13**
39 *Price's Lane **K14**
(Aston Quay)
47 Price's Place (Ranelagh) **K16**
46 Priestfield Cottages **J16**
46 Priestfield Drive **J16**
38 Primrose Avenue **K13**
38 Primrose Grove **Q8**
59 Primrose Hill **T20**
(Dun Laoghaire)
32 Primrose Lane **XX13**
38 *Primrose Street **K13**
(off Wellington Street Upper)
47 Prince Arthur Terrace **K17**
58 Prince Edward Tce Lwr **R20**
58 Prince Edward Tce Upr **R20**
8 Prince of Wales Tce **N16**
(Sandymount)
39 Prince's Street North **K14**
39 Prince's Street South **L14**
56 Princeton **N19**
38 Prior Hall **H15**
17 Priorswood Road **Q8**
57 Priory Avenue **Q19**
65 Priory Ct (Grange Road) **K22**
57 Priory Drive (Stillorgan) **Q20**
25 Priory East **G12**
57 Priory Grove (Stillorgan) **Q20**
53 Priory Hall (Kimmage) **G18**
57 Priory Hall (Stillorgan) **Q20**
25 Priory North **G11**
46 Priory Road **J17**
53 Priory Walk (Kimmage) **G18**
53 Priory Way (Kimmage) **G18**
25 Priory West **G12**
39 Proby Gardens **R20**
73 Proby Hall **V22**
58 Proby Park **V22**
58 Proby Square **R20**
39 Proby's Lane **K14**
40 Promenade Road **N13**
26 Prospect Avenue **K12**
(Finglas Road)
64 Prospect Avenue **H22**
(Stocking Lane)
64 Prospect Court **H23**
64 Prospect Drive **H22**
64 Prospect Glen **H22**
64 Prospect Grove **H22**
64 Prospect Heath **H22**
64 Prospect Heights **H22**
48 Prospect Lane **M18**
71 Prospect Lawn **S23**
64 Prospect Meadows **H22**
26 Prospect Road **K12**
26 Prospect Square **K12**
64 Prospect Terrace **G15**
(Kilmainham)
49 Prospect Terrace **P16**
(Sandymount)
64 Prospect View **H22**
26 Prospect Way **K12**
47 *Protestant Row **K15**
(Wexford Street)
47 Proud's Lane **K15**
38 *Provost Row **J14**
(Arbour Hill)
38 Prussia Street **J14**
7 Purley Park **T4**
47 Purser Gardens **J16**
46 Pyro Villas **J15**

28 **QUARRY COTTAGES P11**
53 Quarry Drive **F18**
38 Quarry Road (Cabra) **H12**
31 Quarry Road **U28**

(Ferndale Road)
43 Quarryfield Court **B17**
39 Quartiere Bloom **K14**
58 Queen's Park **S20**
59 Queen's Road **U20**
38 Queen's Street **J14**
47 Quinn's Lane **L15**
31 Quinn's Road **V27**

19 **RADCLIIFE V9**
7 Radlett Grove **U4**
45 Rafter's Avenue **G16**
46 Rafter's Lane **G16**
47 Rafter's Road **G16**
48 Raglan Hall Apts **M16**
47 Raglan Lane **M16**
48 Raglan Road **M16**
61 Raheen Avenue **B21**
61 Raheen Close **B21**
61 Raheen Court **B21**
61 Raheen Crescent **B21**
40 Raheen Dr (Ballyfermot) **D15**
61 Raheen Drive (Tallaght) **B21**
61 Raheen Green **B21**
44 Raheen Park **D15**
(Ballyfermot)
61 Raheen Park (Tallaght) **B21**
61 Raheen Road **B21**
30 Raheny **R10**
30 Raheny Park **R11**
19 Raheny Road **R9**
19 Railway Ave (Baldoyle) **U9**
45 Railway Ave (Inchicore) **F15**
7 Railway Ave (Malahide) **S2**
18 Railway Close **T8**
48 Railway Cottages **N16**
7 Railway Court **S2**
18 Railway Mews **T8**
73 Railway Road **W22**
18 Railway Rd (Clongriffin) **T8**
39 Railway Street **L13**
39 *Railway Terrace **M15**
(off Macken St)
38 Rainsford Avenue **J15**
72 Rainsford Lane **V24**
38 Rainsford Street **J15**
8 Ralahine **U24**
46 Raleigh Square **G17**
36 Ramillies Road **E15**
48 Ramleh Close **M18**
48 Ramleh Park **M18**
23 Ramor Park **B10**
8 Ranelagh **L16**
48 Ranelagh Avenue **L16**
48 Ranelagh Road **L16**
45 Raphoe Road **G17**
42 Rath Geal **ZZ17**
2 Rathbeale Court **M1**
2 Rathbeale Crescent **M1**
2 Rathbeale Rise **M2**
2 Rathbeale Road **L1**
24 Rathborne Avenue **F11**
24 Rathborne Close **F11**
24 Rathborne Drive **F11**
24 Rathborne Way **F11**
54 Rathdown Avenue **J19**
54 Rathdown Court **J18**
54 Rathdown Crescent **J19**
66 Rathdown Grove **N22**
54 Rathdown Park **J19**
38 Rathdown Road **J13**
66 Rathdown Square **J13**
66 Rathdown Terrace **N22**
54 Rathdown Villas **J19**
46 Rathdrum Road **H16**
54 Rathfarnham **J19**
54 *Rathfarnham Mill **J19**
(Church Lane)
54 Rathfarnham Park **J19**
54 Rathfarnham Road **J19**
54 Rathfarnham Wood **J20**
55 Rathgar **K18**
47 Rathgar Avenue **J18**
47 Rathgar Court **K17**
54 Rathgar Park **J18**
47 Rathgar Place **K17**
47 Rathgar Road **K18**
47 Rathgar Villas **J18**
2 Rathingle Road **L2**
54 Rathland Drive **H18**
11 Rathlin House **C9**
27 Rathlin Road **K11**
63 Rathlyon Grove **F22**
63 Rathlyon Park **F22**
31 Rathmichael Dales **U27**
31 Rathmichael Haven **U27**
72 Rathmichael Manor **U26**
31 Rathmichael Park **V26**
31 Rathmichael Road **U26**

31 Rathmichael Woods **V26**
47 Rathmines **K17**
47 Rathmines Avenue **K17**
47 Rathmines Avenue Court **K17**
47 Rathmines Close **K17**
47 Rathmines Park **K17**
47 Rathmines Road Lower **K17**
47 Rathmines Road Upper **K17**
60 Rathmintan Close **A22**
60 Rathmintan Court **A22**
60 Rathmintan Crescent **A22**
60 Rathmintan Drive **A22**
8 Rathmore **T6**
66 Rathmore Avenue **N21**
30 Rathmore Park **R10**
54 Rathmore Villas **J18**
31 Rathsallagh Avenue **V26**
31 Rathsallagh Drive **V26**
31 Rathsallagh Grove **V26**
31 Rathsallagh Park **V26**
17 Rathvale Avenue **Q9**
17 Rathvale Drive **Q9**
17 Rathvale Grove **Q9**
17 Rathvale Park **Q9**
25 Rathvilly Drive **G10**
25 Rathvilly Park **G10**
13 Ratoath Drive **F9**
25 Ratoath Estate **G10**
25 Ratoath Road (Cabra) **F10**
25 Ratra Park **F12**
25 Ratra Road **F12**
25 Ravens Court **G10**
54 Ravens Rock Road **P22**
54 Ravensdale Drive **H18**
54 Ravensdale Park **H18**
40 Ravensdale Road **M13**
9 Ravenwood Avenue **YY9**
9 Ravenwood Crescent **YY9**
9 Ravenwood Drive **YY9**
9 Ravenwood Estate **YY9**
9 Ravenwood Green **YY9**
9 Ravenwood Lawn **YY9**
9 Ravenwood Rise **YY9**
9 Ravenwood Road **YY9**
9 Ravenwood View **YY9**
47 Raymond Street **J16**
58 *Red Brick Terrace **R21**
(Annaville Avenue)
35 Red Cow Cottages **C13**
44 Red Cow Lane **J14**
44 Red Cow Roundabout **C17**
38 Redberry **XX15**
56 Redesdale Court **P20**
56 Redesdale Crescent **N20**
56 Redesdale Road **N20**
7 Redfern Avenue **T4**
18 Redmond's Court **S9**
47 Redmond's Hill **K15**
51 Redwood Avenue **D20**
51 Redwood Close **D20**
55 Redwood Court **K19**
(Churchtown)
51 Redwood Ct (Tallaght) **C20**
51 Redwood Drive **C20**
57 Redwood Grove **Q19**
52 Redwood Heights **D20**
51 Redwood Lawn **C20**
52 Redwood Park **D20**
52 Redwood Rise **D20**
52 Redwood View **D20**
51 Redwood Walk **C20**
38 *Reginald Square **J15**
(Reginald Street)
38 Reginald Street **J15**
46 Rehoboth Avenue **J16**
46 Rehoboth Place **H16**
46 Reilly's Avenue **H16**
46 Reuben Avenue **H15**
46 Reuben Street **H15**
47 *Rhodaville **K16**
(off Mountpleasant Ave)
46 Rialto Buildings **H15**
46 Rialto Cottages **H15**
46 Rialto Drive **H16**
46 *Rialto Park **H15**
(off Rialto Street)
46 Rialto Street **H15**
29 Ribh Avenue **Q10**
29 Ribh Road **Q10**
49 Richelieu Park **P14**
68 Richmond **R21**
27 Richmond Avenue **L12**
(Fairview)
58 Richmond Avenue **T20**
(Monkstown)
55 Richmond Ave South **L18**
39 Richmond Cottages **L13**
(Summerhill)
27 Richmond Ct (Marino) **L12**
55 Richmond Ct (Milltown) **L18**

STREET INDEX

Page	Street	Grid Ref
39	Richmond Crescent	L13
27	Richmond Estate	M12
58	Richmond Green	T20
58	Richmond Grove	T20
58	Richmond Hill (Monkstown)	T20
47	Richmond Hill (Rathmines)	K16
39	Richmond Lane	L13
27	Richmond Lodge	L12
47	Richmond Mews	K16
39	*Richmond Parade (Richmond Crescent)	L13
58	Richmond Park (Monkstown)	S20
47	Richmond Place (Rathmines)	K16
47	*Richmond Pl South (Sth Richmond St)	K16
27	Richmond Road	L12
47	Richmond Row	K16
39	Richmond Street North	L13
47	Richmond Street South	K16
xxx	Richmond Terrace	
47	Richmond Villas	K16
56	Richview	M18
55	Richview Park	L18
56	Richview Villas	M18
72	Ridge Hall	V25
72	Ridge Hill	V25
2	Ridgewood Avenue	L3
2	Ridgewood Close	L3
2	Ridgewood Court	L3
2	Ridgewood Green	L3
2	Ridgewood Grove	L3
2	Ridgewood Park	L3
2	Ridgewood Place	L3
2	Ridgewood Square	L3
45	Ring Street	F15
45	Ring Terrace	F15
40	Ringsend	N15
40	Ringsend Park	N14
40	Ringsend Road	M15
72	Rinn na Mara	R12
72	River Close	V25
25	River Drive	F11
26	River Gardens	K11
72	River Lane (Loughlinstown)	V26
25	River Road (Ashtown)	G11
23	River Road (Blanchardstown)	C10
23	River Road Cottages	D10
2	River Valley Avenue	M2
2	River Valley Close	L2
2	River Valley Court	L2
2	River Valley Drive	M2
2	River Valley Grove	M3
2	River Valley Heights	M2
2	River Valley Lawn	M2
2	River Valley Park	M2
2	River Valley Rise	M2
2	River Valley Road	L2
2	River Valley View	L2
2	River Valley Way	L2
55	Riverbank (Braemor Rd)	Q19
66	*Riverbank (Dundrum) (Riversdale)	M21
26	Riverbank Hall	JI1
10	Riverpark View	A8
66	Riversdale (Dundrum)	M21
66	*Riversdale (Herbert Hill)	M21
35	Riverside (Palmerstown)	C13
43	Riversdale Avenue (Clondalkin)	B17
35	Riversdale Avenue (Palmerston)	C13
54	Riversdale Avenue (Terenure)	J19
35	Riverside Court	C13
43	Riversdale Crescent	B17
43	Riversdale Drive	B17
43	Riversdale Green	B16
54	Riverside Grove (Kimmage)	H18
35	Riversdale Grove (Palmerstown)	B13
43	Riversdale Park (Clondalkin)	B17
35	Riversdale Park (Palmerstown)	C13
43	Riversdale Road	B17
43	Riverside (Clondalkin)	B17
46	*Riverside (Kimmage) (Hazel Park)	H18
10	Riverside (Mulhuddart)	A8
16	Riverside Avenue	N8
54	Riverside Cottages	H20
16	Riverside Crescent	N8
16	Riverside Dr (Coolock)	P8
35	Riverside Drive (Palmerston)	C13
55	Riverside Drive (Rathfarnham)	K19
16	Riverside Grove	N8
16	Riverside Park	N8
16	Riverside Road	N8
48	Riverside Walk	M18
25	Riverston Abbey	G12
24	Rivervale	F11
39	*Riverview (Macken Street)	M15
62	Riverview (Oldbawn)	D22
35	Riverview (Palmerstown)	C13
36	Riverview Court	E14
22	Riverwood Chase	A11
22	Riverwood Close	A11
22	Riverwood Copse	A11
22	Riverwood Court	A11
22	Riverwood Crescent	A11
22	Riverwood Dale	A11
22	Riverwood Dene	A11
22	Riverwood Drive	A11
22	Riverwood Gardens	A11
22	Riverwood Glebe	A11
22	Riverwood Glen	A11
22	Riverwood Green	A11
22	Riverwood Grove	A11
22	Riverwood Hall	A11
22	Riverwood Heath	A11
22	Riverwood Lawn	A11
22	Riverwood Park	A11
22	Riverwood Place	A11
22	Riverwood Road	A11
22	Riverwood Terrace	A11
22	Riverwood Vale	A11
22	Riverwood View	A11
22	Riverwood Way	A11
38	Robert Emmett Close	JI4
39	Robert Place	L12
38	Robert St (James's St)	JI5
39	Robert St (Jones's Rd)	L12
23	Robin Villas	C13
44	Robinhood Park	E17
44	Robinhood Road	D17
7	Robswall	T3
7	Robswall Path	U3
7	Robswall Walk	U3
69	Rochestown Avenue	T22
69	Rochestown House Apts	T22
69	Rochestown Park	U22
69	Rochfort Avenue	ZZ14
34	Rochfort Close	ZZ14
34	Rochfort Crescent	ZZ15
34	Rochfort Downs	ZZ14
34	Rochfort Green	ZZ14
33	Rochfort Park	ZZ14
34	Rochfort Way	ZZ15
58	Rock Hall	R19
58	Rock Hill	R19
48	*Rock Lane (Baggot St Lower)	L15
73	Rock Lodge	V23
66	Rockfield (Dundrum)	M21
32	Rockfield (Lucan)	XX15
53	Rockfield Avenue (Kimmage)	G18
22	Rockfield Close	A11
50	Rockfield Drive (Clondalkin)	A18
22	Rockfield Dr (Coolmine)	A11
53	Rockfield Dr (Kimmage)	G18
22	Rockfield Pk (Coolmine)	A10
68	Rockford Manor	S21
68	Rockford Park	S21
58	Rockford Terrace	S20
73	Rockfort Avenue	W22
3	Rockingham Terrace	N2
73	Rocklands	W21
45	Rockmeadon Court	G17
21	Rockstown	Z10
66	Rockview	M23
70	Rockville	Q26
58	Rockville Crescent	S20
58	Rockville Drive	S20
70	Rockville Drive	R25
58	Rockville Estate	R20
58	Rockville Park	S20
58	Rockville Road	R20
58	Rockwell Cove Apts	R19
32	Rockwood	XX15
67	Rocwood	Q22
38	Roe Lane	JI4
56	Roebuck Avenue	P19
56	Roebuck Castle	N19
56	Roebuck Crescent	M19
56	Roebuck Downs	M19
53	Roebuck Drive	G18
56	Roebuck Hill	N15
55	Roebuck Lawn	M19
56	Roebuck Park	M20
56	Roebuck Road	M19
48	Roger's Lane	L15
47	Roland Court	KI7
69	Rollins Court	U21
69	Rollins Villas	U21
42	Ronanstown	A16
19	Roncalli Road	T10
64	Rookwood Lodge	H22
64	Rookwood View	H22
25	Roosevelt Cottages	G12
40	*Ropewalk Place (Parkview Place)	N15
68	Rory O'Connor Park	S21
63	Ros Mor View	G22
59	Rosary Gardens East	U20
59	Rosary Gardens West	T20
46	Rosary Road	H15
40	Rosary Tce (Ringsend)	N15
59	*Rosary Terrace (off Library Road)	U20
19	Rosbeg Court	T10
33	Rosberry	YY15
33	Rosberry Avenue	YY15
33	Rosberry Court	YY15
33	Rosberry Lane	YY15
33	Rosberry Park	YY15
33	Rosberry Place	YY15
68	Rose Park	T21
35	Rose View	C13
67	Roseacre	P23
2	Rosebank	D22
43	Rosebank Court	B16
43	Rosebank Hall	A16
43	Rosebank Place	A16
43	Rosebank View	B16
9	Rosedale Close	YY9
9	Rosedale Crescent	YY9
47	*Rosedale Terrace (Lower Clanbrassil St)	JI6
18	Roseglade Avenue	S10
18	Roseglen Road	S10
22	Rosehaven	B11
68	Rosehill	R21
33	Roselawn (Lucan)	YY13
23	Roselawn Avenue	B10
23	Roselawn Close	C10
23	Roselawn Court	C10
23	Roselawn Crescent	B10
23	Roselawn Drive (Blanchardstown)	B10
23	Roselawn Glade	B10
23	Roselawn Grove	B10
23	Roselawn Road	B10
23	Roselawn Road	C10
23	Roselawn View	B10
23	Roselawn Walk	B10
23	Roselawn Way	C10
56	Rosemount (Churchtown)	M20
28	Rosemount (Donnycarney)	N11
29	Rosemount Avenue	P10
57	Rosemount Court (Booterstown)	P19
56	Rosemount Court (Dundrum)	M20
37	Rosemount Court (Inchicore Rd)	G15
56	Rosemount Crescent (Roebuck Road)	M19
56	Rosemount Glade	M20
56	Rosemount Hall	M20
55	Rosemount Park	M20
12	Rosemount Park Drive	D8
11	Rosemount Park Road	D8
38	Rosemount Road	JI5
38	Rosemount Terrace (Arbour Hill)	JI4
57	Rosemount Terrace (Booterstown)	P19
55	Rosemount Terrace (Dundrum)	L20
29	Rosevale Court	Q11
29	Rosevale Mansions	Q11
55	Roseville Terrace	ZZ15
22	Rosewood Grove	ZZ15
59	Rosmeen Gardens	U20
59	Rosmeen Park	K15
38	Ross Road	K15
38	Ross Street	H13
34	Rossaveal Court	D14
34	Rossecourt Avenue	ZZ15
34	Rossecourt Green	ZZ15
34	Rossecourt Grove	ZZ15
34	Rossecourt Heights	ZZ15
34	Rossecourt Lane	ZZ15
34	Rossecourt Rise	ZZ15
34	Rossecourt Square	ZZ15
34	Rossecourt Terrace	ZZ15
34	Rossecourt Way	ZZ15
60	Rossfield Avenue	A21
60	Rossfield Crescent	A21
60	Rossfield Drive	A21
60	Rossfield Gardens	A21
60	Rossfield Green	A21
60	Rossfield Grove	A21
60	Rossfield Park	A21
60	Rossfield Way	A21
35	Rossmore Avenue (Ballyfermot)	D15
53	Rossmore Avenue (Templeogue)	F20
53	Rossmore Close	G20
53	Rossmore Crescent	G20
36	Rossmore Drive (Ballyfermot)	D14
53	Rossmore Drive (Templeogue)	F20
53	Rossmore Grove	G20
53	Rossmore Lawns	G20
53	Rossmore Park	G20
35	Rossmore Road (Ballyfermot)	D14
53	Rossmore Road (Templeogue)	G20
19	Rostrevor Road	K19
39	Rostrevor Terrace (Lr Grand Canal St)	M15
55	Rostrevor Terrace (Orwell Road)	K15
46	Rothe Abbey	H15
66	Rowan Avenue	N20
48	Rowan Hall	N17
58	Rowan Park	S20
58	Rowan Park Avenue	S20
58	Rowanbyrn	S20
66	Rowans Road	N22
34	Rowlagh Avenue	A15
34	Rowlagh Crescent	A15
34	Rowlagh Gardens	A15
34	Rowlagh Green	A15
34	Rowlagh Park	A15
34	Rowserstown Lane	G15
25	Royal Canal Avenue	F11
38	Royal Canal Bank	K12
38	Royal Canal Bank	K13
38	Royal Canal Terrace	JI3
39	Royal Hibernian Way	L15
15	Royal Oak	M8
69	Royal Terrace East	U21
69	Royal Terrace Lane	U21
69	Royal Terrace North	U21
69	Royal Terrace West	U21
38	Royse Road	K12
46	Royston	G18
46	Royston Village	G18
68	Ruby Hall	T22
47	Rugby Road	L17
47	Rugby Villas	L17
23	Rus-in-Urbe Terrace	U21
23	Rushbrook	B10
53	Rushbrook Avenue	F19
53	Rushbrook Court	F20
53	Rushbrook Crescent	F19
53	Rushbrook Drive	F19
53	Rushbrook Grove	F19
53	Rushbrook Park	F19
53	Rushbrook Road	F19
53	Rushbrook View	F19
53	Rushbrook Way	F19
9	Rusheeney Avenue	YY9
9	Rusheeney Close	YY9
9	Rusheeney Court	ZZ9
9	Rusheeney Crescent	ZZ9
9	Rusheeney Green	YY9
9	Rusheeney Grove	YY9
9	Rusheeney Manor	YY9
9	Rusheeney Park	YY9
9	Rusheeney View	ZZ9
9	Rusheeney Way	YY9
60	Russell Avenue (Fortunestown Way)	A21
39	Russell Avenue (Jones's Road)	L13
40	Russell Avenue East	M13
60	Russell Close	A22
60	Russell Court	A22
60	Russell Crescent	A21
60	Russell Downs	A21
60	Russell Drive	A22
60	Russell Green	A22
60	Russell Grove	A22
3	Russell House	P2
60	Russell Lane	A21
60	Russell Lawns	A22
60	Russell Meadows	A21
60	Russell Place	A21
60	Russell Rise	A21
39	Russell Street	L13
60	Russell View	A21

Page   **Grid Ref**

60 Russell Walk **A22**
3 Russell's Mews **P3**
3 Russell's Place **P3**
3 Russell's Terrace **P4**
46 Rutland Avenue **H16**
  (Crumlin Road)
39 Rutland Cottages **L13**
39 Rutland Court **L13**
46 Rutland Grove **J17**
39 Rutland Place North **L13**
39 Rutland Place West **K13**
39 Rutland Street Lower **L13**
47 Rutledge Terrace **J16**
47 Ryan's Cottages **J17**
  (Harold's Cross)
39 Ryder's Row **K14**

39 **SACKVILLE AVE L13**
39 Sackville Gardens **L13**
39 Sackville Place **K14**
10 Saddlers Avenue **A8**
10 Saddlers Close **A8**
47 Saddlers Court **K16**
10 Saddlers Crescent **A8**
10 Saddlers Drive **A8**
10 Saddlers Glade **A8**
10 Saddlers Grove **A8**
10 Saddlers Lawn **A8**
60 Saggart Abbey **ZZ22**
72 Saintsbury Avenue **V24**
56 Salamanca **N20**
47 Salem Court **K17**
15 Sallowood View **L8**
15 Sallowood Walk **L8**
63 Sally Park **F21**
63 Sally Park Close **F21**
69 Sallyglen Road **U22**
48 Sallymount Avenue **L17**
48 Sallymount Gardens **L17**
48 Sallymount Terrace **L17**
69 Sallynoggin **U22**
69 Sallynoggin Park **T22**
69 Sallynoggin Road **T22**
37 Salmon Pool Apts **G14**
53 Salthill **T20**
59 *Salthill Place **U20**
  (off Crofton Road)
56 Saltzburg **N20**
15 Sampson's Lane **K14**
57 Sanderling Apts **P19**
48 Sandford Avenue **M17**
  (Donnybrook)
47 Sandford Avenue **J16**
  (Donore Avenue)
46 Sandford Close **L17**
47 Sandford Gardens **J16**
  (off Donore Avenue)
48 Sandford Gardens **M17**
  (Sandford Avenue)
48 Sandford Lodge **L17**
47 *Sandford Park **L17**
  (off O'Donovan Road)
47 Sandford Park **J16**
  (Sandford Avenue)
48 Sandford Road **L17**
48 *Sandford Row **L17**
  (Collier's Avenue)
48 Sandford Terrace **L17**
2 Sandford Wood **M1**
41 Sandon Cove **P12**
39 Sandwith Street Lower **L14**
39 Sandwith Street Upper **L15**
73 Sandycove Avenue East **V21**
73 Sandycove Avenue Nth **V20**
73 Sandycove Avenue West **V21**
73 Sandycove Lane East **V21**
73 Sandycove Point **V20**
73 Sandycove Road **V21**
66 Sandyford **N22**
66 Sandyford Downs **N23**
66 Sandyford Hall Green **P23**
66 Sandyford Park **N23**
66 Sandyford Road **M21**
66 Sandyford View **B9**
66 Sandyford Village **N23**
14 Sandyhill Avenue **J9**
14 Sandyhill Court **J9**
14 Sandyhill Gardens **J9**
14 Sandyhill Terrace **J9**
14 Sandyhill Way **J9**
49 Sandymount **N16**
49 Sandymount Avenue **N16**
49 Sandymount Castle **N16**
49 Sandymount Castle Dr **N16**
49 Sandymount Castle Park **N16**
49 Sandymount Castle Rd **N16**
49 Sandymount Court **N15**
49 *Sandymount Green **N16**
  (Gilford Road)
49 Sandymount Road **N15**
57 Sans Souci Park **Q19**

20 Santa Sabina Manor **W10**
15 Santry **L9**
15 Santry Avenue **L8**
15 Santry Close **M8**
15 Santry Court **M8**
14 Santry Cross **K8**
15 Santry Villas **L8**
64 Sarah Curran Avenue **J21**
64 Sarah Curran Road **J21**
37 Sarah Place **G14**
36 Sarsfield Ct (Inchicore) **F15**
32 Sarsfield Terrace (Lucan) **XX13**
33 Sarsfield Park **XX13**
38 Sarsfield Quay **J14**
36 Sarsfield Road **F15**
38 Sarsfield Street **K13**
  (Phibsborough)
69 Sarsfield St (Sallynoggin) **U21**
32 *Sarsfield Terrace **XX13**
  (Hanbury Lane)
19 Sarto Lawn **T9**
19 Sarto Park **T9**
19 Sarto Rise **T9**
19 Sarto Road **T10**
46 Saul Road **H17**
73 Saval Grove **V22**
73 Saval Park Crescent **V22**
73 Saval Park Gardens **V22**
73 Saval Park Road **V22**
11 Scariff House **C9**
63 Scholarstown Park **G22**
63 Scholarstown Road **G22**
38 School Avenue **P10**
38 School Street **J15**
15 Schoolhouse Court **L9**
39 Schoolhouse Lane **L15**
  (Kildare Street)
15 Schoolhouse Lane (Santry) **L9**
38 *Schoolhouse Lane West **K15**
  (off High Street)
25 Scribblestown **F10**
24 Scribblestown Road **E11**
6 Sea Road **R2**
73 Seabank Court (Dalkey) **V21**
7 Seabank Court (Malahide) **T2**
49 Seabury **P17**
6 Seabury Avenue **Q2**
6 Seabury Close **Q2**
6 Seabury Court **Q2**
6 Seabury Crescent **Q2**
6 Seabury Dale **Q2**
6 Seabury Downs **Q2**
6 Seabury Drive **R2**
6 Seabuty Gardens **Q2**
6 Seabury Glen **Q2**
6 Seabury Green **Q2**
6 Seabury Grove **Q2**
6 Seabury Heights **Q2**
6 Seabury Lane **Q2**
6 Seabury Lawns **Q2**
6 Seabury Meadows **Q2**
6 Seabury Orchard **Q2**
6 Seabury Parade **Q2**
6 Seabury Park **Q2**
6 Seabury Place **Q2**
6 Seabury Road **Q2**
6 Seabury View **Q2**
6 Seabury Walk **Q2**
6 Seabury Wood **Q2**
19 Seacliff Avenue **T9**
19 Seacliff Drive **T9**
19 Seacliff Road **T9**
29 Seacourt **Q12**
31 Seafield (Shankill) **W26**
19 Seafield (Sutton) **U9**
29 Seafield Ave (Clontarf) **Q12**
58 Seafield Avenue **S20**
  (Monkstown)
57 Seafield Close **P18**
72 Seafield Court **V25**
  (Loughlinstown)
7 Seafield Ct (Malahide) **S2**
57 Seafield Crescent **P18**
41 Seafield Downs **R12**
57 Seafield Drive **P18**
29 Seafield Grove **R12**
57 Seafield Park **P18**
72 Seafield Rd (Ballybrack) **V25**
57 Seafield Road **P18**
  (Booterstown)
72 Seafield Road (Killiney) **V24**
29 Seafield Road East **Q12**
29 Seafield Road West **P12**
73 Seafield Terrace **X22**
49 Seafort Avenue **P16**
49 Seafort Cottages **N16**
49 Seafort Gardens **N15**
57 Seafort Parade **Q19**
49 Seafort Terrace **N16**
49 Seafort Villas **P16**

19 Seagrange Avenue **T9**
19 Seagrange Drive **T9**
19 Seagrange Road **T9**
8 Seagrave **T6**
13 Seagrave Close **H8**
13 Seagrave Court **H8**
13 Seagrave Drive **H8**
13 Seagrave Rise **H8**
14 Seagrave Terrace **H8**
13 Seagrave Way **H8**
57 Seamount **P19**
7 Seamount Drive **T3**
7 Seamount Grove **T3**
7 Seamount Heights **T3**
7 Seamount Park **T3**
7 Seamount Road **T3**
3 Seamount View **P2**
13 Seamus Ennis Road **H9**
39 Sean MacDermott **L13**
  Street Lower
39 Sean MacDermott **L13**
  Street Upper
40 Sean Moore Road **N15**
39 *Sean O'Casey Avenue **L13**
  (Summer Street North)
39 Sean Tracey House **L13**
61 Sean Walsh Memorial Pk **C21**
29 Seapark (Dollymount) **Q12**
7 Seapark (Malahide) **T3**
41 Seapark Drive **Q12**
7 Seapark Hill **T3**
29 Seapark Road **Q12**
19 Seapoint Ave (Baldoyle) **U8**
19 Seapoint Ct (Baldoyle) **U8**
58 Seapoint Tce (Blackrock) **S19**
40 Seapoint Tce (Ringsend) **N15**
3 Seatown Park **N1**
3 Seatown Park The Avenue **N1**
3 Seatown Park The Court **N1**
3 Seatown Pk The Crescent **N1**
3 Seatown Park The Drive **N1**
3 Seatown Park The Green **N1**
3 Seatown Park The Grove **N1**
3 Seatown Road **P1**
3 Seatown Terrace **N2**
3 Seatown Villas **N1**
3 Seatown Walk **N1**
3 Seatown West **N1**
40 Seaview Avenue East **M13**
40 Seaview Avenue North **N12**
72 Seaview Lawn **V26**
31 Seaview Park **V26**
48 Seaview Terrace **N17**
  (Donnybrook)
59 Seaview Terrace **T20**
  (Dun Laoghaire)
21 Seaview Terrace (Howth) **Y10**
72 Seaview Wood **V26**
39 Second Ave (Seville Pl) **M14**
51 Second Ave (Tallaght) **C20**
69 Sefton **T22**
69 Sefton Green **T22**
67 *Sefton Hall **R22**
  (Kelston Hall)
47 Selskar Terrace **L16**
48 Serpentine Avenue **N16**
48 Serpentine Park **N16**
49 Serpentine Road **N16**
49 Serpentine Terrace **N16**
62 Seskin View Avenue **D22**
62 Seskin View Drive **D22**
62 Seskin View Park **D22**
62 Seskin View Road **D22**
39 Setanta Place **L15**
15 Seven Houses **U21**
37 Seven Oaks (Inchicore) **F15**
27 Seven Oaks (Whitehall) **L11**
44 Seventh Lock Cottages **D16**
44 Seventh Lock Place **D16**
39 Seville Place **L13**
15 Seville Terrace **L13**
70 Shaldon Grange **Q26**
15 Shamrock Cottages **L13**
48 Shamrock Hill Mews **M17**
15 Shamrock Place **L13**
38 *Shamrock Street **K13**
  (Auburn Street)
39 Shamrock Terrace **L13**
47 Shamrock Villas **J17**
55 Shanagarry **L18**
15 Shanard Avenue **K9**
15 Shanard Road **K9**
15 Shanboley Road **M9**
34 Shancastle Avenue **A14**
34 Shancastle Close **A14**
34 Shancastle Crescent **A14**
34 Shancastle Drive **A14**
34 Shancastle Lawns **A14**
34 Shancastle Park **A14**
26 Shandon Crescent **J12**

26 Shandon Drive **J12**
26 Shandon Gardens **J12**
26 Shandon Green **J12**
26 Shandon Mill **J12**
58 Shandon Park **S20**
  (Monkstown)
26 Shandon Park **J12**
  (Phibsborough)
38 Shandon Road **J12**
15 Shangan Avenue **L9**
15 Shangan Court **K9**
15 Shangan Crescent **K9**
15 Shangan Drive **L9**
15 Shangan Gardens **L9**
15 Shangan Green **L9**
15 Shangan Park **L9**
15 Shangan Road **K9**
31 Shanganagh Cliffs **V26**
31 Shanganagh Grove **V27**
31 Shanganagh Road **V26**
72 Shanganagh Terrace **V24**
71 Shanganagh Vale **U24**
31 Shanganagh Wood **V26**
15 Shanglas Road **M9**
47 Shand Road **J18**
31 Shankill **V27**
15 Shanliss Avenue **L9**
15 Shanliss Drive **L9**
15 Shanliss Gardens **K9**
15 Shanliss Park **L9**
15 Shanliss Road **K9**
15 Shanliss Walk **L9**
15 Shanliss Way **L9**
37 Shannon Terrace **H15**
15 Shanowen Avenue **K9**
15 Shanowen Crescent **L9**
15 Shanowen Drive **L9**
15 Shanowen Grove **K9**
15 Shanowen Park **K9**
15 Shanowen Road **L9**
15 Shanowen Square **L9**
15 Shanrath Road **L9**
15 Shantalla Avenue **M9**
28 Shantalla Drive **M10**
28 Shantalla Park **M10**
28 Shantalla Road **M10**
15 Shanvarna Road **L9**
69 Sharavogue **V22**
39 Shaw Street **L14**
48 Shaw's Lane **M15**
38 Shea's Court **J13**
72 Sheelin Avenue **V25**
72 Sheelin Drive **V25**
72 Sheelin Grove **V25**
72 *Sheelin Hill **V25**
  (Ridge Hill)
72 Sheelin Walk **V25**
11 Sheephill Avenue **C8**
11 Sheephill Green **C8**
11 Sheephill Park **C8**
10 Sheepmoor Avenue **A10**
10 Sheepmoor Close **A9**
10 Sheepmoor Crescent **A9**
10 Sheepmoor Gardens **A9**
10 Sheepmoor Green **A9**
10 Sheepmoor Grove **A9**
10 Sheepmoor Lawn **A9**
10 Sheepmoor Way **A9**
48 Shelbourne Avenue **M16**
48 Shelbourne Lane **M16**
40 Shelbourne Park Mews **M15**
48 Shelbourne Road **M16**
40 Shelbourne Village **M15**
22 Shelerin Road **ZZ10**
41 Shellys Banks Road **P15**
40 Shelmalier Road **M13**
27 Shelmartin Avenue **M12**
27 Shelmartin Terrace **M12**
53 Shelton Drive **G18**
53 Shelton Gardens **G18**
53 Shelton Grove **G18**
53 Shelton Park **G18**
54 Sherborne **K18**
39 Sheriff Street Lower **L14**
40 Sheriff Street Upper **M14**
27 Sherkin Court **L11**
27 Sherkin Gardens **L11**
39 Sherrard Avenue **K13**
39 *Sherrard Court **K13**
  (off Portland Place)
39 Sherrard Street Lower **K13**
39 Sherrard Street Upper **K13**
39 *Sherrards Court **K13**
  (Portland Place)
20 Shielmartin Drive **W11**
20 Shielmartin Park **W11**
20 Shielmartin Road **W11**
39 Ship Street Great **K15**
39 Ship Street Little **K15**
49 Shrewsbury **N16**

Page		Grid Ref
31	Shrewsbury Hall	V27
71	Shrewsbury House	T24
71	Shrewsbury Lawn	T24
69	Shrewsbury Lodge	T23
49	Shrewsbury Park	N16
49	Shrewsbury Road	N16
	(Ailesbury Road)	
31	Shrewsbury Rd (Shankill)	V27
71	Shrewsbury Woods	T24
48	Sibthorpe Lane	L16
38	Sigurd Road	J14
69	Silchester Court	U21
69	Silchester Crescent	U21
69	Silchester Park	U21
69	Silchester Road	U21
69	Silchester Wood	U21
14	Silloge Avenue	K9
14	Silloge Crescent	K9
14	Silloge Gardens	K9
14	Silloge Road	J9
56	Silver Birches	M20
	(Dundrum)	
67	Silver Pines	Q22
32	Silverberry	XX15
32	Silverdale	XX15
33	Silverwood	XX15
54	Silverwood Drive	H20
54	Silverwood Road	H20
48	Simmon's Court	N17
47	*Simmon's Place	L13
	(Rutland Place North)	
48	Simmonscourt Avenue	N17
48	Simmonscourt Castle	N17
48	Simmonscourt Road	N16
48	Simmonscourt Terrace	M17
66	Simons Ridge	M23
40	*Simpsons Lane	N15
	(Bath Street)	
57	Sion Hill	Q19
47	Sion Hill Avenue	J17
27	Sion Hill Court	M11
27	Sion Hill Road	M11
69	Sion Road	U22
67	Sir Ivor Mall	Q22
47	Sir John Rogerson's Qy	M14
38	*Sitric Place	J14
	(off Sitric Road)	
38	Sitric Road	J14
11	Skelligs Court	C9
28	Skelly's Lane	N10
37	Skreen Road	G13
38	Slade Row	J14
17	Slademore Avenue	Q9
17	Slademore Close	Q9
17	Slademore Court	Q9
17	Slademore Drive	Q9
46	Slane Road	H16
26	Slaney Close	H11
26	Slaney Road	H11
37	Slemish Road	G13
66	Slieve Rua Drive	N21
45	Slievebloom Park	F17
45	Slievebloom Road	F17
45	Slievemore Road	G16
46	Slievenamon Road	G15
59	Sloperton	T20
38	Smithfield	J14
38	*Smithfield Terrace	J14
	(Smithfield)	
48	Smith's Cottages	L17
	(Donnybrook)	
47	*Smith's Lane	JI7
	(Ryan's Cottages)	
59	Smith's Villas	T20
59	Smyth Gardens	T20
17	Snowdrop Walk	Q8
11	Snugborough Road	C8
22	Snugborough Road	A10
	(Extension)	
40	*Somerset Street	M15
	(Doris Street)	
69	Somerton	T22
26	Somerton Lane	B12
45	Somerville Avenue	F17
45	Somerville Drive	G17
45	Somerville Park	F17
55	Sommerville	M20
26	Sonesta	R2
56	Sophie Baret Residence	N20
56	Sorbonne	N20
22	Sorrel Dale	A10
22	Sorrel Drive	ZZ10
22	Sorrel Heath	ZZ10
22	Sorrel Park	ZZ10
73	Sorrento Close	W22
73	Sorrento Court	W21
73	Sorrento Drive	W22
73	Sorrento Heights	W22
73	Sorrento Lawn	W22
73	Sorrento Mews	W22
73	Sorrento Park	X22

Page		Grid Ref
73	Sorrento Road	W22
73	Sorrento Terrace	X22
57	South Avenue	P20
3	South Bank (Swords)	N1
40	South Bank Road	P15
46	South Circular Road	J16
	(Dolphin's Barn)	
37	South Circular Road	G14
	(Islandbridge)	
46	South Circular Road	H15
	(Kilmainham)	
47	South Circular Road	K16
	(Portobello)	
39	*South City Market	K15
	(on South Great Georges St)	
40	South Dock Place	M15
40	South Dock Road	M15
40	South Dock Street	M15
39	South Great George's St	K15
20	South Hill (Howth)	X11
55	South Hill (Milltown)	L18
57	South Hill Avenue	P19
57	South Hill Park	P19
40	South Lotts Road	M15
68	South Park (Cornelscourt)	S22
68	South Park Drive	S22
73	South Winds	W21
57	South Wood Park	Q19
58	Southdene	S20
45	Southern Cross Avenue	G15
65	Southern Cross Route	L23
66	Southmede	M21
38	Southview Terrace	H15
45	Spa Road (Inchicore)	F15
37	Spa Rd (Phoenix Park)	G13
49	Spafield Terrace	N16
53	Spawell Cottages	F20
39	Spencer Dock	M14
40	*Spencer Place	M13
	(off Spencer Street Nth)	
40	Spencer Row	L14
40	Spencer Street North	M13
47	*Spencer Street South	K16
	(St Vincent Street South)	
47	*Spencer Terrace	J15
	(off Cork Street)	
69	Spencer Villas	V21
45	Sperrin Road	G16
44	Spiddal Park	C15
44	Spiddal Road	C15
25	Spire View	G12
38	Spire View	K13
25	Spire View Lane	K17
38	*Spitalfields	JI5
	(Carman's Hall)	
39	Spring Garden Lane	L14
40	Spring Garden Street	L13
29	Springdale Court Apts	Q10
29	Springdale Road	Q10
61	Springfield (Cabra)	G13
61	Springfield (Tallaght)	C21
54	Springfield Avenue	H20
54	Springfield Crescent	H20
54	Springfield Drive	H20
70	Springfield Lane	R25
68	Springfield Park	R22
	(Deans Grange)	
54	Springfield Park	H20
	(Templeogue)	
54	Springfield Road	H19
68	Springhill Avenue	R21
68	Springhill Cottages	S21
73	Springhill Park (Dalkey)	V22
68	Springhill Park	S21
	(Deans Grange)	
23	Springlawn	B10
23	Springlawn Close	B10
23	Springlawn Court	B10
22	Springlawn Drive	B10
23	Springlawn Heights	B10
22	Springlawn Park	B10
23	Springlawn Road	B10
23	Springmount Apts	G10
64	Springvale	H22
66	Spruce Avenue	N22
39	*St Agatha Court	L13
	(off William Street North)	
45	St Agnes Park	G17
45	St Agnes Road	G17
45	St Agnes Terrace	G17
	(on St Agnes Rd)	
54	St Agnes Terrace	JI9
	(Rathfarnham)	
56	St Aidan's Drive	N20
60	St Aidan's Halting Site	A21
28	St Aidan's Park	M12
28	St Aidan's Park Avenue	M12
28	St Aidan's Park Road	M12
49	St Alban's Park	P17
47	St Alban's Road	J16
27	St Alphonsus Avenue	K12

Page		Grid Ref
27	St Alphonsus Rd	K12
39	St Andrew Street	K15
33	St Andrews	ZZ14
33	St Andrews Drive	ZZ14
33	St Andrews Fairway	ZZ14
33	St Andrews Green	ZZ14
8	St Andrew's Grove	S3
39	*St Andrew's Lane	K15
	(off Exchequer Street)	
2	St Andrews Park	M1
33	St Andrews Wood	ZZ14
53	St Anne's (Kimmage)	H18
55	St Anne's (Ranelagh)	L16
29	St Anne's Avenue	R11
29	St Anne's Court	R11
29	St Anne's Drive	R11
31	St Anne's Park	V27
39	St Anne's Road North	K12
46	St Anne's Road South	J16
58	St Anne's Square	R19
	(Blackrock)	
8	St Anne's Square	T6
	(Portmarnock)	
29	St Anne's Terrace	R11
	(Raheny)	
48	St Ann's Tce (Ranelagh)	L16
8	St Ann's Square Lower	T6
43	St Anthony's Avenue	B18
52	St Anthony's Crescent	E18
39	*St Anthony's Place	K13
	(off Temple Street North)	
46	St Anthony's Road	H15
52	St Aongus Court	E20
52	St Aongus Crescent	E20
52	St Aongus Green	E20
52	St Aongus Grove	E20
52	St Aongus Lawn	E20
52	St Aongus Park	E20
52	St Aongus Road	E20
30	St Assam's Avenue	R10
30	St Assam's Drive	R10
30	St Assam's Park	R10
30	St Assam's Road East	S10
30	St Assam's Road West	R10
26	St Attracta Road	J12
72	St Aubyn's Court	V25
38	*St Audoen's Terrace	K15
	(off High Street)	
38	St Augustine Street	J14
67	*St Augustine's Park	R21
	(Obelisk Grove)	
40	St Barnabas Gardens	M13
73	St Begnet's Villas	V20
39	St Benedicts Gardens	K13
52	St Brendan's Avenue	P10
40	St Brendan's Cottages	M15
52	St Brendan's Crescent	E18
29	St Brendan's Drive	P10
29	St Brendan's Park	P10
27	St Brendan's Road	K12
17	St Brendan's Terrace	P9
	(Coolock)	
59	*St Brendan's Terrace	T20
	(St Mary's Street)	
38	St Bricin's Park	H14
40	St Bridget's Avenue	M13
	(North Strand)	
52	St Bridget's Drive	E18
56	St Bridget's Flats	M18
8	St Brigid's Avenue	T6
69	St Brigid's Church Road	Q21
23	St Brigid's Cottages	C10
	(Blanchardstown)	
43	St Brigid's Cottages	C18
	(Clondalkin)	
39	St Brigid's Cottages	M13
	(North Strand)	
28	St Brigid's Court	P10
29	St Brigid's Crescent	P10
43	St Brigid's Drive	B18
	(Clondalkin)	
28	St Brigid's Dr (Killester)	P11
28	St Brigid's Green	P10
28	St Brigid's Grove	P10
28	St Brigid's Lawn	P10
23	St Brigid's Park	C10
	(Blanchardstown)	
43	St Brigid's Park	B18
	(Clondalkin)	
48	St Brigid's Park	S23
	(Cornelscourt)	
43	St Brigid's Rd (Artane)	P10
43	St Brigid's Road	A18
	(Clondalkin)	
39	St Brigid's Road Lwr	K12
23	St Brigid's Road Upr	K12
48	St Broc's Cottages	M17
13	St Canice's Court	F9
26	St Canice's Park	J10
25	St Canice's Road	K10
25	St Canice's Square	H10

Page		Grid Ref
46	St Catherine's Avenue	JI6
42	St Catherines Grove	ZZ17
38	St Catherine's Lane West	J15
73	St Catherine's Park	V21
73	St Catherine's Road	V22
20	St Catherine's Terrace	V9
47	St Clare's Avenue	JI6
27	St Clement's Road	K12
62	St Colmcille's Way	P22
55	St Columbanus Avenue	L19
55	St Columbanus Place	L19
55	St Columbanus Road	L19
2	St Columbas Heights	M2
2	St Columbas Rise	M2
52	St Columba's Road	E18
39	St Columba's Road Lwr	K12
27	St Columba's Road Upr	K12
3	St Columcille's Crescent	N2
3	St Columcille's Drive	N2
3	St Columills Park	N2
53	St Conleth's Road	F18
2	St Cronan's Avenue	L1
2	St Cronan's Close	L2
2	St Cronan's Cottages	M2
2	St Cronan's Court	L1
2	St Cronan's Grove	M1
2	St Cronan's Lawn	L1
2	St Cronan's View	L2
2	St Cronan's Way	L2
5	St David's	N10
41	St David's Court	P12
28	St David's Park	N10
38	St David's Terrace	H13
	(Blackhorse Avenue)	
26	St David's Tce	K11
	(Glasnevin)	
28	St David's Wood	N10
28	St Declan's Road	M10
28	St Declan's Terrace	M10
19	St Domhnach's Well St	U9
62	St Dominic's Avenue	D21
62	St Dominic's Court	D21
62	St Dominic's Road	D21
62	St Dominic's Terrace	D21
18	St Donagh's Crescent	S9
18	St Donagh's Park	S9
18	St Donagh's Road	S9
26	St Eithne Road	J12
38	St Elizabeth's Court	JI3
64	St Enda's Drive	J21
64	St Enda's Park	J21
54	St Enda's Road	JI8
26	St Finbarr's Court	H12
52	St Finbarr's Close	E19
26	St Finbarr's Road	H12
33	St Finian's Avenue	XX14
33	St Finian's Close	XX14
33	St Finian's Crescent	XX14
33	St Finian's Grove	XX14
26	St Fintan Road	J12
20	St Fintan Terrace	J12
20	St Fintan's Crescent	W11
20	St Fintan's Grove	W11
68	St Fintan's Park	S21
	(Dean's Grange)	
20	St Fintan's Pk (Sutton)	W10
20	St Fintan's Road	W11
35	St Fintan's Terrace	C13
68	St Fintan's Villas	S21
38	St Francis Square	K15
69	St Gabriel's	T23
29	St Gabriel's Court	Q12
29	St Gabriel's Road	Q12
55	St Gall Gardens North	L19
55	St Gall Gardens South	L19
64	St Gatien Road	J21
39	St George's Avenue	K12
	(Clonliffe Road)	
72	St George's Avenue	V23
	(Killiney)	
37	St George's Villas	F15
	(Inchicore)	
53	St Gerard's Road	F18
25	St Helena's Court	H10
25	St Helena's Drive	H10
25	St Helena's Road	H10
36	St Helen's	V21
57	St Helen's Road	P18
45	*St Helen's Terrace	G15
	(Connolly Avenue)	
57	St Helen's Villas	P18
57	St Helen's Wood	P19
57	St Helier's Copse	Q20
39	St Ignatius Avenue	K12
39	St Ignatius Road	K12
27	St Ita's Road	K11
7	St Ives	S2
39	St James Avenue	L13
	(Clonliffe Road)	
49	*St James Place	N15
	(Sandymount Road)	

STREET INDEX

Page		Grid Ref
49	St James Terrace (Sandymount)	N15
37	St Jame's Wood	G15
28	St James's	P12
38	St James's Avenue (James's Green)	J15
45	St James's Pl (Inchicore)	F15
52	St James's Road	E18
46	St James's Terrace (Dolphin's Barn)	H16
26	St Jarlath Road	J12
47	St John Street	J15
28	St John's Court (Donnycarney)	N11
49	St John's	P17
43	St John's Avenue (Clondalkin)	A18
38	*St John's Avenue (The Coombe)	J15
42	St John's Close	A18
37	St John's Cottages	H15
16	St John's Ct (Beaumont)	N9
42	St John's Ct (Clondalkin)	A18
50	St John's Crescent	A18
50	St John's Drive	A18
50	St John's Gate	A18
42	St John's Green	A18
38	St John's Grove	A18
49	*St John's Lane (off Strand Road)	P16
50	St John's Lawn	A18
59	St John's Park (Dun Laoghaire)	T20
43	St John's Park East	A18
43	St Johns Park West	A18
43	St John's Road	A18
49	St John's Road East	P17
42	St John's Road West (Clondalkin)	A18
37	St John's Road West (Islandbridge)	H14
38	St John's Terrace (Mount Brown)	H15
37	St. John's Well Way	H15
43	St John's Wood (Clondalkin)	A18
29	St John's Wood (Clontarf)	P12
42	St John's Wood West	A18
39	St Joseph Street	K13
25	St Joseph's	F10
39	St Joseph's Avenue (Ballybough)	L12
27	St Joseph's Avenue (Drumcondra)	K12
24	St Joseph's Cottages	F12
38	St Joseph's Court	J13
55	St Joseph's Grove	M20
39	St Joseph's Mansions	L13
39	St Joseph's Parade	K13
38	St Joseph's Place (Dorset Street Lower)	K13
38	St Joseph's Place (Prussia Street)	J14
38	St Joseph's Road (Aughrim Street)	J14
53	St Joseph's Road (Walkinstown)	F18
41	St Joseph's Square	Q12
39	*St Joseph's Street (off Leo Street)	K13
17	St Joseph's Tce (Fairview)	M12
39	St Joseph's Terrace (Mountjoy Parade)	L13
46	*St Joseph's Terrace (off Dolphin's Barn)	H16
40	*St Joseph's Terrace (off Pembroke Street)	N15
59	*St Joseph's Terrace (on Tivoli Road)	U20
39	St Joseph's Villas (Summerhill)	L13
47	*St Kevin's Avenue (off Blackpitts)	J15
47	St Kevin's Cottages	K16
55	St Kevin's Court	K18
55	St Kevin's Gardens	K18
47	St Kevin's Parade	K16
55	St Kevin's Pk (Rathgar)	K18
66	St Kevin's Park (Stillorgan)	P21
47	St Kevin's Road	K16
47	*St Kevin's Terrace (New Bride St)	K15
69	St Kevin's Villas	U21
52	St Killian's Avenue	E18
43	St Killian's Park	B17
52	St Laurence Grove	E14
57	St Laurence Park	Q20
36	St. Laurence Court	E14

Page		Grid Ref
38	*St Laurence Place (Fontenoy Street)	K13
38	*St Laurence Place (Lr Sheriff Street)	K12
36	St Laurence Road	E14
36	St Laurence Terrace (Chapelizod)	E14
36	St Lawrence Glen	E15
8	St Lawrence O'Toole Ave	T6
21	*St Lawrence Quay (Harbour Road)	Y9
28	St Lawrence Road (Clontarf)	N12
21	St Lawrence Rd (Howth)	Y9
28	St Lawrence's Court	N12
21	St Lawrence's Terrace (Howth)	Y10
34	St Loman's Road	ZZ14
38	St Luke's Avenue	J15
16	St Luke's Court	N9
38	St Luke's Crescent	L18
38	*St Luke's Gate (The Coombe)	J15
62	St Maelruans Park	D21
37	St Maignenn's Terrace	H15
52	St Malachy's Drive	F18
27	St Malachy's Road	K11
73	St Margaret's Close	V21
57	St Margaret's (Booterstown)	Q19
18	St Margaret's Avenue (Kilbarrack)	T10
7	St Margaret's Avenue (Malahide)	S3
38	*St Margaret's Avenue (off Pimlico)	J15
39	*St Margaret's Ave North (Mountjoy Parade)	L13
13	St Margaret's Court	G18
14	St Margaret's Halting Site	J8
7	St Margaret's Pk (Ballymun)	S3
14	St Margaret's Road	K8
13	St Margaret's Rd (Finglas)	G8
7	St Margaret's Road (Malahide)	S3
46	St Mark's Terrace	J15
34	St Mark's Avenue	A14
34	St Mark's Crescent	A15
34	St Mark's Drive	A15
34	St Mark's Gardens	A15
34	St Mark's Green	A15
34	St Mark's Grove	A15
8	St Marnock's Avenue	T6
46	St Martin's Drive	H18
46	St Martin's Park	H18
39	*St Mary's Ave North (Mountjoy Street)	K13
54	St Mary's Avenue (Rathfarnham)	J20
37	St Mary's Avenue West	J15
45	St Mary's Crescent	F17
45	St Mary's Drive	F17
48	St Mary's Lane	M15
39	St Mary's Mansions	L14
25	St Mary's Park (Crumlin)	F17
21	St Mary's Park (Finglas)	F10
39	St Mary's Place (Howth)	Y10
39	St Mary's Place North	K13
45	St Mary's Rd (Crumlin)	G17
21	St Mary's Road (Howth)	Y10
40	St Mary's Road North (East Wall)	M13
48	St Mary's Road South (Ballsbridge)	M16
59	St Mary's Street	T20
38	St Mary's Terrace (Arbour Hill)	J14
40	*St Mary's Terrace (Bath Street)	N15
36	St Mary's Terrace (Chapelizod)	E14
39	St Mary's Terrace (Mountjoy Street)	K13
54	St Mary's Terrace (Rathfarnham)	J20
72	St Mathias Wood	U24
52	St Mel's Avenue	E19
38	*St Michael's Close (off High Street)	K15
45	St Michael's Estate	G15
38	*St Michael's Hill (off High Street)	K15
56	St Michael's House	M20
38	*St Michael's Road (Wellington Street Upper)	K13
27	St Michael's Road	K11
47	St Michael's Terrace (Blackpitts)	J15
59	*St Michael's Terrace (York Terrace)	T20

Page		Grid Ref
38	*St Michan's Place (off Chancery Street)	K14
38	St Michan's Street	K14
22	*St Mobhi Avenue (on St. Mobhi Road)	A11
26	St Mobhi Boithirin	K11
26	St Mobhi Drive	K11
26	St Mobhi Grove	K11
27	St Mobhi Road	K11
22	St Mochtas Avenue	A11
22	St Mochtas Chase	A10
22	St Mochtas Drive	A11
22	St Mochtas Green	A11
22	St Mochtas Grove	A11
22	St Mochtas Lawn	A10
22	St Mochtas Road	A11
22	St Mochtas Vale	A11
40	St Mura's Terrace	M13
55	*St Nathy's House (Airfield Drive)	L20
55	*St Nathy's Villas (Camberly Oaks)	L20
21	St Nessan's Apts	Z10
21	St Nessan's Close	Y10
21	*St Nessans Court (Main Street)	Y10
21	St Nessan's Terrace	Y10
38	St Nicholas Place	K15
43	St Oliver's Park	B15
26	St Pappin's Green	J10
26	St Pappin's Road	J10
14	St Pappin's Street	K8
43	*St Patrick's Avenue (St Patrick's Park)	A17
73	*St Patrick's Ave (St Patrick's Square)	W22
39	St Patrick's Avenue (Fairway)	M13
8	St Patrick's Avenue (Portmarnock)	T6
38	St Patrick's Close (Kevin Street Upper)	K15
69	St Patrick's Close (Kill O' the Grange)	T21
54	St Patrick's Cottages	J20
69	St Patrick's Crescent (Kill O' the Grange)	T21
27	St Patrick's Parade	K12
23	St Patrick's Park (Blanchardstown)	B10
43	St Patricks Park (Clondalkin)	A17
38	*St Patrick's Place (off Royal Canal Bank)	K12
43	St Patrick's Road (Clondalkin)	A16
73	St Patrick's Rd (Dalkey)	W22
27	St Patrick's Road (Drumcondra)	K12
53	St Patrick's Road (Walkinstown)	F18
73	St Patrick's Sq (Dalkey)	W22
37	St Patrick's Tce (Inchicore)	F15
69	St Patrick's Terrace (Kill O' the Grange)	T21
38	*St Patrick's Terrace (Nth Brunswick St)	J14
39	*St Patrick's Terrace (off Fitzroy Avenue)	L12
39	*St Patrick's Terrace (Russell Street)	L13
40	St Patrick's Villas	N15
69	St Paul's Terrace	V21
38	St Peter's Avenue	J13
38	*St Peter's Close (Royal Canal Bank)	K12
53	St Peter's Crescent	F18
53	St Peter's Drive	F18
38	St Peter's Road (Phibsborough)	J13
45	St Peter's Road (Walkinstown)	F18
38	St Peter's Square	K12
69	St Peter's Terrace (Dun Laoghaire)	V21
21	St Peter's Tce (Howth)	Y10
53	St Peter's Terrace (Walkinstown)	F18
11	St Philomenas	C8
11	St Philomena's Court	C7
11	St Philomena's Park	C7
26	St Philomena's Road	J12
42	St Ronan's Avenue	A15
42	St Ronan's Close	A15
43	St Ronan's Crescent	A15
42	St Ronan's Drive	A15
43	St Ronan's Gardens	A15
43	St Ronan's Green	A15
43	St Ronan's Grove	A15
42	St Ronan's Park	A15

Page		Grid Ref
42	St Ronan's Way	A15
18	*St Samson Court	R7
18	St Samson Square	R7
47	St Stephen's Green East	K15
47	St Stephen's Green Nth	K15
47	St Stephen's Green Sth	K15
47	St Stephen's Green West	K15
7	St Sylvester Villas	S3
46	St Teresa's Gardens	J15
52	St Teresa's Place	K12
45	St Teresa's Rd (Crumlin)	G18
26	St Teresa's Road (Glasnevin)	K12
57	St Thomas Mead	P19
47	St Thomas Road (Ardee Street)	J15
57	St Thomas's Road (Mount Merrion)	P19
47	St Ultan's Flats	K16
38	*St Vincent Street North (Goldsmith Street)	K13
47	St Vincent Street South	K16
45	St Vincent Street West	G15
25	St Vincent's Cottages	F12
28	St Vincent's Court	M11
28	St Vincent's Court	N11
58	St Vincent's Park	R20
3	St Werburghs	P2
47	Stable Lane (Harcourt Street)	K15
47	Stable Lane (Leeson St Lwr)	K15
38	Stable Lane (Smithfield)	J14
47	Stamer Street	K16
45	Stanford Green	F17
38	Stanhope Street	J14
38	Stanley Street	J14
46	Stannaway Avenue	G18
36	Stannaway Court	G18
46	Stannaway Drive	H17
46	*Stannaway Road	H17
19	Stapolin Lawns	T8
43	Station Close	A16
69	Station Rd (Glenageary)	V21
72	Station Road (Killiney)	V24
43	Station Road (off Clover Hill Road)	A16
8	Station Road (Portmarnock)	S6
29	Station Road (Raheny)	R10
31	Station Road (Shankill)	V26
20	Station Road (Sutton)	V9
22	*Station View Apts (Oldfarm)	B11
18	Station Way	S8
22	Stationcourt	A11
22	Stationcourt Hall	A11
22	Stationcourt Park	A11
22	Stationcourt View	A11
22	Stationcourt Way	A11
38	Steeven's Lane	H14
27	Stella Avenue	K11
40	Stella Gardens	N15
39	Stephen Street Lower	K15
39	Stephen Street Upper	K15
48	Stephen's Lane	L15
39	Stephen's Place	L15
46	Stephen's Road	G15
67	Stillorgan	Q21
67	Stillorgan Court	P21
57	Stillorgan Grove	Q21
67	Stillorgan Heath	P21
57	Stillorgan Park	Q20
57	Stillorgan Park Avenue	Q20
48	Stillorgan Road (Donnybrook)	N17
68	Stillorgan Rd (Foxrock)	R22
57	Stillorgan Road (Mount Merrion)	P19
67	Stillorgan Rd (Stillorgan)	Q21
67	Stillorgan Wood	P21
55	Stirling Park	K19
38	*Stirrup Lane (off Church Street)	J14
4	Stockhole	N6
4	Stockhole Lane	M5
63	Stocking Lane	G23
23	Stockton Court	D11
23	Stockton Drive	D11
23	Stockton Green	D11
23	Stockton Grove	D11
23	Stockton Lawn	D11
23	Stockton Park	D11
65	*Stone Masons Green	K22
65	Stone Masons Way	K22
38	Stone Mews	K17
9	Stonebridge	YY10
9	Stonebridge Avenue	YY10
31	Stonebridge Close	V27
9	Stonebridge Drive	YY10

STREET INDEX

Page		Grid Ref

31 Stonebridge Lane U26
9 Stonebridge Rd YY10
(Clonsilla)
31 Stonebridge Road U26
(Shankill)
54 Stonepark Abbey J20
54 Stonepark Court J22
54 Stonepark Orchard J20
59 Stoneview Place U20
56 Stoney Road (Dundrum) M20
40 Stoney Road (East Wall) M13
38 Stoneybatter J14
39 Store Street L14
26 Stormanstown Road K10
68 Stradbrook Close S21
58 Stradbrook Gardens S20
58 Stradbrook Grove S20
58 Stradbrook Hall S20
68 Stradbrook Hill S21
58 Stradbrook Lawn S20
58 Stradbrook Park S20
58 Stradbrook Road S20
9 Stralem Court YY9
9 Stralem Crescent YY9
9 Stralem Grove YY9
9 Stralem Mews YY9
9 Stralem Terrace YY9
49 Strand Lane P17
19 Strand Road (Baldoyle) U8
72 Strand Road (Ballybrack) V25
49 Strand Road (Merrion) P17
8 Strand Rd (Portmarnock) T6
8 Strand Rd (Portmarnock) U5
8 Strand Rd (Portmarnock) U4
49 Strand Rd (Sandymount) P16
20 Strand Road (Sutton) W10
7 Strand Street Great S2
40 Strand Street (Ringsend) N1
39 Strand Street Great K14
39 Strand Street Little K14
55 *Strand Terrace L18
(Milltown Hill)
8 Strandmill Avenue T6
8 Strandmill Park U6
8 Strandmill Road U6
39 Strandville Avenue M13
(North Strand)
28 Strandville Avenue East N12
(Clontarf)
28 Strandville House N12
39 Strandville Place M13
40 Strangford Gardens M13
40 Strangford Road M13
40 Strasburg Terrace N15
55 Stratford K18
72 Strathmore Road V24
6 Streamatown Lane Q4
72 Streamville Court V25
18 Streamville Road R9
39 *Strong's Court Q14
(Findlater Place)
39 Suffolk Street K15
46 Suir Road G15
39 Sullivan Street H14
39 *Summer Arch L13
(off Summer Street North)
39 Summer Place L13
39 *Summer Row L13
(off Summer Street North)
39 Summer Street North L13
38 Summer Street South J15
22 Summerfield B10
(Blanchardstown)
40 Summerfield (Ringsend) N15
62 Summerfield (Tallaght) D22
22 Summerfield Avenue B10
22 Summerfield Close B10
73 Summerfield Close W22
22 Summerfield Green B10
22 Summerfield Lawns B10
22 Summerfield Meadows B10
22 Summerfield Rise B10
39 Summerhill L13
59 Summerhill Court V20
59 Summerhill Parade U20
(Dun Laoghaire)
39 Summerhill Parade L13
(Summerhill)
39 Summerhill Place L13
59 Summerhill Road U20
(Dun Laoghaire)
41 Summerville P13
47 Summerville Park K17
73 *Summerville Terrace W22
(on Dalkey Ave)
55 Sunbury Court K18
55 Sunbury Gardens K18
8 Suncroft Avenue T6
60 Suncroft Drive A22
60 Suncroft Park A22
60 Sundale Avenue A22

60 Sundale Close A21
60 Sundale Crescent A21
60 Sundale Green A21
60 Sundale Grove A21
60 Sundale Heights A21
60 Sundale Lawn ZZ21
60 Sundale Meadows A21
60 Sundale Parade A21
60 Sundale Park A22
60 Sundale Road A22
60 Sundale Villas A21
60 Sundale Walk A21
46 Sundrive Park H17
46 Sundrive Road H16
55 *Sunnybank Court M20
(Ophaly Court)
45 Sunville Green G17
47 Susan Terrace J15
39 Susanville Road L12
48 Sussex Road L16
59 Sussex Street U20
48 Sussex Terrace L16
20 Sutton V9
20 Sutton Castle Apts W11
19 Sutton Court U9
19 Sutton Downs U9
19 Sutton Grove U9
19 Sutton Lawns U9
19 Sutton Park U9
9 Swallowbrook ZZ8
9 Swallowbrook Crescent ZZ8
9 Swallowbrook View ZZ8
38 Swan Alley J15
47 Swan Grove L16
48 Swan Place L16
39 *Swan Yard K15
(off Harry Street)
18 Swan's Nest Apts S9
18 Swan's Nest Avenue S9
18 Swan's Nest Road S9
47 Swanville Place K17
46 Swanward Court J16
47 Sweeney's Terrace J15
58 Sweetbriar Lane N21
58 Sweetman's Avenue R19
58 *Sweetman's Avenue R19
(St Anne's Square)
55 Sweetmount Avenue L20
65 Sweetmount Drive L21
55 *Sweetmount House L20
(Weston Close)
55 Sweetmount Park L20
71 Swift Hall S24
xxx Swiftbrook (Saggart)
60 Swiftbrook (Tallaght) A21
60 Swiftbrook Avenue A21
60 Swiftbrook Close A21
60 Swiftbrook Drive A21
60 Swiftbrook Park A21
38 Swift's Alley J15
16 Swift's Grove N7
38 *Swift's Row K14
(off Ormond Quay)
37 Swilly Road H12
3 Swords S24
2 Swords Manor Ave L1
2 Swords Manor Court L1
2 Swords Manor Cres L1
2 Swords Manor Drive L1
2 Swords Manor Grove L1
2 Swords Manor View L1
2 Swords Manor Way L1
4 Swords Road M6
(Collinstown)
6 Swords Road (Malahide) R3
15 Swords Road (Santry) L9
38 Swords Street H14
29 Sybil Hill Avenue Q11
29 Sybil Hill Road Q11
68 Sycamore Avenue S23
(Cabinteely)
22 Sycamore Avenue B11
(Castleknock)
51 Sycamore Ave (Tallaght) C19
71 Sycamore Close S23
(Cornelscourt)
51 Sycamore Close C19
(Kilnamanagh)
69 Sycamore Court T23
68 Sycamore Crescent S23
(Cabinteely)
57 Sycamore Crescent P20
(Mount Merrion)
71 Sycamore Drive S23
(Cabinteely)
22 Sycamore Drive B11
(Castleknock)
65 Sycamore Dr (Dundrum) L21
51 Sycamore Dr (Tallaght) C19

71 Sycamore Green S23
(Cabinteely)
71 Sycamore Grove S24
(Cabinteely)
68 Sycamore Gro (Foxrock) R22
31 *Sycamore House V26
(Eaton Wood Grove)
19 Sycamore House U9
(Sutton)
68 Sycamore Lawn S23
(Cabinteely)
23 Sycamore Lawn B11
(Castleknock)
23 Sycamore Park B11
(Castleknock)
14 Sycamore Pk (Finglas) H9
52 Sycamore Pk (Tallaght) D19
65 Sycamore Rd (Dundrum) L21
14 Sycamore Rd (Finglas) H9
44 Sycamore Road D17
(Fox & Geese)
57 Sycamore Road P20
(Mount Merrion)
39 Sycamore Street K14
22 Sycamore View B11
71 Sycamore Walk S24
59 Sydenham U20
66 *Sydenham Place N21
(on Kilmacud Rd Upr)
48 Sydenham Road N16
(Ballsbridge)
56 Sydenham Road M20
(Dundrum)
66 Sydenham Villas M21
(Dundrum)
57 Sydney Avenue R19
49 Sydney Parade Avenue P17
57 Sydney Terrace R19
51 Sylvan Avenue D19
51 Sylvan Close C19
51 Sylvan Drive C19
55 Synge House K19
47 Synge Lane K16
47 Synge Place K16
47 Synge Street K16
43 Synge Way C16
39 Synnott Place K13
39 Synnott Row K13
59 Synnott Terrace T20

39 **TAAFFE'S PLACE M13**
6 Talbot Q3
6 Talbot Avenue Q3
23 Talbot Court C10
(Blanchardstown)
6 Talbot Court (Malahide) R2
23 Talbot Downs C10
69 Talbot Lane (Killiney) V23
39 Talbot Lane (Talbot St) L14
57 Talbot Lodge Q20
6 Talbot Park Q3
39 Talbot Place L14
73 Talbot Road (Killiney) V23
6 Talbot Road (Swords) Q3
39 Talbot Street L14
61 Tallaght C21
61 Tallaght Bypass C21
53 Tallaght Road F20
62 Tallaght Road E21
61 *Tallow Hall C21
(Belgard Square)
52 Tamarisk Avenue D19
52 Tamarisk Close D19
52 Tamarisk Court D19
52 Tamarisk Dale D19
52 Tamarisk Drive D19
52 Tamarisk Grove D19
52 Tamarisk Heights D19
52 Tamarisk Lawn D19
52 Tamarisk Park D19
52 Tamarisk View D19
52 Tamsrisk Walk D19
52 Tamarisk Way D19
32 Tandys Lane WW14
32 Tandys Lane WW14
56 Taney Avenue M20
56 Taney Court M20
56 Taney Crescent M20
56 Taney Drive M20
56 Taney Grove M20
56 Taney Lawn M20
56 Taney Manor M20
56 Taney Park M20
56 Taney Rise M20
56 Taney Road M20
39 *Tangier Lane K15
(off Grafton Street)
54 Tara Crescent E22
54 Tara Hill Crescent J20
54 Tara Hill Grove J20
54 Tara Hill Road J20

18 Tara Lawn R9
39 Tara Street L14
65 Taylor's Hill K23
64 Taylor's Lane J21
(Ballyboden)
38 Taylor's Lane (Pimlico) J15
38 Temple Bar K14
38 Temple Buildings K13
38 Temple Cottages K13
38 Temple Ct (Arbour Hill) H14
58 *Temple Court R19
(St Anne's Square)
39 *Temple Court L15
(Off Hogan Place)
55 Temple Court Apts L7
58 Temple Crescent S20
47 Temple Gdns (Milltown) L18
15 Temple Gdns (Santry) L8
58 Temple Hill S20
54 Temple Hill H18
(on Terenure Road West)
39 Temple Lane North L13
39 Temple Lane South K14
53 Temple Manor F19
(Greenhills)
53 Temple Manor Ave F19
53 Temple Manor Close F19
53 Temple Manor Court F19
53 Temple Manor Drive F19
53 Temple Manor Green F19
53 Temple Manor Way F19
15 Temple Park L18
15 Temple Park Apts L8
58 Temple Park Avenue S19
48 Temple Place L16
55 Temple Road (Blackrock) R19
55 Temple Road (Rathgar) L18
18 Temple Square L18
39 Temple Street North K13
55 Temple Street West H14
55 *Temple Terrace W22
38 *Temple Villas J14
(Arbour Hill)
47 *Temple Villas L17
(on Palmerston Road)
55 Templemore Avenue K18
53 Templeogue L20
53 Templeogue Lodge L20
53 Templeogue Road G20
53 Templeogue Wood G20
63 Templeroan G20
63 Templeroan Avenue G21
63 Templeroan Close G21
63 Templeroan Court G21
63 Templeroan Crescent G21
64 Templeroan Downs H21
63 Templeroan Drive G21
63 Templeroan Green G22
63 Templeroan Grove G21
63 Templeroan Lodge G22
64 Templeroan Meadows H21
63 Templeroan Mews G21
63 Templeroan Park G21
63 Templeroan Road G21
63 Templeroan View G21
63 Templeroan Way G21
18 Templeview Avenue R8
17 Templeview Close R8
18 Templeview Copse R8
17 Templeview Court R8
18 Templeview Crescent R8
17 Templeview Downs R8
18 Templeview Drive R8
18 Templeview Green R8
17 Templeview Grove R8
17 Templeview Lawn R8
18 Templeview Park R8
17 Templeview Place R8
17 Templeview Rise R8
17 Templeview Row R8
18 Templeview Square R8
18 Templeview Vale R8
18 Templeview Walk R8
18 Templeview Way R8
53 Templeville Avenue G19
54 Templeville Drive G19
54 Templeville Park H19
54 Templeville Road G19
54 Terenure J18
54 Terenure Park J18
54 Terenure Place J18
54 Terenure Road East J18
54 Terenure Road North J18
54 Terenure Road West H18
41 Terminal Road North Q14
41 Terminal Road South Q14
39 Termon Court J8
39 *Terrace Place L13
(off Bella St)
6 Texas Lane R2
58 The Alders S20

Page	Street	Grid Ref
59	The Anchorage	T20
48	The Appian Way	L16
65	The Avenue (Ballinteer)	M22
63	The Avenue (Ballyboden)	H22
70	The Avenue (Carrickmines)	R25
33	The Avenue (Grange Manor)	XX15
9	The Avenue (Manorfields)	YY9
10	The Avenue (Mulhuddart)	A8
51	The Avenue (Tallaght)	C19
53	The Avenue (Templeogue)	G19
7	The Bawn	S3
7	The Bawn Grove	S3
72	*The Beeches (The Rowans)	V25
18	The Beeches (Donaghmede)	R9
66	The Beeches (Kilmacud)	N21
58	The Beeches (Monkstown)	S20
64	The Beeches (Willbrook)	J21
60	The Belfry (Citywest Road)	ZZ22
37	The Belfry (Inchicore)	G15
18	The Belfry (Kilbarrack)	S9
66	*The Birch (Riversdale)	M21
67	The Birches	R23
66	*The Blackthorn (Riversdale)	M21
28	The Bramblings	P11
35	The Briars	C13
31	The Bridge	V27
73	The Burgage	W22
54	The Castlelands	J20
72	*The Cedars (Abberley) (The Elms)	V25
58	The Cedars (Monkstown)	S20
15	*The Charter (Ballymun Main Street)	K8
67	The Chase	Q22
65	The Cherries	K22
15	*The Claremont Apts (Ballymun Main Street)	K8
27	The Cloisters (Grace Park Road)	L11
46	The Cloisters (Mount Tallant Avenue)	J18
65	The Close (Ballinteer)	M22
63	The Close (Ballyboden)	H22
16	The Close (Beaumont)	M9
33	The Close (Grange Manor)	XX15
9	The Close (Manorfields)	YY9
57	The Close (Mount Merrion)	P19
51	The Close (Tallaght)	C19
62	The Close (Tallaght)	D22
53	The Close (Templeogue)	G19
38	The Coombe	J15
35	The Coppice (Palmerston)	C13
68	The Coppins (Foxrock)	R23
65	The Copse (Ballinteer)	L22
27	The Copse (Drumcondra)	L11
65	The Court (Ballinteer)	L22
72	The Court (Ballybrack)	V24
71	The Court (Carrickmines)	S24
40	The Court (Clontarf)	N12
48	The Court (Donnybrook)	M17
70	The Court (Glenamuck Road)	R25
16	The Court (Larch Hill)	M8
10	The Court (Mulhuddart)	A8
30	The Court (Raheny)	S11
31	The Court (Shankill)	V27
51	The Court (Tallaght)	C20
51	The Court (Tallaght)	C19
53	The Court (Templeogue)	G19
27	The Court (Whitehall)	M10
22	The Courtyard (Clonsilla)	A11
67	The Courtyard (Leopardstown)	P22
54	The Courtyard (Rathfarnham)	J20
54	The Courtyard (Templelogue)	H19
68	The Coutryard (Foxrock)	R22
6	The Cove	R2
35	The Covert	C13
65	The Crescent (Ballinteer)	L22
63	The Crescent	H22
70	The Crescent (Ballyboden)	R25
70	The Crescent (Carrickmines)	R25
23	The Crescent (Castleknock)	C12
48	The Crescent (Donnybrook)	M17
33	The Crescent (Grange Manor)	XX15
16	The Crescent (Larch Hill)	M8
32	The Crescent (Lucan)	WW13
7	The Crescent (Malahide)	U3
10	The Crescent (Mulhuddart)	A8
28	The Crescent (off Beaumont Rd)	M10
48	The Crescent (Ranelagh)	L17
3	The Crescent (Swords)	N2
51	The Crescent (Tallaght)	B20
51	The Crescent (Tallaght)	C19
62	The Crescent (Tallaght)	D21
54	The Crescent (Templelogue)	H19
27	The Crescent (Whitehall)	L11
65	The Dale (Ballinteer)	L22
51	The Dale (Belgard)	C20
70	The Dale (Carrickmines)	R25
51	The Dale (Kilnamanagh)	C19
9	The Dale (Manorfields)	YY9
65	The Dell	K22
35	The Dingle	B14
64	The Drive (Ballyboden)	H21
33	The Drive (Grange Manor)	XX15
51	The Drive (Kilnamanagh)	C19
9	The Drive (Manorfields)	YY9
10	The Drive (Mulhuddart)	A8
62	The Drive (Tallaght)	D22
31	The Drive (Woodbrook Glen)	W29
64	*The Drive Apts (The Drive Ballyboden)	H21
8	The Dunes	U5
66	The Elm (Rockfield)	M21
56	The Elm (Elm Park)	P18
72	The Elms (Loughlinstown)	V25
31	The Fairways (Woodbrook Glen)	W29
54	The Falls	J19
67	The Forum	P22
57	The Fosters	P19
65	The Gables (Dundrum)	L21
67	*The Gables (Foxrock) (The Hedgerows)	R23
42	The Gables (Grange View Road)	YY17
65	The Gables (Nutgrove)	K21
55	The Gables (Rathgar)	K18
70	The Gardens	R25
51	The Garth (Coliemore)	B20
51	The Garth (Kingswood Heights)	C19
43	The Gate	A17
21	The Gate Lodge	Z11
65	The Glade (Ballinteer)	L22
51	The Glade (Kingswood Heights)	C20
35	The Glade (Palmerston)	B14
33	The Glebe	YY14
65	The Glen (Ballinteer)	L22
64	The Glen (Ballyboden)	H21
69	The Glen (Glenageary Rd)	U21
30	The Glen (Raheny)	S11
70	The Glen	R25
15	The Goulding Apts	K8
38	The Granary	J15
68	The Grange (Deans Grange)	S21
7	The Grange (Malahide)	S4
54	The Grange (Terenure)	J18
65	The Green (Ballinteer)	L22
63	The Green (Ballyboden)	H21
16	The Green (Beaumont)	M9
70	The Green (Carrickmines)	R25
16	The Green (Larch Hill)	M8
7	The Green (Malahide)	S2
9	The Green (Manorfields)	YY9
10	The Green (Mulhuddart)	A8
51	The Green (Tallaght)	C19
53	The Green (Templeogue)	G19
73	The Green Road	X22
54	The Greenlands	J20
65	The Grove (Ballinteer)	L22
65	The Grove (Dundrum)	K21
33	The Grove (Grange Manor)	XX15
30	The Grove (Raheny)	S11
51	The Grove (Tallaght)	B20
51	The Grove (Tallaght)	C19
62	The Grove (Tallaght)	D21
27	The Grove (Whitehall)	L11
21	The Haggard (Howth)	Y10
54	The Hall	J18
15	*The Hampton (Ballymun Main Street)	K8
26	The Haven (Glasnevin)	K11
6	The Haven (Malahide)	S2
72	The Hawthorns (Abberley)	V25
51	The Heath (Tallaght)	C20
53	The Heath (Templeogue)	G19
65	The Heath (The Heath)	M21
67	The Hedgerows	R23
65	The Heights (Ballinteer)	L22
65	The Hill (Ballinteer)	M22
7	The Hill (Malahide)	S3
59	The Hill (Monkstown)	T20
10	The Hill (Mulbuddart)	A8
57	The Hill (Stillorgan)	Q21
18	The Hole in the Wall Rd	S8
66	The Holly (Rockfield)	M21
36	The Island	E14
15	The Kilmore Apts	K8
8	The Kilns	S6
54	The Lakelands	J20
72	The Larches (Abberley)	V25
45	The Laurels (Bluebell)	E16
55	The Laurels (Dundrum)	L20
54	The Laurels (Rathfarnham)	J20
62	*The Laurels (Tallaght) (Main Street)	D1
54	The Laurels (Terenure)	J18
65	The Lawn (Ballinteer)	L22
63	The Lawn (Ballyboden)	H22
25	The Lawn (Finglas)	H10
3	The Lawn (Kinsaley)	P3
51	The Lawn (Tallaght)	B20
7	The Lighthouse	U3
66	The Linden	M21
8	The Links	T6
28	The Lodge (Clontarf)	N12
69	The Lodge (Glenageary)	U21
15	*The Maieston (Ballymun Main Street)	K8
19	The Mall (Baldoyle)	U8
32	The Mall (Lucan)	XX13
7	The Mall (Malahide)	S2
53	The Manor (Templeogue)	G19
56	The Maples (Bird Avenue)	M19
58	The Maples (Monkstown)	S20
65	The Meadow	L22
29	The Meadow (Killester)	Q11
68	The Meadows (Newtownpark Ave)	R23
51	The Meadows East	C20
51	The Meadows West	B20
28	The Mews (Clontarf)	P12
28	The Mews (Killester)	P11
47	The Mews (Rathmines)	K17
54	The Mews (Templelogue)	H19
43	The Mill Pond Apts	A17
23	The Mills	C10
36	The Moorings (Chapelizod)	E14
7	The Moorings (Malahide)	T3
12	The New Road	E9
72	The Nurseries (Ballybrack)	V24
10	The Nurseries (Mulhuddart)	A8
2	The Nurseries (Swords)	M3
72	*The Oaks (Abberley) (The Rowans)	V25
65	The Oaks (Ballinteer)	L22
51	The Oaks (Belgard)	C20
55	The Oaks (Churchtown)	L20
30	The Oaks (Dollymount)	R12
72	The Oaks (Loughlinstown)	U25
66	The Oaks (Rockfield)	M21
2	The Oaks (Swords)	L3
33	The Old Forge	XX15
7	The Old Golf Links	T3
33	The Old Hill	XX13
22	The Orchard (Carpenterstown)	B11
68	The Orchard (Deans Grange)	R21
29	The Orchard (Killester)	P11
53	The Orchard (Kimmage)	H18
32	The Orchard (Lucan)	XX13
35	The Orchard (Palmerston)	B13
35	The Orchard Apts	B15
35	The Oval	C14
45	The Paddock (Ashtown)	F11
40	The Paddock's (Clontarf)	P12
73	The Paddocks (Dalkey)	W21
46	The Paddocks (Kilmainham)	G15
3	The Paddocks (Swords)	N2
56	The Palms	N19
28	The Park (Beaumont)	M9
33	The Park (Grange Manor)	XX15
18	The Park (Larch Hill)	M8
51	The Park (Tallaght)	C19
62	The Park (Tallaght)	D22
53	The Park (Templeogue)	G19
65	The Pines (Ballinteer)	L22
23	The Pines (Castleknock)	D11
29	The Pines (Killester)	P11
66	The Pines (Kilmacud)	N21
70	The Place (Carrickmines)	R25
58	The Poplars	S20
25	The Priory (Cabra)	G12
64	The Priory (Grange Rd)	J21
7	*The Priory (Malahide) (Killeen Terrace)	S2
65	The Rise (Ballinteer)	L22
64	The Rise (Ballyboden)	H22
70	The Rise (Carrickmines)	R25
73	The Rise (Dalkey)	V22
27	The Rise (Glasnevin)	K10
7	The Rise (Malahide)	S3
9	The Rise (Manorfields)	YY9
57	The Rise (Mount Merrion)	P19
51	The Rise (Tallaght)	B20
51	The Rise (Tallaght)	C19
9	The Road (Manorfields)	YY9
63	The Rookery	G22
66	The Rowan (Rockfield)	M21
72	The Rowans (Abberley)	V25
23	The Sand Holes	C12
59	The Slopes	T20
40	The Square (Irishtown)	N15
16	The Square (Larch Hill)	M8
32	The Square (Lucan)	XX13
61	The Square (Tallaght)	C21
57	The Stables	P19
36	The Steeples	E15
28	The Stiles Road	P12
21	The Summit (Howth)	Z11
48	The Sweepstakes	N16
72	*The Sycamores (The Elms Loughlinstown)	V25
66	The Sycamores (Rockfield)	M21
70	The Terrace	R25
27	The Thatch Road	M10
70	The Thicket	R23
14	The Turnpike	K8
35	The Vale	C13
65	The View (Ballinteer)	L22
70	The View (Carrickmines)	R25
16	The View (Larch Hill)	M8
9	The View (Manorfields)	YY9
51	The View (Tallaght)	C19
62	The View (Tallaght)	E22
22	The Village (Clonsilla)	ZZ11
27	The Village (Drumcondra)	L11
30	The Village (Raheny)	S11
32	The Village Centre	XX13
32	*The Village Court (The Village Centre)	XX13
73	The Village Gate	W22
65	The Walk (Ballinteer)	L22
70	The Walk (Carrickmines)	R25
9	The Walk (Manorfields)	YY9
62	The Walk (Tallaght)	D22
53	The Walk (Templeogue)	G19
6	The Warren	Q3
3	The Water Rill	P2
36	The Weir	E14
64	The Wicklow Way	J23
66	The Willow (Rockfield)	M21
72	*The Willows (Abberley) (The Rowans)	V25
26	The Willows (Glasnevin)	J11
58	The Willows (Monkstown)	S20
55	The Willows (Orwell Road)	K19
70	The Wood (Carrickmines)	R25
62	The Wood (Tallaght)	D22
54	The Woodlands (Rathfarnham)	J20

Page		Grid Ref
54	Theresa House	J20
39	Third Avenue	M14
	(Seville Place)	
51	Third Avenue (Tallaght)	C20
38	*Thirlestane Terrace	J15
	(Hanbury Lane)	
38	Thomas Court	J15
38	*Thomas Davis St South	J15
	(Francis Street)	
45	Thomas Davis St West	F15
39	Thomas Lane	K14
45	Thomas Moore Road	F17
38	Thomas Street	J15
38	Thomas Street West	J15
69	Thomastown Crescent	U22
69	Thomastown Road	U23
72	Thomond	V26
36	Thomond Road	E15
39	*Thompson's Cottages	L13
	(Rutland Place North)	
38	Thor Place	H14
21	*Thormanby Grove	Y10
	(Thormanby Road)	
21	Thormanby Lawns	Y10
21	Thormanby Lodge	Z10
21	Thormanby Road	Y10
21	Thormanby Woods	Z10
57	Thorn Wood	P19
10	Thornberry Apts	ZZ8
40	Thorncastle Court Apts	M14
40	Thorncastle Street	N14
55	Thorncliff	L18
55	Thorncliffe Park	L19
28	Thorndale Avenue	N10
27	Thorndale Court	M10
28	Thorndale Crescent	N10
28	Thorndale Drive	N11
28	Thorndale Grove	N11
28	Thorndale Lawns	N10
28	Thorndale Park	N10
43	Thornfield Square	B17
29	Thornhill Lane	R12
57	Thornhill Rd (Kilmacud)	P20
18	Thornville Avenue	S9
18	Thornville Drive	S10
18	Thornville Park	T9
18	Thornville Road	S9
18	Thornville Terrace	S10
52	Three Rock Close	E19
65	Three Rock Grove	L23
67	Three Rock Road	P22
38	Thundercut Alley	J14
52	Tibradden Close	E18
52	Tibradden Drive	E18
52	Tibradden Grove	E19
64	Tibradden Road	J23
71	Ticknick	S26
65	Ticknock Dale	M23
65	Ticknock Grove	M23
65	Ticknock Hill	M23
65	Ticknock Road	L23
28	Timber Mills Apts	P10
36	Tinkler's Path	E13
47	Tivoli Avenue	J17
59	Tivoli Close	T21
59	Tivoli Road	U20
59	Tivoli Terrace East	U20
59	Tivoli Terrace North	T20
59	Tivoli Terrace South	T20
58	Tobernea Terrace	S19
26	Tolka Cottages	J11
26	Tolka Estate	J10
26	Tolka Estate Road	J11
40	Tolka Quay	N14
40	Tolka Quay Road	N13
27	Tolka Road	L12
26	Tolka Vale	H11
25	Tolka Valley Road	G11
25	Tolka Valley View	G10
39	Tom Clarke House	L12
47	Tom Kelly Road	K16
28	Tonduff Close	E19
46	Tonguefield Road	H17
17	Tonlegee Avenue	Q9
17	Tonlegee Drive	Q9
17	Tonlegee Road	R9
33	Tor an Ri Close	ZZ15
33	Tor an Ri Court	ZZ15
33	Tor an Ri Lane	ZZ15
42	Tor an Ri Parade	ZZ15
33	Tor an Ri Terrace	ZZ15
33	Tor an Ri Walk	ZZ15
73	Torca Road	W22
73	Torca View	W22
7	Torcaill	T4
27	Torlogh Gardens	M12
28	Torlogh Parade	M11
67	Torquay Road	Q22
67	Torquay Wood	Q22
11	Tory Square	C9
27	Tourmakeady Road	L10

Page		Grid Ref
54	Tourville Lodge	J19
54	Tower Avenue	J18
23	Tower Rd (Castleknock)	C12
43	Tower Rd (Clondalkin)	A17
37	*Tower Terrace	H15
	(off Kilmainham Lane)	
26	Tower View Cottages	J12
39	Townsend Street	L14
7	Townyard Lane	S2
59	Traders Wharf	T19
58	Trafalgar Lane	S20
58	Trafalgar Tce (Blackrock)	S19
19	Tramway Court (Sutton)	V9
62	Tramway Ct (Tallaght)	D21
16	Tranquility Grove	N9
69	Traverslea Close	U21
69	*Traverslea Woods	U21
37	*Traynor Place	H15
	(O'Reilly Avenue)	
52	Treepark Avenue	D19
52	Treepark Close	D19
52	Treepark Drive	D19
52	Treepark Road	D19
57	Trees Avenue	P20
57	Trees Road Lower	P20
56	Trees Road Upper	P20
57	Treesdale	Q20
30	Tresilian	R23
16	Trim Road	N9
56	Trimleston Apts	
57	Trimleston Avenue	P18
57	Trimleston Drive	P18
57	Trimleston Gardens	P18
57	Trimleston Park	P18
57	Trimleston Road	P18
39	Trinity Street	K14
39	Trinity Terrace	K13
36	*Tristan House Apts	E14
	(Hibernia Terrace)	
49	Tritonville Avenue	N15
49	Tritonville Close	N15
49	Tritonville Court	N16
49	Tritonville Crescent	N15
49	Tritonville Road	N15
61	Tuansgate Apts	C21
32	Tubber Lane Road	VV14
73	Tubbermore Avenue	W22
73	Tubbermore Road	W22
21	Tuckett's Lane	Y10
1	Tudor Court	Q2
67	Tudor Lawns	Q22
48	Tudor Road	L17
17	Tulip Court	Q8
33	Tullyhall	XX16
33	Tullyhall Avenue	XX16
33	Tullyhall Close	XX16
33	Tullyhall Court	XX16
33	Tullyhall Crescent	YY16
33	Tullyhall Drive	XX16
33	Tullyhall Green	XX16
33	Tullyhall Park	XX16
33	Tullyhall Rise	YY16
33	Tullyhall Way	XX16
71	Tullyvale	T25
16	Turnapin Cottages	M7
15	Turnapin Green	M7
16	Turnapin Grove	M7
15	Turnapin Lane	M7
17	Turnberry	U9
19	Turnberry Square	U9
44	Turnpike Road	D18
57	Turnstone Apts	P19
35	Turret Road	C14
47	Turrets Flats	K17
37	Turvey Avenue	G15
30	Tuscany Downs	R10
19	Tuscany Park	U9
58	Twin Cottages	R20
61	Tymon Close	D22
61	Tymon Crescent	C22
61	Tymon Grove	D22
62	Tymon Heights	E22
61	Tymon Lane	E20
52	Tymon Lane	E19
61	Tymon Lawn	D22
52	Tymon Lodge Apts	E19
52	Tymon North	E20
52	Tymon North Avenue	E20
52	Tymon North Court	E20
52	Tymon North Gardens	E20
52	Tymon North Green	E20
52	Tymon North Grove	E20
52	Tymon North Lawn	E20
52	Tymon North Park	E20
52	Tymon North Place	E20
52	Tymon North Road	E20
52	Tymonville Avenue	E20
52	Tymonville Court	D20
52	Tymonville Crescent	D20
52	Tymonville Drive	D20
52	Tymonville Grove	E20

Page		Grid Ref
52	Tymonville Lawn	E20
52	Tymonville Park	E20
52	Tymonville Road	D20
51	Tynan Hall	C19
51	Tynan Hall Avenue	C19
51	Tynan Hall Grove	C19
51	Tynan Hall Park	C19
45	Tyrconnell Park	F15
45	Tyrconnell Road	F15
45	Tyrconnell Street	F15
45	Tyrconnell Villas	F15
45	Tyrone Place	G15
39	Tyrrel Place	L13
40	*Tyrrel's Lane	N15
	(off Fitzwilliam St Ringsend)	
56	**UCD VILLAGE**	**N19**
73	**BELGROVE**	
73	Ullardmor	W22
38	Ulster Street	J12
38	Ulster Tce (North Strand)	L13
67	Ulster Terrace	Q21
	(Stillorgan Grove)	
73	Ulverton Close	W21
73	Ulverton Court	W21
73	Ulverton Road	W21
21	Upper Cliff Road	Z20
36	Upper Glen Road	D13
34	Uppercross	ZZ13
62	Uppercross Court	D21
46	Uppercross Road	H15
21	Urney Grove	V22
38	Usher Street	J14
38	Usher's Island	J14
38	Usher's Quay	J14
68	**VALE VIEW AVENUE**	**S23**
68	Vale View Close	S23
68	Vale View Grove	S23
68	Vale View Lawn	S23
39	Valentia Parade	K13
27	Valentia Road	L11
25	Valeview Crescent	G10
25	Valeview Drive	G10
25	Valeview Gardens	G10
71	Valley Avenue	U25
71	Valley Close	U25
	(Loughlinstown)	
25	Valley Park Avenue	F10
25	Valley Park Drive	F10
25	Valley Park Road	F10
2	Valley View	L1
71	Valley View	U25
71	Valley Walk	U25
71	Vally Drive	T25
	(Loughlinstown)	
46	Vauxhall Avenue	H15
28	Vavasour Square	M15
28	Venetian Hall	P11
25	Ventry Park	G12
25	Ventry Road	H12
30	Verbena Ave (Foxrock)	R23
25	Verbena Ave (Kilbarrack)	T9
18	Verbena Grove	T9
18	Verbena Lawn	T9
18	Verbena Park	T9
22	Verdemont	A10
48	Vergemount	M17
48	Vergemount Hall	M17
48	Vergemount Park	M17
29	Vernon Avenue	Q12
29	Vernon Court (Clontarf)	Q12
41	Vernon Court	Q13
	(Vernon Avenue)	
29	Vernon Drive	Q11
41	Vernon Gardens	Q12
29	Vernon Grove (Clontarf)	Q12
47	Vernon Grove (Rathgar)	K18
29	Vernon Heath	Q12
29	Vernon Park	Q12
29	Vernon Rise	Q11
41	Vernon Street	K15
41	Vernon Wood	Q13
40	*Veronica Terrace	N15
	(off Oliver Plunket Ave)	
60	Verschoyle Avenue	ZZ22
60	Verschoyle Close	ZZ22
60	Verschoyle Crescent	ZZ22
60	Verschoyle Drive	ZZ22
60	Verschoyle Glen	ZZ22
60	Verschoyle Green	ZZ22
60	Verschoyle Heights	ZZ22
60	Verschoyle Park	ZZ22
39	Verschoyle Place	L15
	(off Lwr Mount St)	
60	Verschoyle Rise	ZZ22
60	Verschoyle Vale	ZZ22
29	Verville Court	P12
59	Vesey Mews	T20
32	Vesey Park	XX14

Page		Grid Ref
59	Vesey Place	T20
32	Vesey Terrace	XX13
38	Vicar Street	J15
72	Vico Road	W23
72	*Vico Terrace	W23
	(Off Vico Road)	
48	Victoria Avenue	M17
	(Donnybrook)	
49	*Victoria Cottages	N15
	(off Irishtown Rd)	
27	Victoria Lane	L20
54	*Victoria Lane	K18
	(off South Zion Road)	
38	Victoria Quay	J14
73	Victoria Road (Clontarf)	P12
73	Victoria Road (Dalkey)	W22
72	Victoria Road (Killiney)	V23
54	Victoria Rd (Terenure)	J18
47	Victoria Street	K16
73	Victoria Tce (Dalkey)	W22
59	Victoria Terrace	U20
	(Dun Laoghaire)	
55	Victoria Tce (Dundrum)	M20
47	Victoria Village (Rathgar)	K18
29	Victoria Villas (Clontarf)	N12
47	Victoria Villas (Rathgar)	J18
38	Viking Place	J14
38	Viking Road	J14
38	*Villa Bank	K13
	(Royal Canal Bank)	
23	Villa Blanchard	C10
47	*Villa Building Apts	Y9
	(Harbour Road)	
57	Villa Nova	Q20
37	Villa Park Avenue	G12
25	Villa Park Drive	G12
25	Villa Park Gardens	G12
25	Villa Park Road	G12
54	Village Court Apts	J20
53	Village Green	J19
	(Rathfarnham)	
62	Village Green (Tallaght)	D21
10	Village Heights	A8
53	Village Sq (Tallaght)	D21
32	Village Weir	XX13
69	Villarea Park	V21
47	Villiers Road	K18
26	Violet Hill Drive	J11
26	Violet Hill Park	J11
26	Violet Hill Road	J11
25	Virginia Drive	G10
61	*Virginia Hall	C21
	(Belgard Square)	
61	Virginia Heights	C21
25	Virginia Park	G10
15	Viscount Avenue	M8
26	**WADELAI GREEN**	**K10**
26	Wadelai Road	K10
29	Wade's Avenue	R11
53	Wainsfort Avenue	G19
53	Wainsfort Crescent	G19
53	Wainsfort Drive	G18
53	Wainsfort Gardens	G19
53	Wainsfort Grove	H19
53	Wainsfort Manor	G19
53	Wainsfort Manor Cr	G19
53	Wainsfort Manor Drive	G19
53	Wainsfort Manor Green	G19
53	Wainsfort Manor Grove	G19
53	Wainsfort Park	H19
53	Wainsfort Road	G19
47	Waldemar Terrace	L20
47	Walker's Cottages	K16
45	Walker's Court	K16
45	Walkinstown	E17
45	Walkinstown Avenue	E17
45	Walkinstown Close	E17
45	Walkinstown Crescent	E17
45	Walkinstown Cross	F18
45	Walkinstown Drive	E17
45	Walkinstown Green	E17
45	Walkinstown Parade	E17
45	Walkinstown Park	E17
45	Walkinstown Road	E17
47	Wallace Road	F17
51	Walnut Ave (Clondalkin)	C19
27	Walnut Ave (Whitehall)	L11
51	Walnut Close	C19
27	Walnut Court	L10
51	Walnut Drive	C19
27	Walnut Lawn	L11
27	Walnut Park	L11
27	Walnut Rise	L11
64	Walnut View	H22
27	Walsh Road	K11
67	Waltersland Road	Q21
47	Waltham Terrace	Q19
47	*Walworth Road	K16
	(Victoria Street)	
47	Ward's Hill	J15

Page		Grid Ref

48 Warner's Lane **L16**
22 Warren Avenue **B11**
22 Warren Close **B11**
19 Warren Court **U9**
22 Warren Crescent **B11**
22 Warren Green **B11**
(Carpenterstown)
19 Warren Green (Sutton) **U9**
22 Warren Park **B11**
47 Warren Street **K16**
19 Warrenhouse Road **U9**
47 Warrenmount **J15**
47 Warrenmount Place **J15**
40 Warrenpoint **P12**
11 Warrenstown Close **B8**
10 Warrenstown Court **B8**
10 Warrenstown Drive **B8**
10 Warrenstown Garth **B8**
11 Warrenstown Green **B8**
11 Warrenstown Grove **B8**
10 Warrenstown Lawn **B9**
10 Warrenstown Park **B8**
10 Warrenstown Place **B8**
11 Warrenstown Rise **B8**
10 Warrenstown Row **B8**
10 Warrenstown Vale **B8**
10 Warrenstown View **B8**
10 Warrenstown Walk **B8**
10 Warrenstown Way **B8**
48 Warrington Lane **M15**
48 Warrington Place **M15**
48 Warwick Terrace **L16**
54 Wasdale Grove **J18**
54 Wasdale House **J19**
54 Wasdale Park **J19**
54 Washington Lane **H20**
54 Washington Park **H20**
47 Washington Street **JI6**
27 Waterfall Avenue **L12**
29 Waterfall Road **R11**
61 Watergate Estate **C21**
39 Waterloo Avenue **M13**
48 Waterloo Lane **M16**
48 Waterloo Road **L16**
61 Watermeadow Drive **C22**
61 Watermeadow Park **C22**
30 Watermill Avenue **R11**
62 Watermill Close **D22**
29 Watermill Drive **R11**
62 Watermill Grove **D22**
30 Watermill Lawn (Raheny) **R11**
60 Watermill Lawn **D22**
(Tallaght)
29 Watermill Park **R11**
30 Watermill Road **R11**
25 *Watermint Court **G11**
(Lockkeeper's Walk)
40 Waterside Apts **M15**
3 Waterside Avenue **P2**
3 Waterside Close **P3**
3 Waterside Court **P2**
7 Waterside Crescent **T4**
(Portmarnock)
3 Waterside Cres (Swords) **P2**
3 Waterside Drive **P2**
3 Waterside Green **P3**
3 Waterside Grove **P2**
3 Waterside King's Hall **P2**
3 Waterside Lawn **P2**
3 Waterside Park **P3**
3 Waterside Place **P3**
3 Waterside Rise **P2**
3 Waterside Road **P2**
3 Waterside Walk **P2**
3 Waterside Way **P2**
35 Waterstown Avenue **C13**
11 Waterville Road **C9**
11 Waterville Row **B9**
11 Waterville Terrace **C9**
43 Watery Lane **B17**
(Clondalkin)
2 Watery Lane (Swords) **M1**
38 *Watkins Buildings **J15**
(Ardee Street)
38 Watling Street **J14**
72 Watson Avenue **U24**
72 Watson Drive **U24**
72 Watson Park **U24**
69 Watson Road **U23**
69 Watson's Estate **U23**
27 Waverley Avenue **M12**
47 Waverley Terrace **J17**
38 Weaver Lane **K13**
38 Weaver's Close **J15**
22 Weaver's Row **ZZ10**
(Clonsilla)
47 Weavers Row **J15**
(The Coombe)
47 Weaver's Square **J15**
38 Weaver's Street **J15**
9 Weavers Walk **ZZ10**

58 Webster's Cottages **R20**
66 Wedgewood Estate **N22**
32 Weirview **XX13**
67 Weirview Drive **Q21**
19 Weldon's Lane **U8**
3 Well Road **N2**
39 Wellesley Place **L13**
53 Wellington Cottages **F19**
47 Wellington Court **G18**
47 *Wellington Gardens **L17**
(off Oakley Road)
48 Wellington House **M16**
53 Wellington Lane **F20**
(Tallaght)
48 Wellington Lane **M16**
(Wellington Road)
53 Wellington Park **G19**
48 Wellington Place **M16**
(Leeson Street)
38 Wellington Place North **K13**
53 Wellington Quay **K14**
48 Wellington Road **M16**
(Ballsbridge)
37 Wellington Road **G14**
(Phoenix Park)
53 Wellington Road **G19**
(Templeogue)
59 Wellington Street **U20**
(Dun Laoghaire)
39 Wellington St Lower **K13**
38 Wellington St Upper **K13**
25 Wellmount Avenue **G10**
25 Wellmount Court **G10**
25 Wellmount Crescent **G10**
25 Wellmount Drive **G10**
25 Wellmount Green **G10**
25 Wellmount Parade **G10**
25 Wellmount Park **G10**
25 Wellmount Road **G10**
27 Wellpark Avenue **L11**
10 Wellview Avenue **A7**
10 Wellview Crescent **A7**
10 Wellview Green **A7**
10 Wellview Grove **A7**
10 Wellview Park **A7**
7 Wendell Avenue **U4**
38 Werburgh Street **K15**
67 Wesbury **P2**
66 Wesley Heights **M22**
48 Wesley House **L16**
66 Wesley Lawns **M22**
47 Wesley Place **J16**
54 Wesley Road **K18**
26 West Park Drive **J10**
59 West Pier **T19**
(Dun Laoghaire)
21 West Pier (Howth) **Y9**
40 West Road **M13**
45 West Terrace **F15**
42 Westbourne Close **ZZ17**
54 Westbourne Court **J19**
42 Westbourne Drive **ZZ17**
42 Westbourne Grove **ZZ17**
63 Westbourne Lodge **G21**
42 Westbourne Rise **ZZ17**
54 Westbourne Road **J19**
42 Westbourne View **ZZ17**
53 Westbrook **G18**
60 Westbrook Lawns **ZZ22**
32 Westbrook Park **WW14**
55 Westbrook Road **L19**
32 Westbury **WW14**
32 Westbury Avenue **XX15**
32 Westbury Close **XX15**
32 Westbury Drive **XX14**
32 Westbury Grove **WW15**
32 Westbury Park **XX15**
22 Westend Village **B10**
52 Western Park Way **E19**
23 Western Parkway **B12**
Motorway
46 Western Road **J16**
38 Western Way **K13**
65 Westerton Rise **M21**
32 Westfield Avenue **VV13**
47 Westfield Road **J17**
57 Westfield Terrace **N15**
54 Westhampton Place **J18**
39 Westhaven **Z8**
39 Westland Row **L15**
67 *Westminster Court **R23**
(The Hedgerows)
67 Westminster Lawns **Q22**
39 Westminster Park **R22**
68 Westminster Road **R23**
67 Westmoreland Park **L17**
39 Westmoreland Street **K14**
55 Weston Avenue **L20**
55 Weston Cl (Churchtown) **L20**
32 Weston Close (Leixlip) **VV13**

32 Weston Court **VV13**
32 Weston Crescent **VV14**
32 Weston Drive **VV13**
32 Weston Green **VV13**
55 Weston Grove **L20**
32 Weston Heights **VV14**
32 Weston Lawn **VV13**
32 Weston Meadow **VV14**
55 Weston Pk (Churchtown) **L20**
32 Weston Park (Leixlip) **VV13**
55 Weston Road **L20**
55 Weston Terrace **L20**
32 Weston Way **VV14**
29 Westpark (Coolock) **Q10**
61 Westpark (Tallaght) **D21**
11 Westway Close **C8**
11 Westway Grove **C8**
11 Westway Lawns **C9**
11 Westway Park **C8**
11 Westway Rise **C8**
11 Westway View **C8**
25 Westwood Ave **F10**
25 Westwood Road **F10**
47 Wexford Street **K15**
67 Whately Place **P21**
7 Wheatfield Grove **U4**
35 Wheatfield Road **C14**
(Palmerstown)
7 Wheatfield Road **U4**
(Portmarnock)
34 Wheatfields Avenue **B15**
34 Wheatfields Close **B15**
34 Wheatfields Court **B15**
34 Wheatfields Crescent **B15**
34 Wheatfields Drive **B15**
34 Wheatfields Grove **B15**
34 Wheatfields Park **B15**
37 Wheaton Court **F15**
40 Whelan House Flats **M15**
58 Whelan's Terrace **R19**
38 *Whitaker Hall **K13**
(Western Way)
51 White Hall **C19**
56 White Oak **M19**
15 Whiteacre Close **L9**
15 Whiteacre Court **L9**
15 Whiteacre Crescent **L9**
15 Whiteacre Place **L9**
15 Whitebank Road **P15**
55 Whitebarn Road **K20**
56 Whitebeam Avenue **M18**
55 Whitebeam Road **M18**
66 Whitebeams Road **N22**
61 Whitebrook Park **B21**
22 Whitechapel Avenue **A10**
22 Whitechapel Court **A10**
22 Whitechapel Crescent **A10**
22 Whitechapel Green **A10**
22 Whitechapel Grove **A10**
22 Whitechapel Lawn **A10**
22 Whitechapel Park **A10**
22 Whitechapel Road **A10**
64 Whitechurch Abbey **J21**
64 Whitechurch Close **J22**
64 Whitechurch Court **J22**
64 Whitechurch Crescent **J22**
64 Whitechurch Drive **J22**
64 Whitechurch Green **J22**
64 Whitechurch Grove **J22**
64 Whitechurch Hill **J22**
64 Whitechurch Lawn **J22**
64 Whitechurch Park **J22**
64 Whitechurch Pines **J21**
64 Whitechurch Place **J22**
54 Whitechurch Road **J20**
64 Whitechurch Stream **J21**
64 Whitechurch View **J22**
64 Whitechurch Walk **J22**
64 Whitechurch Way **J22**
39 *Whitefriar Gardens **K15**
(off Whitefriar St)
39 Whitefriar Place **K15**
39 Whitefriar Street **K15**
27 Whitehall **L10**
53 Whitehall Close **G19**
53 Whitehall Gardens **G18**
68 Whitehall Mews **R22**
53 Whitehall Park **G19**
53 Whitehall Road **K20**
(Churchtown)
53 Whitehall Rd **G18**
(Kimmage)
45 Whitehall Road West **G18**
53 Whitehall Square **F18**
38 White's Lane North **K13**
24 White's Road **E12**
73 White's Villas **W21**
10 Whitestown **A9**
10 Whitestown Avenue **A9**

10 Whitestown Crescent **A9**
10 Whitestown Drive **A9**
(Blanchardstown)
61 Whitestown Dr (Tallaght) **B22**
10 Whitestown Gardens **A9**
10 Whitestown Green **A9**
10 Whitestown Grove **A9**
10 Whitestown Park **A9**
61 Whitestown Road **C22**
10 Whitestown Walk **A9**
61 Whitestown Way **C22**
28 Whitethorn **N10**
28 Whitethorn Avenue **N10**
28 Whitethorn Close **N10**
28 Whitethorn Cr (Artane) **N10**
35 Whitethorn Crescent **B15**
(Coldcut Road)
35 Whitethorn Drive **B15**
35 Whitethorn Gardens **B15**
28 Whitethorn Gro (Artane) **N10**
28 Whitethorn Pk (Artane) **N10**
35 Whitethorn Park **B15**
(Coldcut Road)
28 Whitethorn Rise **N10**
28 Whitethorn Rd (Artane) **N10**
55 Whitethorn Road **M18**
(Milltown)
68 Whitethorn Wk (Foxrock) **R22**
69 Whitethorn Walk **T22**
(Kill O' the Grange)
35 Whitethorn Way **B15**
54 Whitton Road **J18**
39 Whitworth Avenue **K14**
39 *Whitworth Parade **K12**
(off Saint Patrick's Road)
39 Whitworth Place **K12**
39 Whitworth Road **K12**
39 *Whitworth Terrace **L13**
(off Russell Ave)
39 *Wicklow Lane **K15**
(off Wicklow Street)
39 Wicklow Street **K15**
26 Wigan Road **K12**
53 Wilderwood Grove **F20**
49 Wilfield **N16**
49 Wilfield Park **N16**
49 Wilfield Road **N16**
47 Wilfrid Road **JI7**
47 Wilfrid Terrace **JI7**
9 Willans Avenue **XX9**
9 Willans Drive **XX9**
9 Willans Green **XX9**
9 Willans Rise **XX9**
9 Willans Row **XX9**
9 Willans Way **XX9**
54 Willbrook **N16**
64 Willbrook Downs **J21**
64 Willbrook Estate **J20**
54 Willbrook Grove **J20**
47 Willbrook House **L16**
54 Willbrook Lawn **J20**
54 Willbrook Park **J20**
54 Willbrook Road **J20**
54 Willbrook Street **J20**
54 *William Pallister House **J20**
(Stonepark Court)
39 William Street North **L13**
39 William Street South **K15**
39 William's Lane **K14**
47 William's Park **K17**
39 *William's Place Lwr **K13**
(off Portland Place)
47 William's Place South **K15**
39 William's Place Upper **K13**
37 *Willie Bermingham Pla **H15**
(Kilmainham Lane)
19 Willie Nolan Road **U8**
53 Willington Avenue **F19**
53 Willington Court **F19**
53 Willington Crescent **F19**
53 Willington Drive **F19**
53 Willington Green **F19**
53 Willington Lawn **F19**
53 Willington Park **F19**
50 Willow Ave (Clondalkin) **A18**
71 Willow Avenue **U25**
(Loughlinstown)
59 Willow Bank **T20**
64 Willow Bank Drive **H21**
64 Willow Bank Park **H21**
50 Willow Ct (Clondalkin) **A18**
71 Willow Court **U25**
(Loughlinstown)
71 Willow Crescent **U25**
50 Willow Drive **A18**
65 Willow Gate **L21**
50 Willow Gro (Clondalkin) **A18**
68 Willow Grove **S23**
(Cornelscourt)
69 Willow Grove **T22**

Page		Grid Ref	Page		Grid Ref	Page		Grid Ref	Page		Grid Ref
	(Kill O'The Grange)		38	Wood Lane	J14	69	Woodlawn Park	T21	47	Wynnefield Park	K17
23	Willow Lodge	D12	38	Wood Quay	K14		(Dun Laoghaire)		47	Wynnefield Road	K17
49	Willow Mews	P17	47	Wood Street	K15	63	Woodlawn Pk (Tallaght)	F22	56	Wynnsward Drive	M18
68	Willow Pk (Foxrock)	R22	25	Woodbank Avenue	F10	62	Woodlawn Park Ave	E21	56	Wynnsward Park	M18
71	Willow Park	U25	25	Woodbank Drive	F10	62	Woodlawn Park Drive	F21	18	Wyteleaf Grove	R8
	(Loughlinstown)		23	Woodberry	B11	62	Woodlawn Park Grove	F22	73	Wyvern Estate	V23
14	Willow Park Ave	J9		(Carpenterstown)		16	Woodlawn Rise	M8			
14	Willow Park Close	J9	32	Woodberry (Lucan)	XX15	55	Woodlawn Terrace	L20	39	XAVIER AVENUE	M13
14	Willow Park Cres	J9	57	Woodbine Avenue	P18	16	Woodlawn View	M8			
14	Willow Park Drive	K9	18	Woodbine Close	R9	69	Woodlawn Villas	T21	56	YALE	N19
14	Willow Park Grove	J9	29	Woodbine Drive	R9	16	Woodlawn Walk	M8	58	Yankee Terrace	R20
14	Willow Park Lawn	J9	56	Woodbine House	P18	16	Woodlawn Way	M8	38	*Yarnhall Street	K14
14	Willow Park Road	J9	57	Woodbine Park	P18	55	Woodleigh	K18		(Henrietta Place)	
57	Willow Pl (Booterstown)	Q19		(Booterstown)		66	Woodley Court	N21	71	Yeates Hall	S24
71	Willow Place	U25	29	Woodbine Pk (Raheny)	R9	66	Woodley Park	N21	43	Yeates Way	C16
	(Loughlinstown)		56	Woodbine Road	P18	69	Woodley Road	U23	43	Yellow Meadows Ave	B17
65	Willow Road (Dundrum)	L21		(Booterstown)		65	Woodpark (Ballinteer)	L22	43	Yellow Meadows Drive	B17
44	Willow Road	D17	18	Woodbine Road (Raheny)	R9	23	Woodpark	C10	43	Yellow Meadows Estate	C17
	(Fox & Geese)		55	Woodbine Terrace	M20		(Blanchardstown)		43	Yellow Meadows Grove	B17
57	Willow Terrace	Q19		(Dundrum)		23	Woods End	C10	43	Yellow Meadows Lawn	B17
72	Willow Vale	U24	22	Woodbrook Court	A11	32	Woodscape	XX15	43	Yellow Meadows Park	B17
9	Willow Wood Close	ZZ10	22	Woodbrook Crescent	A11	29	Woodside (Clontarf)	Q12	43	Yellow Meadows Vale	B17
9	Willow Wood Downs	ZZ10	31	Woodbrook Downs	V28	21	Woodside (Howth)	Y10	27	Yellow Road	M10
9	Willow Wood Green	ZZ10	22	Woodbrook Hall	A11	55	Woodside	K19	6	Yellow Walls	R2
9	Willow Wood Grove	ZZ10	22	Woodbrook Park	A11		(Rathfarnham)		6	Yellow Walls Road	R2
9	Willow Wood Lawn	ZZ10		(Carpenterstown)		55	Woodside Drive	K19	69	Yellowwood Avenue	T23
9	Willow Wood Park	ZZ9	53	Woodbrook Park	G20	55	Woodside Grove	K19	54	Yewland Terrace	J18
9	Willow Wood Rise	ZZ9		(Templeogue)		48	Woodstock Court	L17	47	York Avenue	K17
9	Willow Wood View	ZZ10	22	Woodbrook Square	A11	48	Woodstock Gardens	L17	59	York Rd (D/Laoghaire)	T20
9	Willow Wood Walk	ZZ9	21	Woodcliff Heights	Z10	63	Woodstock Park	G21	47	York Road (Rathmines)	K17
66	Willow	M21	35	Woodfarm Avenue	C14	63	Woodstown	F22	40	York Road (Ringsend)	N14
49	Willowfield	P16	35	Woodfarm Cottages	C13	63	Woodstown Abbey	F22	58	York Street	K15
56	Willowfield Avenue	M20	35	Woodfarm Drive	C14	63	Woodstown Abbey	G22	59	York Terrace	T20
56	Willowfield Park	M20	63	Woodfield	G22	63	Woodstown Avenue	F22			
57	Willowmount	Q19	37	Woodfield Cottages	F15	63	Woodstown Close	F22	54	ZION ROAD	K18
9	Willows Court	ZZ10	37	Woodfield Place	F15	63	Woodstown Court	F22	37	Zoo Road	G14
9	Willows Drive	ZZ10	67	Woodford	P22	63	Woodstown Crescent	F22	47	*Zuma Terrace	J16
9	Willows Green	ZZ10	43	Woodford Avenue	C17	63	Woodstown Dale	F22		(on Mount Drummond Ave)	
9	Willows Road	ZZ10	43	Woodford Close	C17	63	Woodstown Drive	F22			
33	Willsbrook Avenue	YY14	47	Woodford Court	J17	63	Woodstown Gardens	F22			
33	Willsbrook Crescent	ZZ13		(Harold's Cross)		63	Woodstown Green	F22			
33	Willsbrook Drive	YY13	43	Woodford Court	C17	63	Woodstown Heath	F22			
33	Willsbrook Gardens	YY13		(Monksfield)		63	Woodstown Heights	F23			
33	Willsbrook Green	YY14	43	Woodford Crescent	B17	63	Woodstown Hill	F22			
33	Willsbrook Grove	YY13	43	Woodford Downs	C17	54	*Woodstown House	J20			
33	Willsbrook Park	YY14	43	Woodford Drive	B17		(Stonepark Court)				
33	Willsbrook Place	YY13	43	Woodford Garth	B17	63	Woodstown Lane	G22			
33	Willsbrook Road	YY14	43	Woodford Green	C17	63	Woodstown Lawn	F22			
33	Willsbrook View	YY14	43	Woodford Grove	C17	63	Woodstown Meadow	F22			
33	Willsbrook Way	YY13	43	Woodford Heights	C17	63	Woodstown Parade	F22			
73	Wilmont Avenue	V21	43	Woodford Hill	C17	63	Woodstown Park	F22			
56	Wilson Crescent	N20	43	Woodford Lawn	C17	63	Woodstown Place	F22			
56	Wilson Road	P20	43	Woodford Meadows	B17	63	Woodstown Rise	F22			
38	Wilson Terrace	J15	43	Woodford Parade	B17	63	Woodstown Road	F22			
39	Wilson's Place	L15	43	Woodford Park	C17	63	Woodstown Vale	F22			
48	Wilton Place	L16	43	Woodford Park Road	B17	63	Woodstown Walk	F22			
48	Wilton Terrace	L16	43	Woodford Rise	C17	63	Woodstown Way	F23			
27	Windele Road	K11	43	Woodford Road	B17	67	Woodthorpe	P21			
9	Windermere	YY10	43	Woodford Terrace	C17	63	Woodtown Way	G23			
21	Windgate Rise	Y11	43	Woodford Ved	C17	10	Woodvale Avenue	ZZ9			
21	Windgate Road	Y11	43	Woodford Villas	B17	10	Woodvale Crescent	ZZ9			
46	Windmill Ave (Crumlin)	G17	43	Woodford Walk	B17	10	Woodvale Drive	ZZ9			
2	Windmill Ave (Swords)	M2	43	Woodford Way	C17	10	Woodvale Garth	ZZ9			
46	Windmill Cr (Crumlin)	G17	55	Woodhaven	M18	10	Woodvale Green	ZZ9			
2	Windmill Lands	L2	15	Woodhazel Close	K9	10	Woodvale Grove	ZZ9			
39	Windmill Lane	L14	15	Woodhazel Terrace	K9	10	Woodvale Park	ZZ9			
45	Windmill Park	G17	10	Woodlands	A9	10	Woodvale Way	ZZ9			
2	Windmill Rise	M2		(Blakestown Road)		32	Woodview (Lucan)	WW14			
45	Windmill Road	G17	8	Woodlands (Malahide)	T5	18	Woodview Close	R9			
31	Windrush	V26	55	Woodlands (Rathgar)	K18	54	Woodview Cottages	J19			
27	Windsor Avenue	M12	69	Woodlands Avenue	T23	67	Woodview Ct (Stillorgan)	Q21			
68	Windsor Court	S21		(Cornelscourt)		32	Woodview Court Apts	WW14			
58	Windsor Drive	S2	57	Woodlands Avenue	P20	22	Woodview Grove	B10			
7	*Windsor Mews	S3		(Stillorgan)		32	Woodview Heights	WW14			
	(St Margaret's Avenue)		8	Woodlands Court	U5		(Lucan)				
58	Windsor Park	S21	69	Woodlands Drive	T23	18	Woodview Park	R9			
47	Windsor Place	L15		(Johnstown Road)			(Ardara Avenue)				
47	Windsor Road	L17	57	Woodlands Dr (Stillorgan)	P20	23	Woodview Park	D11			
59	Windsor Terrace	U20	69	Woodlands Park	T23		(Castleknock)				
	(Dun Laoghaire)			(Johnstown Road)		33	Woodville Avenue	YY13			
7	Windsor Tce (Malahide)	S3	57	Woodlands Park	Q20	33	Woodville Close	YY13			
47	Windsor Tce (Ranelagh)	K16		(Mount Merrion)		16	Woodville Court	P9			
27	Windsor Villas	M12	69	Woodlands Road	T23	33	Woodville Green	YY13			
55	Windy Arbour	M19	16	Woodlawn	M8	33	Woodville Grove	YY13			
38	Winetavern Street	K14	16	Woodlawn Avenue	M8	16	Woodville House	N9			
47	Winton Avenue	K18	16	Woodlawn Close	M8	33	Woodville Lawn	YY13			
54	Winton Grove	J18	16	Woodlawn Court	M8	27	Woodville Road	K12			
48	Winton Road	L16	55	Woodlawn Crescent	L20	33	Woodville Walk	YY13			
59	Wolfe Tone Avenue	U20		(Churchtown)		38	*Wormwood Gate	J14			
38	Wolfe Tone Quay	H14	16	Woodlawn Crescent	M8		(off Bridge Street Lower)				
39	Wolfe Tone Street	K14		(Coolock Lane)		72	Wyattville	U25			
47	Wolseley Street	J16	16	Woodlawn Drive	M8	72	Wyattville Close	U25			
73	Wolverton Glen	V22	16	Woodlawn Green	M8	72	Wyattville Hill	U25			
42	Wood Avens	A15	55	Woodlawn Grove	L20	72	Wyattville Park	U25			
62	Wood Dale Close	E22		(Churchtown)		72	Wyattville Road	U25			
62	Wood Dale Crescent	E22	16	Woodlawn Grove	M8	65	Wyckham Grove	M21			
62	Wood Dale Drive	E22		(Coolock Lane)		65	Wyckham Park Road	L21			
62	Wood Dale Green	E22	55	Woodlawn Park	L20	66	Wyckham Place	M21			
63	Wood Dale Grove	F22		(Churchtown)		65	Wyckham Way	M22			
63	Wood Dale Oak	F22	16	Woodlawn Park	M8	58	Wynberg Park	S20			
62	Wood Dale View	F22		(Coolock Lane)		47	Wynnefield House	K17